MW00748636

THE

Birder's Guide

BRITISH COLUMBIA

A Walking Guide to Bird Watching Sites

KEITH TAYLOR

Birder's Guide
to
BRITISH
COLUMBIA

copyright © 1998 Keith Taylor
revised second edition
First published in 1993

All rights reserved.
No part of this work may be reproduced
or used in any form or by any means -
graphic, electronic, or mechanical -
without prior permission from the
publisher.

Published by Steller Press Limited
13 - 4335 West 10th Avenue
Vancouver, British Columbia V6R 2H6

Designed by Paul Thomas,
Graphic Design

Canadian Cataloguing in Publication
Data
Taylor, K. (Keith), The birder's guide,
British Columbia
(Steller guides) includes index
ISBN 1-894143-00-0
1. Birding sites - British Columbia -
Guidebooks.
2. Bird watching - British Columbia -
Guidebooks.
3. British Columbia - Guidebooks. I.
Title II. Series
QL685.5.B7T39 1998
598Ō.07Ō234711 C98-900291-8

Printed in Canada

*This book is dedicated to the tens of millions
who have, or will, suffer from a debilitating
episode of depression in the course of their lives.
The stigma often placed on the mentally ill must
be replaced with understanding and compassion
for in reality these illnesses are caused by
inherited biochemical imbalances - and rank
among the most painful experiences a human can
endure.*

KT

PREFACE

This is the fourth book in a series of bird-finding guides that I have written. The writing of these books has not been for profit or recognition, but rather for helping fellow "independent" birders in their world-wide quests of birds. It is hoped that in some small way these books have helped to influence the saving of rainforest through the promotion of the concept of "eco-tourism".

In particular I wish to thank the following people:

David Mark, who pioneered birdfinding in B.C. with - "Where to Find Birds in British Columbia" - and proved to be imperial while discovering the birding sites within the province, Barbara Adams, Robert Butler, Colin Butt, Jim Burbridge, Joan Burbridge, E. Callin, R. Wayne Campbell, R.A. Cannings, R.J. Cannings, S.G. Cannings, Arnie Chadock, John Clague, Gary S. Davidson, Yorke Edwards, Al Grass, Jude Grass, Tony Greenfield, D.V. George, Paul Goossen, Ken Hall, Larry Halverson, Robert Hay, Margo Hearne, Jerry Herzig, Rick Howie, Tom Jacobson, the late Brian Kautesk, Jane King, the late Francis King, Doug Kragh, Mark Lightbody, Alan MacLeod, Jo Ann MacKenzie, Hue MacKenzie, Blake Maybank, Bill Merilees, Barb McGrenere, Ed McMackin, Dave Mossop, Hank Van der Pol, Doug Powell, Wilma Robinson, Christopher Sandham, Madelon Schouten, Chris Siddle, Denise Skwarock, Tom Smallwood, David Sterling, Rick Toochin, Mike Toochin, Robin Yellowlees, Wayne Weber, John G. Woods, Tim Zurowski, the American Birding Association, Kallahin Expeditions, the Okanagan Naturalists Club, and several birding tour groups based in the United States and England.

TABLE OF CONTENTS

NOTES & OBSERVATIONS

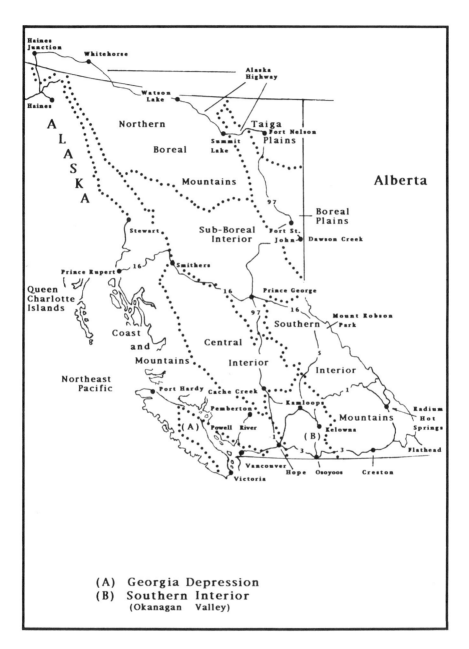

(A) Georgia Depression
(B) Southern Interior
      (Okanagan   Valley)

MAP 1   ECO ZONES AND ROAD SYSTEMS OF BRITISH COLUMBIA

INTRODUCTION

Wild. Mysterious. Spectacular. Immense. British Columbia covers 952,263 square kilometers of awe-inspiring, unspoilt country. Within British Columbia's boundaries lie some of the most photogenic countryside which can compete with any of the most scenic areas of the planet!

British Columbia is a land of climatic contrasts - unrivalled for its tremendous range of life zones - a veritable feast of ornithological riches. A series of massive mountain ranges and alternating rainshadow trenches running northwest to southeast form a succession across the province, creating a complex geography and an accompaniment of great habitat diversity. The topography and the prevailing winds from the Pacific Ocean create a series of wet and dry regimes between the coast and the Rockies: western mountain slopes hold a huge, irregular strip of wet coniferous forest, while eastern slopes hold semi-arid steppe plateaus of scattered pines and grasslands. Far to the north, cold polar continental air pours across the boreal forests of the intermontane lowlands and the extensive corrugated plateaus, further modifying the province's climate. The mountain ranges in the northern portion of the province are generally lower where wet and dry regions are not so pronounced.

Four eco-regions will be concentrated on in this guide, collectively producing all of the bird species to be found in British Columbia: the Georgia Depression, the Okanagan Valley, the Peace River Parklands, and a small portion of the Northern Boreal Forest - Haines Road area. The journey is a fascinating experience, taking you through the whole spectrum of habitats found throughout the province from sea level to over 10,000 feet in elevation.

Nowhere in the world can one watch birds in such an idyllic and spectacularly varied environment, virtually everything from arid, windswept grasslands to vast swathes of unbroken, verdant forests, from jagged, snow-encrusted peaks to shallow, reed-fringed wetlands, from desert salton basins to turquoise-coloured alpine lakes, from endless expanses of stunted boreal forest and dwarf-willows to coastal fjords notched and scalloped by countless bays, from flower-strewn meadows to a citadel of mountain woodlands laced with cool, shady canyons, from pine-clad ridges to endless dunes basked in warm sunshine.

As in any developed country, British Columbia has a well-maintained highway and road network covering limitless kilometers. Many of the better birding areas can be attained on paved roads with excellent roadside birding opportunities. Also many birding sites are easily accessible by public transport.

British Columbia is blessed with an range of National and Provincial Parks, strategically located for thoroughly satisfying flora and fauna experiences.

There are 336 of these diverse and exquisite reserves, ranging in size from less than one to over a million hectares, yielding unlimited birding opportunities.

British Columbia is a veritable treasure trove of natural wonders, a living natural history museum. Early summer (June through early July) is the best time as the weather is at its best and all of the 249 breeding species are singing throughout the province.

Although there are no endemics, birdlife is prolific here with 456 species, including some of the world's most beautiful and exotic; incredible birds from the large, pre-historic looking American White Pelican to the iridescent and diminutive Calliope Hummingbird. While most American birders come exclusively to list the locally introduced Eurasian Skylark and Crested Myna, there are many focal points for Canadian birders looking for specialities of the Great Basin and dry cordilleran forest and the wind-swept Pacific coast.

Names to entice the mind of any birder: Yellow-billed Loon, Buller's Shearwater, White-tailed Ptarmigan, California Quail, Wandering Tattler, Surfbird, Rock Sandpiper, South Polar Skua, Heermann's Gull, Marbled Murrelet, Cassin's Auklet, Horned Puffin, Flammulated Owl, Spotted Owl, Common Poorwill, White-throated Swift, Anna's Hummingbird, Williamson's Sapsucker, White-headed Woodpecker, Gray Flycatcher, Bushtit, Pygmy Nuthatch, Canyon Wren, Black-throated Gray Warbler, Townsend's Warbler, Black-headed Grosbeak, and Smith's Longspur. For foreign birders, there is a vast array of species in a tremendous array of colour and shape that will not fail to compete for your attention. Flashes of colour will announce: hummingbirds, sapsuckers, kingbirds, swallows, jays, bluebirds, waxwings, vireos, warblers, tanagers, grosbeaks, crossbills, and finches. Even a novice birder (not knowing songs and calls) should see 240 species in a three week trip.

Note: For reading ease, the index and species are listed individually through the text and lack "S's" (i.e. not Long-toed, Red-necked and Little Stints, but Long-toed Stint, Red-necked Stint and Little Stint).

HOW TO USE THIS BOOK

BIRDING

The main purpose of this guide is to help the independent birder to locate the best places to find all 470 species of birds in British Columbia - "A self-made tour for the independent birder".

A quick inspection of the book will show that it is divided into sixteen trips along loop routes through the better birding areas, via the shortest distances possible. Each loop-trip has a designated starting point where the kilometerage is indicated as (00.0). Each point of interest or importance thereafter will be followed by the kilometerage from the starting point and the last point mentioned. Starting points change occasionally en route so that you may join the loop, or change to other loops, where you wish. The Alaska Highway has kilometerage posts which are used for reference in that region of B.C. With the directions in this guide and a copy of the "British Columbia Recreational Atlas", finding locations will be easy.

Helpful Icons:

Driving Directions   Where to Find Birds   Bird Listing

A complete checklist of the birds of British Columbia with bargraphs is found in the back of this guide. A quick inspection of these (along with the National Geographic's "Field Guide to Birds of North America's" colour-coded range maps showing the seasonal distribution of birds) will give you all of the information of seasonal occurrence and relative abundance of the avifauna for B.C. Outstanding birding spots are given headings. If you are in a hurry, stop only at those places so indicated.

If you are looking for a particular species, simply look for the species you desire in the index, then find it listed in the text under the locales it should be found. Then consult the checklist and bar-graphs to see what your chances are of finding it (its relative abundance in that area), and its seasonal occurrence (does it occur in that month?). For example: a quick inspection of the the National Geographic's guide will show that the Rock Sandpiper only occurs coastally in winter, the checklist and bar-graphs tells you that the Rock Sandpiper is local or rare, and can be found rarely from mid-July, usually from late September, through early May, rarely mid-May. (also see Birding below and the Checklist and Bar-Graphs at the back of this book).

The common names and order in this guide follows the National Geographic Society's "Field Guide to the Birds of North America".

BIRDING

Of the 470 species of birds found in British Columbia, 298 are known to breed in the province. The following occur only as rare or local winter migrants or are quite rare outside of the winter months: Yellow-billed Loon, Clark's Grebe, Emperor Goose, Tufted Duck, King Eider, Rock Sandpiper, Glaucous Gull, Snowy Owl, Brambling, and Hoary Redpoll. A further 106 are vagrants or strictly accidental. Many waterbirds that winter coastally, leave in early to late April and move into the interior (or to the arctic) to breed. As it is not possible to indicate all of the small seasonal arrival and departure dates that can, and do, occur throughout a province as vast as British Columbia, the checklist and Bargraphs in the back of this book only show the four regions that birders will need to visit to see all of B.C.'s birds.

Birding is best in the cooler early morning hours of summer, especially in the southern interior where temperatures climb quickly. The dawn chorus is certainly the best time to find those less common species while they sing. During the winter, birds often join into mixed species flocks, feeding together in small groups. In the interior, especially in the far north, long periods of time may pass before you encounter one of these flocks.

Squeeking and pishing (calling) is an excellent way of attracting birds for closer views, as well as using the taped songs and calls on a" Field Guide to Western Bird Songs", which work very well on nocturnal species, especially owls.

For up-to-date information on rare species telephone the Vancouver Rare Bird Alert at (604) 737-3074 and the Victoria Rare Bird Alert at (250) 592-3381.

Please! If you have any corrections or suggestions for a more useful guide, especially exact locations for rare or local species to further specialize the content of this guide, contact the publisher.

Time to Bird Watch

The species you desire to see will determine the best season to visit. Simply consult the bar-graphs in the back of this book for this information. For those who need many species spread over the entire year, the best all-around birding is during late April and early May (a month later in the far north) when there is an overlapping of winter and summer birds, plus the spring migrants in full colour. However, the greatest number of rare and accidental species are usually found during the fall migration (September - late November). Early summer (June through July) is a very good time for first-time visitors to North America (or to this region) as the weather is at its best and all of the breeding species are singing throughout the province; shorebirds begin to return in late June, although are not prolific in species until mid-August and September.

Winter is the dullest season, but still rewarding; the only season for several species of finch. If you are in an area during a Christmas count (coastal counts produce 135 - 150 species) you have a better chance of finding uncommon species pin-pointed during the count and rarities are often produced.

For pelagic birding, you must arrive in early September onwards for organized tours or take the various ferries for a much smaller list of species.

What To Take Along
PACKING

Packing for a bird watching trip involves common sense and forethought. Pack economically but take into account all the your possible needs both for the terrain and the weather. The items on this list represent a sampling of what you might need on your trip.

Remember that in winter daily temperatures will vary considerably from the coast to the northern interior. Coastal temperatures are usually above freezing, while the northern interior could be -25 C. or more. Rain is prevalent in the winter season on the coast, from October through late April, while summers throughout B.C. are usually very dry and sunny with daily temperatures from 20 - 30 C. on the coast and in the northern interior, and between 30 - 38 C in the dry southern interior. Suitable footwear is required for muddy trails, while running shoes are adequate for most trails in the summer months. A spotting scope is necessary for raptors, waterbirds and shorebirds, and useful for closer views of those more difficult species. A tape recorder and the tape of the "Field Guide to Western Bird Songs" is very valuable for learning songs and to draw-in birds; (and of course your field guides, and tourist guides).

If you are camping , you will be in some of the cleanest, well-maintained parks in the world. All have toilets; many have excellent washrooms with mirrors and washbasin, though most do not have showers. You will need: towel, washcloth, soap, shaving gear, deodorant and flashlight (for nocturnal species), a moderately warm sleeping bag (nights seldom get below 55'F. in summer, although in the far north it will get cooler), sleeping mat and tent. Make sure your tent is equiped with a very fine netting to keep out gnats ("no see 'em's").

All birders (especially campers) will require a "Deet" mosquito repellent.

ITINERARIES

To ensure that your birding expedition is successful, it is important to plan carefully. You can lose time in areas where birds are not occurring or in getting to difficult spots.

Planning an itinerary for a province as vast as British Columbia is very difficult. Driving distances in British Columbia are great: from Vancouver to Haines Alaska, using the Alaskan Highway route, is 2,918.5 kilometers one-way or 5,837 kilometers return! Four major itineraries are suggested for those wishing to get a maximum number of species and each itinerary can be broken down into shorter trips.

(A) For those with unlimited time and driving their own vehicle, especially a camper, the following itinerary is suggested to cover the entire province with the least amount of driving: ferry to Vancouver Island, birding the Victoria area for two or three days, then take the two ferries one-way from Port Hardy through to Haines, Alaska (or directly from Bellingham). Bird the Haines Road for the specialities and proceed south on the Alaska Highway with a brief stop around Fort Nelson, especially for the Yellow-bellied Flycatcher.

Drive directly from Fort Nelson to Fort St. John, arriving a little over one week into your holidays. Bird the sites around Fort St. John and Dawson Creek, allowing four or five days to get all of the Peace River Parklands specialities. Drive directly from Dawson Creek to the Okanagan Valley (with a brief stop for White Pelican en route), arriving at Vaseux Lake at the end of week two or the begining of week three of your holidays.

Allow at least five days to "get" all of the Okanagan specialities, and a day's side-trip to Creston for Forster's Tern and Wild Turkey. Leave the Okanagan, driving directly to Vancouver, birding the "Lower Mainland" for the Crested Myna and any coastal specialities that you may have missed on Vancouver Island. This trip should be completed after four and a half weeks.

(B) The second itinerary is for those driving either their own vehicle or a rented vehicle, involving a round-trip from Vancouver. If you wish, a brief side-trip can be made to Victoria for the Sky Lark etc.

Bird the "Lower Mainland" for three days, based in the Delta area. Drive to Cathedral Park, spending the minimum two days at the lodge getting the alpine specialities, or a night at Manning Park Lodge. Proceed to Vaseux Lake in the southern Okanagan, birding the area with a day's side-trip to Creston for the Forster's Tern and Wild Turkey. Allow five days to get all of the Okanagan specialities.

Mid-way into week two of your holidays, drive toward the Peace River Parklands with brief stops en route for White Pelican (Stum Lake), and Yellow-bellied Flycatcher (Prince George). The drive to the Peace River Parklands, with stops, will take two days. Allow five days to bird Moberly Lake, and the sites around both Dawson Creek and Fort St. John, using motels as bases at each location. If you wish to visit the Haines Road, you should fly from Dawson Creek (see below). At the end of day 19 or 20, drive directly back to Vancouver.

(C)   The third itinerary is basically the same trip as (B), but involves using flights to/from Vancouver to the Okanagan (Kelowna), then to the Peace River Parklands (either Dawson Creek or Fort St. John), and using rental cars at each location. Those wishing to get into the Haines Road for the few specialities found there should fly to/from Whitehorse. Another alternative is to use the return ferry to Haines and rent a car there.

(D)   A fourth separate trip to the Queen Charlotte Islands involves a relatively expensive flight to/from the town of Sandspit, or a long drive to Prince Rupert and a ferry trip from there to Skidegate. As the Queen Charlottes do not have any birds that cannot be seen anywhere else in the province, except for the Horned Puffin, only the most avid B.C. or Canada lister looking for the puffin or possible Asian vagrants will visit these islands. Anyone wishing to take the ferry trip is advised to fly to Prince Rupert and use the ferry as a foot passenger, both the flight and ferry fees will be less expensive!

MAPS

Without a doubt, travellers in British Columbia should purchase a copy of the British Columbia Recreational Atlas. It contains over 88 full colour maps and 10,000 places, creeks, rivers, lakes, and mountains; all Wildlife Management Units are clearly outlined and numbered; locations of the BC Forest Service Recreation sites (over 1000); an index with descriptions of over 100 wildlife viewing areas and Wildlife Reserves, nature conservancies and bird sanctuaries; locations of National and Provincial Parks, with a comprehensive index listing of facilities.

SUGGESTED REFERENCE MATERIALS

A Birders Guide to Vancouver Island (1993), by Keith Taylor, 168 pages

Field Guide to the Birds of North America 2nd Edition(1987), by National Geographic Society; 464 pages; 220 colour plates; distribution maps

British Columbia Recreational Atlas 2nd Edition (1995), 130 pages

Field Guide to Western Bird Songs , Cornell Laboratory of Ornithology with Roger T. Peterson, Houghton Mifflin (1992); 3 C60 cassettes (or 2 CD's) with 28 page booklet; calls and songs of 500 species.

Biitish Columbia Accommodations Guide; approx.130 pages; this free comprehensive accommodations guide published yearly by the Ministry of Tourism, Recreation and Culture lists all of the hotels, motels, private campgrounds, and a few choice Bed and Breakfasts (you will need to buy a book for a more complete listing) available throughout B.C. The guide is arranged by districts, then towns within districts, then a listing of all of the available accommodations and Travel InfoCentres in each community. There is an index of the communities, district maps. This guide is a must for travellers to B.C.!

The MilePost .. 45th Edition (1993); 656 pages; Vernon Publications; available in many bookshops. A must for anyone birding the Alaska Highway! All of the northern highways in B.C., Alberta, Alaska, Yukon and Northwest Territories are logged kilometer-by-kilometer with comprehensive information on gas stations, restaurants, accommodation, camping, ferry schedules and price listings, full-colour photographs, and points of interest; includes road and town maps and advertisments.

ADDITIONAL READING

The Birds of British Columbia Vol. 1, 2 and 3, by R.W. Campbell et al; comprehensive treatise of the provinces nonpasserine birds and passerines

Birds of the Okanagan Valley, British Columbia (1987), by R. Cannings, R.Cannings, S. Cannings; 420 pages of regional biology of the 307 species in this major birding destination

PESTS

Infectious ticks that may carry Lyme Disease or "Rocky Mountain Fever", though rare, could be picked up in brushy areas. These are best avoided by staying on paths and roadways and using insect sprays. Check yourself and remove any ticks immediately. Ticks are a minor problem in British Columbia.

Mosquitoes and Blackflies can be intolerable in northern British Columbia. Elsewhere you will find mosquitoes to be nonexistent or of moderate annoyance, or only intolerable in the twilight hours and after dark around marshes or other wet areas. These biting insects are at their worse in June; cover your skin with light clothing and wear a deet repellent. If you are camping, be sure to have "no see 'em" screening on your tent to keep out gnats. Mosquito coils or a campfire will keep mosquitoes away when they emerge in the evening. Mosquitoes do not carry any diseases in Canada.

There are poisonous snakes in British Columbia (as there are almost everywhere), just use common sense and a little caution. Pacific Rattlesnakes are frequently observed in talus and other rock debris areas of the Okanagan.

The Regions of British Columbia

An Overview

To fully appreciate the birding experience, it is valuable to have an understanding of the geography of the province and the general regions in which bird species can be found. Such an understanding can assist in planning trips and in ensuring that you see the as many species as you can.

GEOGRAPHY AND CLIMATE

British Columbia's topography varies significantly and may be divided into ten separate eco-regions: The Northeast Pacific Ocean (pelagic waters), Georgia Depression, Humid Maritime Coast and Mountains (coastal regions, wet forest and alpine), Southern Interior or Okanagan Valley, Central Interior or Cariboo Parklands, Southern Interior Mountains, Sub-Boreal Interior, Boreal Plains and Taiga Plains, (the last two known collectively as the Peace River Parklands), and Northern Boreal Mountains.

Four of these eco-regions will be concentrated on in this guide, collectively producing all of the bird species to be found in British Columbia: The Georgia Depression, the Okanagan Valley, the Peace River Parklands and a small portion of the Northern Boreal Forest - the Haines Road area.

Northeast Pacific Ocean or Pelagic Waters

The oceanic portion of the province is divided into the cooler Alaska current, reaching the northern Queen Charlotte Islands in summer, and the warmer California current, reaching northern Vancouver Island during summer.

Organized pelagic birding trips during the fall off Vancouver Island produce most of the predictable, but exciting species that occur in our waters (see Pelagics). Pelagic birds are rarely or impossible to see from shore and and a seaworthy boat capable of voyaging 50 kilometers offshore is required. An individual will find that hiring such a vessel will be very expensive indeed, requiring a reservation on an organized trip, or using one of the many ferries plying the B.C. coast; the ferries, however, will produce only a fractional number of species. As access to this habitat is limited by season, the distance travelled offshore, and by the number of trips available, serious pelagic birders will find that such rare species as Laysan Albatross, Short-tailed Albatross, Mottled Petrel, Parakeet Auklet, and even a recently recorded Murphy's Petrel, are unattainable in Canada. If you are planning a pelagic trip, a half-days drive to Westport in Washington State will give you more opportunities to find unusual pelagics.

Georgia Depression

The Georgia Depression is a large basin containing the East Coast of Vancouver Island (with the Southeast Coastal Lowlands), and the "Lower Mainland", the coastal lowlands surrounding the city of Vancouver, north to include the Sunshine Coast, and eastward along the Fraser Valley.

Although the Georgia Depression is in the Humid Maritime Highlands Ecodivision (see below), it is distinguished from the adjacent wet coast forests and high mountains by an expansive, fertile, marshy alluvial floodplain Ð the Fraser Delta (and other adjacent lowlands). This interesting coastal plain holds a juxtaposition of varied habitats including drier deciduous forests of arbutus and garry oak communities, drier extensive mixed forests of red alder, black cottonwood, bigleaf maple, western red-cedar and Douglas-fir, urban parks and agricultural communities, urban development, open sandy shore, rocky coastlines, picturesque lagoons, huge intertidal mudflats, freshwater marshes and saltwater marshes.

Human impact is evident almost everywhere with a population of well over two million inhabitants. The "Lower Mainland" and the Saanich Peninsula on adjacent Vancouver Island, although containing most of the urbanized land in the province, have many excellent birding sites. The concentrated birding in the region by numerous experienced people has produced many of the province's most exciting accidental species.

Many bird species are most common or best looked for here than elsewhere in the province: Black-crowned Night-Heron, Green Heron, Cattle Egret (rare late fall), Trumpeter Swan and Tundra Swan (winter), Mute Swan, Snow Goose (winter), Brant (spring), Eurasian Wigeon (winter), Black Scoter (mainly winter), White-winged Scoter, Surf Scoter, Harlequin Duck, shorebirds (see below), Heermann's Gull, Little Gull (rare), Mew Gull, Thayer's Gull (fall-winter), Western Gull, Glaucous-winged Gull, Common Tern (fall), Caspian Tern (summer), Common Murre, Pigeon Guillemot, Marbled Murrelet, Ancient Murrelet (Victoria-winter), Rhinoceros Auklet, Tufted Puffin (Vancouver Island-summer), Band-tailed Pigeon, Barn Owl, Western Screech Owl, Anna's Hummingbird (Victoria), Tropical Kingbird (rare, late fall), Ash-throated Flycatcher (rare), Pacific-slope Flycatcher, Sky Lark (Victoria-local), Purple Martin (Vancouver Island-local), Northwestern Crow, Chestnut-backed Chickadee, Bushtit, Bewick's Wren, Crested Myna (Vancouver-local), Hutton's Vireo, Black-throated Gray Warbler, Spotted Towhee, Golden-crowned Sparrow (migration, winter), Western Tanager, and House Finch.

Migration of shorebirds is quite spectacular and the Fraser Delta supports huge intertidal mudflats and other wetland habitats. As such, it has an unparalleled variety of shorebirds along its nutrient-rich shores. The sewage treatment settling ponds at Iona Island are internationally recognized as one of the world's best sites for shorebirds; Eurasian vagrants occur with regularity in late summer through the fall months. American Avocet, Black-necked Stilt, Snowy Plover, Marbled Godwit, Bar-tailed Godwit, Hudsonian Godwit, Bristle-thighed Curlew, Far Eastern Curlew, Willet, Spotted Redshank, Terek Sandpiper, Stilt Sandpiper, Red Knot, Curlew Sandpiper, White-rumped Sandpiper, Baird's Sandpiper, Little Stint, Temminck's Stint, Rufous-necked Stint, Spoonbill Sandpiper, Sharp-tailed Sandpiper, Ruff, Upland Sandpiper, and Buff-breasted Sandpiper are among the specialities or rarest of shorebirds that have appeared in the Georgia Depression. Both Pacific and American Golden-Plovers and Semipalmated Sandpiper are recorded in numbers annually.

Black Oystercatcher, Wandering Tattler, Black Turnstone, Surfbird, and Rock Sandpiper are shorebirds that associate with rocky shorelines and, although found locally at Lighthouse Park in West Vancouver, are more easily located on Vancouver Island and along the Sunshine Coast.

The Georgia Depression is also a major flyway for a wealth of migrant waterfowl and continues to be of international importance as a wintering area with huge annual concentrations. Many loons, grebes, and duck species that summered and breed in the interior (or the arctic) are found to winter along the rich marine shores or neighbouring unfrozen agricultural fields, marshes, lakes, and pools. The Fraser Delta in particular is winter home to tens of thousands of waterfowl, including a large proportion of the world's Greater Snow Geese population, some 20,000 individuals. Littoral species such as wintering Pacific Loon, Red-throated Loon, Western Grebe, Red-necked Grebe, Horned Grebe, Eared Grebe, Double-crested Cormorant, Brandt's Cormorant and Pelagic Cormorant, and wintering Greater White-fronted Geese (uncommon), Gadwall, Green-winged Teal, American Wigeon, Northern Pintail, Northern Shoveler, Ruddy Duck, Wood Duck, Canvasback, Redhead, Ring-necked Duck, Tufted Duck (rare), Greater Scaup, Lesser Scaup, Oldsquaw, Barrow's Goldeneye, Common Goldeneye, Bufflehead and Red-breastd Merganser are expected.

The Fraser Delta is also a noteworthy area for wintering raptors with Bald Eagle, Northern Harrier, Red-tailed Hawk, Rough-legged Hawk, American Kestrel, Merlin, Peregrine Falcon, and an occasional Gyrfalcon (or even Prairie Falcon) hunting over the expansive fallow agricultural fields. The Fraser Delta is also the best area in Canada for locating Barn Owl, here at their northern limits. Short-eared Owl, Long-eared Owl, Great Horned Owl, Snowy Owl (winter), Western Screech-Owl and Northern Saw-whet Owl are also found with regularity.

The Georgia Depression has the best climate in Canada, basically a climate of moderately dry, warm springs between the months of March and June, with dry, sunny summers between the months of July and late October. The Georgia Depression lies in the lee of the Vancouver Island and Olympic Peninsula Ranges. The subsequent rainshadow created by these mountains produces drier conditions than the adjacent coastal areas. Summer temperatures range from cool nights of 15 C to mid-day highs of 20 C to 30 C, rarely hotter. Winters are wet with endless drizzle and cloud cover, temperatures are usually above freezing with little snowfall at sea level. Temperatures range between 1 C and 8 C.

Humid Maritime Highlands (Coast and Mountains)

Along the Pacific Coast, the Coast Mountains, Nass Basin, and Nass Ranges hold a huge, irregular strip of wet coniferous forest dominated by Douglas-fir, western red-cedar, yellow-cedar, western hemlock, Sitka spruce and amabilis fir. The region includes the windward side of these mountains, the west coast of Vancouver Island, and all of the Queen Charlotte Islands. Here, among the world's densest coniferous forests, are towering monolithic Douglas-firs; high overhead, sunlight penetrates the canopy in a cathedral manner, filtering beams of silky-light across their immense trunks. Along watercourses and in disturbed (burned, logged) areas the successional species are broad-leafed maple and red alder; the latter is paramount for breeding Warbling Vireo. These wet forests are akin to the wet forests of the Southern Interior Mountains, neither is especially noted for having a richness in bird species in the conifer belts. A few species associated with these forests are Band-tailed Pigeon, Spotted Owl, Western Screech-Owl, Red-breasted Sapsucker, Pacific-slope Flycatcher, Steller's Jay, Northwestern Crow, Chestnut-backed Chickadee, Winter Wren, Varied Thrush, and Townsend's Warbler. The coastal mountains have large areas of alpine (most of which is inaccessible) that hold the characteristic birds of this region.

The littoral waters of the coastal straits, inlets, shores, and the adjacent lowlands are rich in species, however. The coastline is a major flyway for a plenitude of species including a wide variety of waterbirds and shorebirds to a mixture of passerines. As this habitat is representative of the Georgia Depression, it is treated more fully under that heading.

The climate of this region at lower elevations is temperate; temperatures being influenced by the relative proximity to the sea. As one accends the spectacular peaks to alpine, temperatures drop accordingly. Temperatures along the coast are generally above freezing in winter months with little snowfall, midday summer temperatures are seldom warmer than 20 C to 30 C with cool nights. Precipitation and cloud cover are abundant for much of year, with torrential rains during the winter. A brief reprieve of dry weather with plenty of sunshine usually occurs during July through early September.

Southern Interior or Okanagan Valley

The dry interior of British Columbia is the northernmost extension of the great semi-arid steppe plateaus of the western United States, known collectively as "The Great Basin". The region includes the leeward ranges of the Coast Mountains, the Thompson Plateau, the Clear Range, the Okanagan Range, and the western side of the Okanagan and Shuswap highlands.

The Okanagan Valley, one of the only desert-like habitats in Canada, lies close to the Washington state-border in southern British Columbia. The Okanagan is a "must" on anyone's itinerary to British Columbia. The Okanagan Valley provides an excellent illustration of the altitudinal zonation of vegetation and altitudinal segregation of bird species in British Columbia, the diversity of habitats produces an unusual richness of accompanying avifauna, some 308 species have occurred with 193 species known to breed regularly of which 107 are resident.

Typical steppe or bunchgrass prairie dominated by arid-zone plants including sagebrush, bluebunch wheatgrass, cheat grass, knapweed, antelope-brush, red threeawn grass, rabbitbrush and prickly-pear cactus predominate in the valleys, basins, and on the lower slopes and benchlands. This habitat has been, and continues to be encroached upon by cattle grassing, human habitation, and the planting of orchards. Where habitat remains, characteristic birds such as Long-billed Curlew, Mountain Bluebird, Grasshopper Sparrow (local or rare), Vesper Sparrow, Lark Sparrow, and Western Meadowlark are still found. In areas where sagebrush is dominant Sage Thrasher (local and rare) and Brewer's Sparrows are still found. In winter these areas are quite unproductive except for a few Gray Partridge, Northern Shrike, Horned Lark and Snow Bunting.

In the arid valley bottoms are a string of lakes, and throughout the region several mineral-rich sloughs; both harbour many species of migrant and nesting grebes, ducks, and migrant shorebirds. Surrounding these watercourses are marshes and narrow bands of dense riparian growth: in the red-osier, dogwood, willows, chokecherry and mountain alder are found Ruffed Grouse, Long-eared Owl, Western Screech-Owl, Eastern Kingbird, Willow Flycatcher, Tree Swallow, Black-capped Chickadee, Veery, Gray Catbird, Red-eyed Vireo, Yellow Warbler, Yellow-breasted Chat, American Redstart and Black-headed Grosbeak. Yellow-headed Blackbird are found among the other common widespread species breeding in the marshes.

Several crags or rocky bluffs with talus slopes are found along the Okanagan Valley. Characteristic birds found are Chukar, White-throated Swift, Violet-green Swallow, Canyon Wren and Rock Wren. Cliff faces may harbour an eyrie of a Golden Eagle or possibly Prairie Falcon. In the brushy patches near these bluffs are Say's Phoebe, Nashville Warbler, Lazuli Bunting, and possibly a Calliope Hummingbird feeding on thistle flowers.

The arid lower elevations of the valley floor soon gives way to the lower edge of the lower montane forest, where generally cooler and moister conditions permit. Here, in the scattered ponderosa pines, are American Kestrel, Lewis' Woodpecker, Western Kingbird, and Mountain Bluebird. In continuous tracts are Common Poorwill, White-headed Woodpecker (rare),

Clark's Nutcracker, White-breasted Nuthatch, Pygmy Nuthatch, and Western Bluebird. These forests are usually open, with little or no underbrush except along streams; treeless areas support sagebrush and bunchgrass. In juxtaposition to this habitat along the permanent streams, draws, and ravines there is a shady habitat of trembling aspen with dense thickets of ground story herbage that attracts Cooper's Hawk, Ruffed Grouse, Black-chinned Hummingbird, Calliope Hummingbird, Rufous Hummingbird, Red-naped Sapsucker, Western Wood-Pewee, House Wren, Veery, Warbling Vireo, Nashville Warbler, and MacGillivary's Warbler.

Higher, where Douglas-fir begins to invade the larger stands of ponderosa pine, the uncommon Flammulated Owl will be found nesting in summer.

With an ever-increasing elevation, and with decreasing numbers of ponderosa pine, montane forests of Douglas-fir become the dominant sight and trembling aspen and lodgepole pine appear. Where there are western larch look for Williamson's Sapsucker. Others in this much cooler and wetter zone include: Great Horned Owl, Northern Pygmy-Owl, Northern Saw-whet Owl, Dusky Flycatcher, Steller's Jay, Mountain Chickadee, Red-breasted Nuthatch, Townsend's Solitaire, Swainson's Thrush, Cassin's Vireo, Western Tanager and Cassin's Finch.

Still higher, in the sub-alpine (above 1,250 m.), Engelmann spruce, lodgepole pine, and subalpine fir support Northern Goshawk, Spruce Grouse, Blue Grouse, Boreal Owl (rare), Three-toed Woodpecker, Olive-sided Flycatcher, Hammond's Flycatcher, Gray Jay, Clark's Nutcracker, Mountain Chickadee, Boreal Chickadee, Winter Wren, Golden-crowned Kinglet, Ruby-crowned Kinglet, Townsend's Solitaire, Hermit Thrush, Varied Thrush, American Robin, Yellow-rumped Warbler, Northern Waterthrush, Dark-eyed Junco, White-crowned Sparrow, Fox Sparrow, Pine Siskin, Red Crossbill, White-winged Crossbill, and Pine Grosbeak.

At timberline white-bark pines and low stature sub-alpine fir become scattered and dwarfed, invaded by numerous small wet meadows. Above the treeline in the alpine meadows of Mount Baldy, Apex Mountain, and Brent Mountain at 2,200 m. are White-tailed Ptarmigan (rare), Horned Lark and American Pipit.

The Okanagan Valley has long been a focal point for birders looking for the specialities of the Great Basin and dry cordilleran forest that barely reach north into Canada: White-headed Woodpecker, Canyon Wren, Sage Thrasher, and Gray Flycatcher are restricted in Canada to the Okanagan Valley. Birds such as Long-billed Curlew, Wilson's Phalarope, Prairie Falcon, Chukar, Gray Partridge, Flammulated Owl, Burrowing Owl, Common Poorwill, White-throated Swift, Black-chinned Hummingbird, Calliope Hummingbird, Lewis' Woodpecker, Williamson's Sapsucker, Pygmy Nuthatch, Rock Wren, Gray Catbird, Nashville Warbler, Yellow-breasted Chat, Lazuli Bunting, Grasshopper Sparrow, Lark Sparrow, Brewer's Sparrow, Bobolink, and Cassin's Finch are most easily found here.

The Okanagan lies in a rain-shadow, cast by the Coast and Cascade Ranges. The valleys are quite dry with 10 inches of rain a year, there is ever-increasing precipitation with higher elevation. June is a fairly wet month, followed by very dry and hot summers. High temperatures reach 30 C to 38 C at mid-day. Winters are cold, falling below freezing by early December. Low temperatures are highly variable depending on Arctic fronts with lows between - 2 C to - 15 C. Snow is usually on the ground intermittently. Altitude as well as seasons effect the temperatures here with high temperatures as low as 5 C on the alpine tundra above 2,200 m.

Southern Interior Mountains

The Southern Interior Mountains, lying east of the interior plateaus in the southeastern portion of the province, consists of the Columbia and Continental Ranges of the Rocky Mountains and the southern Rocky Mountain Trench. These series of massive mountains and alternating trenches create a complex geography and an accompaniment of great habitat diversity because of the combinations of very wet mountains and very dry rainshadow valleys.

There are seven vegetation zones including the dry southeastern area on either side of the East Kootenay Trench where ponderosa pine is the main seral species. Noteworthy are the extensive marshes along the upper reaches of the Columbia River and the wetlands associated with the Creston valley. The coniferous forest in the Southern Interior Mountains is arranged in striking belts. At lower elevations there is a montane belt of Douglas-fir and western larch. Floodplains often have black cottonwood, spruce, and red-osier dogwood, whilst grasslands are practically nonexistent. In the sub-alpine belt, Engelmann spruce and subalpine fir dominate with western hemlock and western redcedar where there is more precipitation. The uppermost belt, alpine, is dominated by rock and glaciers with patches of heath vegetation and sedge-grass meadows.

This biotic region is very similar to the Humid Coast Forest avifauna and the only interior region that supports Chestnut-backed Chickadee. Steller's Jay and Varied Thrush are also among the similar species that share these wetter forests. This region claims the only breeding colony of Forster's Tern, located at Creston, which is also one of the few places that Western Grebe and the rare Clark's Grebe nest. Creston-Lister is the centre of abundance for Wild Turkey in the province. Black-billed Cuckoo, although rare, occurs regularly.

There are cold snowy winters, ranging from just below freezing to well-below freezing with Arctic fronts. Warm summers with ample precipitation are the rule with mid-day temperatures of 20 C to 35 C. Temperature is higher and rainfall lower in the rainshadow region of the Rocky Mountain Trench.

Central Interior or Cariboo Plateau

The Central Interior Mountains lie to the east of the Coast Mountains, between the Fraser Basin and the Thompson Plateau; the region containing the Chilcotin, Cariboo, and Nechako plateaus. The Chilkotin Ranges lie along the east side of the Pacific Ranges, their serrated peaks rising progressively higher as they approach the granite ranges to the west. Between the ranges lies gently sloping areas of undissected upland plateaus and parklands. The Cariboo Parklands of central British Columbia are characteristically a patchwork of open forests of lodgepole pine and Douglas-fir, with smaller groves of white spruce and quaking aspen nestled among gently rolling foothills; dominant are major grasslands. Blue and Spruce Grouse inhabit the forests with the rare Great Gray Owl found in the ecotone between the forest edge and grasslands. In the grasslands of sagebrush, rabbitbrush, bluebunch wheatgrass, and needlegrass are Swainson's Hawk, Sharp-tailed Grouse, Horned Lark, Western Meadowlark, and Savannah Sparrow. This region has a mixture of bird species that may be classified as "southwestern" and "northwestern"

Meandering streams and low depressions have created the numerous small lakes and marshes that dot the area. These wetlands contain concentrations of breeding waterfowl, some of which may have spent the winter along the British Columbia coast, leaving in April for the interior. Noteworthy is the only breeding colony of the American White Pelican in the province, nesting at Stum Lake on the Chilcotin Plateau. The "prairie sloughs" and surrounding grasslands are also centres of importance for the breeding of Eared Grebe, Sandhill Crane, Barrow's Goldeneye, Long-billed Curlew, Greater Yellowlegs, Ring-billed Gull, Herring Gull, Black Tern, and Yellow-headed Blackbird.

Climbing higher, the upland regions have sub-boreal zones and limited sub-alpine and alpine habitats.

The region has a typical continental climate: cold winters and warm summers. Lying in the rainshadow of the Coast Mountains, precipitation mainly falls in early summer with convective showers. Warm summers are the rule with intense surface heating; mid-day temperatures range from 30 - 40 C. Winter temperatures range from just below freezing to well-below freezing with Arctic fronts and snow cover is generally moderate.

Sub-Boreal Interior

The Sub-Boreal Interior is the northernmost extension of the humid continental uplands. It lies adjacent to the northern edge of the Cariboo Parklands and Southern Interior Mountains in the north-central part of the province; the towns of Quesnel, Prince George, and Mackenzie lie within its boundaries. The region consists of the large Fraser Basin, and the southern portion of the Skeena, Omineca, Muskwa, and Hart Ranges.

An expanse of gently rolling country in the interior plateaus are punctuated with a labyrinth of rivers, lakes and wetlands. Around these are extensive regions of coniferous forests dominated by white spruce and subalpine fir. Floodplains have black cottonwood and white spruce, with a lush understory of red-osier dogwood and deciduous brush. Boreal Owl, Yellow-bellied Flycatcher (a small population around Prince George), Magnolia Warbler, and Rusty Blackbird are three typical inhabitants of these boreal forests, while Herring Gull and Black Tern nest in the widely available bogs created by the poor drainage in the Fraser Basin.

The complex series of mountain ranges rising from the Fraser Basin have long, rounded ridges that eventually become jagged and serrated in profile, created by alpine glaciation eons ago. Lower slopes contain edaphic grassy areas, grading into Engelmann spruce, lodgepole pine, and sub-alpine fir forests, then extensive rocky alpine tundra at higher elevations. The multiple hues of the rocks of the alpine peaks are a testimony to their turbulent geological past.

Winters are very cold, well below freezing, with moderately warm summers. Precipitation is ample all year and snow can cause road closures.

Boreal and Taiga Plains or Peace River Parklands

A small portion of the Boreal Plains (that extend eastward across Alberta to Saskatchewan) lies in the northeast portion of British Columbia. The boreal component of the Peace River Parklands (three-quarters of the region) is centered around the towns of Fort St. John and Dawson Creek, east of the Rocky Mountains. The semi-open country of deep river valleys, moist shrub-grasslands, and groves of trembling aspen has an appearance much like that of the Cariboo Parklands, but with a different avifauna. Dominating the higher elevations are white and black spruce and lodgepole pine.

The Taiga Plains (or sub-arctic ecodivision) lies to the north of the boreal forests, extending from the Fort Nelson River Basin to the border of the Northwest Territories and beyond. Dominant in lower elevation riparian areas are balsam poplar, while white and black spruce, lodgepole pine and tamarack replace the poplars in the well drained upland sites. Wetlands and muskeg occur extensively with the poor drainage that occurs throughout the region. The area is known for its breeding Lesser Yellowlegs and Solitary Sandpipers and abundant Spruce Grouse. This is one of the better regions for breeding Yellow-bellied Flycatcher, Black-and-white Warbler, Cape May Warbler, Bay-breasted Warbler, Canada Warbler, Le Conte's Sparrow, Swamp Sparrow, and Rose-breasted Grosbeak.

The Peace River Parklands, lying northeast of the Rocky Mountains' Hart and Muskwa Ranges, is an interesting area in British Columbia to the birder because the breeding ranges of several "eastern" birds terminate here: Upland Sandpiper, Broad-winged Hawk, Eastern Phoebe, Philadelphia Vireo,

Black-and-white Warbler, Cape May Warbler, Bay-breasted Warbler, Palm Warbler, Mourning Warbler, Connecticut Warbler, Canada Warbler, Rose-breasted Grosbeak, Le Conte's Sparrow, Nelson's Sharp-tailed Sparrow (local), and Common Grackle. It is also the best region of the province to concentrate on finding Sandhill Crane, White-rumped Sandpiper (migration), Sharp-tailed Grouse, Northern Hawk-Owl, Boreal Owl, Yellow-bellied Sapsucker, Black-backed Woodpecker, Three-toed Woodpecker, Least Flycatcher, Alder Flycatcher, Yellow-bellied Flycatcher, Blue Jay, Bohemian Waxwing, Tennessee Warbler, Magnolia Warbler, Black-throated Green Warbler, Blackpoll Warbler, Ovenbird, Clay-colored Sparrow, White-throated Sparrow, Swamp Sparrow, Rusty Blackbird, and in winter Hoary Redpoll. Winter finds this region virtually devoid of any bird life except for a few Spruce Grouse, Three-toed Woodpecker, Gray Jay, Common Raven, Boreal Chickadee, and a few winter finches.

The climate of the Peace River Parklands is typically continental, generally dry with sunny skies. The region is very cold in winter, well below zero, due to latitude and the lack of barriers to stop Arctic air masses. Winters are long and summers brief and moderately warm with midday highs usually around 20 - 30 C. There are short daylight hours in winter and long hours of daylight in summer. There is little precipitation throughout the year, although roads will have times of snow closures. The Taiga plains in summer are often covered in cloud with unstable weather.

Northern Boreal Mountains

The Northern Boreal Mountains (or sub-arctic highlands) extend from northern British Columbia, east of the Boundary Ranges of the Coast Mountains, beyond to the Yukon, Northwest Territories, and Alaska. Intermontane lowlands, high mountains, and plateaus are characteristic of the region and are strongly influenced by Arctic air. Muskeg and black spruce are found in low-lying areas of poor drainage, while drier low valleys may have willow-birch shrublands. Higher, on middle elevation slopes, are white spruce and sub-alpine fir with brakes of trembling aspen. The highest elevations support alpine, the wind-swept barrens of lichen-covered rock supporting White-tailed Ptarmigan and Rock Ptarmigan. Below these summits are alpine grasslands and twisted and dwarfed willows where Willow Ptarmigan appear.

The Alaska Highway traverses through the region to higher elevations at Summit Pass in Stone Mountain Park and along the Haines Road where three species of ptarmigan can be seen just off the highway right-of-way. Pacific Loon, Semipaimated Plover, American Golden Plover (probable), Hudsonian Godwit (rare), Greater Yellowlegs, Lesser Yellowlegs, Solitary Sandpiper, Wandering Tattler (rare), Red-necked Phalarope, Short-billed Dowitcher, Least Sandpiper, Arctic Tern, Gyrfalcon, Short-eared Owl, Say's Phoebe, Gray-cheeked Thrush, Northern Shrike, American Tree Sparrow, Brewer's "Timberline" Sparrow, Golden-crowned Sparrow, Lincoln's Sparrow, Smith's Longspur, Snow Bunting, Common Redpoll, Gray-crowned Rosy Finch, and Rusty Blackbird are all breeding specialities along the Haines Road. The Gray-cheeked Thrush and Smith's Longspur are rarely seen away from this site in B.C.

Spruce Grouse, Northern Hawk-Owl, Boreal Owl, Three-toed Woodpecker, Black-backed Woodpecker, Gray Jay, Boreal Chickadee, Bohemian Waxwing, Red Crossbill, White-winged Crossbill, Pine Grosbeak, and Blackpoll Warbler are widespread characteristic species of boreal and sub-alpine forests.

Winters are long and extremely cold, well below zero due to both elevation and latitude, summers are short and cool. Precipitation varies little throughout the year because the region lies in a rainshadow; although snowfall during the winter can block all roads but the Alaska Highway, continuously.

Alpine

Alpine scenery is spectacular! Vistas present fantastic views of the surrounding precipitous crags, distant valleys, and emerald alpine lakes. At dawn, mountain peaks often poke through the early morning clouds, resembling islands in a white sea.

Alpine is widespread in British Columbia on the highest peaks, most of which are unaccessible. The few areas that are attainable are on gravel or logging roads, at ski developments, and at communication installations, or, as is the case for the Haines area, on paved road. Characteristic birds of the alpine are Golden Eagle, Gyrfalcon, White-tailed Ptarmigan, Rock Ptarmigan and Willow Ptarmigan (mainly northern), Horned Lark, Gray Jay, American Pipit, American Tree Sparrow (northern), Golden-crowned Sparrow, Fox Sparrow, and Gray-crowned Rosy Finch. Pacific Loon, American Golden Plover, Wandering Tattler, Red-necked Phalarope, Arctic Tern, Gyrfalcon, Brewer's ("Timberline") Sparrow, Smith's Longspur, and Snow Bunting are restricted to the Haines Road.

COMMON, CONSPICUOUS ROADSIDE SPECIES:

The following partial list of species may be seen en route to destinations, commonly viewed flying across roads, in fields, on roadside poles and wires, or in roadside pools and marshes.

Great Blue Heron
Canada Goose
Mallard
Killdeer
Glaucous-winged Gull (coast)
Red-tailed Hawk
American Kestrel(interior)
Common Pheasant
Rock Dove
Rufous Hummingbird
Belted Kingfisher
Northern Flicker
Downy Woodpecker
Eastern Kingbird interior)
Western Kingbird (interior)
Violet-green Swallow

Barn Swallow
Steller's Jay
Black-billed Magpie (interior)
American Crow (interior)
Northwestern Crow (coast)
Common Raven
Mountain Bluebird (interior)
American Robin
European Starling
Savannah Sparrow
Song Sparrow
Western Meadowlark (interior)
Red-winged Blackbird
Brewer's Blackbird
House Sparrow and House Finch
American Goldfinch

PELAGICS

Albatross
Short-tailed Albatross   R
Black-footed Albatross
Laysan Albatross   R

Gadfly Petrels

Mottled Petrel   R

Storm-Petrels
Leach's Storm-Petrel
Fork-tailed Storm-Petrel
Skuas, Gulls, Terns
South Polar Skua
Pomarine Jaeger
Parasitic Jaeger
Long-tailed Jaeger
Black-legged Kittiwake
Red-legged Kittiwake   Acc
Sabine's Gull
Arctic Tern
Aleutian Tern   Acc
Thick-billed Murre   R

Shearwaters and Petrels
Northern Fulmar
Flesh-footed Shearwater
Sooty Shearwater
Short-tailed Shearwater
Pink-footed Shearwater
Streaked Shearwater   H
Buller's Shearwater
Black-vented Shearwater   R

Frigatebirds
Magnificent Frigatebird   Acc
Tropicbirds
Red-tailed Tropicbird   Acc

Phalaropes
Red-necked Phalarope
Red Phalarope

Alcids
Xantus' Murrelet   Acc
Cassin's Auklet
Parakeet Auklet   R
Horned Puffin   R
Tufted Puffin

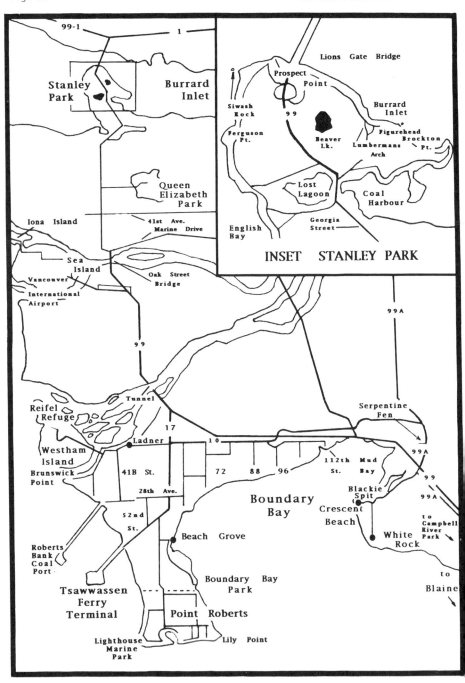

MAP 2   VANCOUVER   LOOPS 1-2

LOOP 1   DELTA - WHITE ROCK

TSAWWASSEN FERRY TERMINAL

We begin our tour at the Tsawwassen Ferry Terminal.

After leaving the ferry terminal, pull over onto the wide shoulder of the road along the three kilometer stretch of the man-made spit.

There are large rafts of sea ducks present during the winter months and tens of thousands of Dunlin on the vast mudflats at the head of the bay. Loons, grebes, cormorants, and gull species are well represented. Heermann's Gull are seen fairly regularly as post-breeding wanderers in late summer and fall. A small population of Brant winter in offshore waters, while numbers can be seen during the spring migration period. The rock jettys at the terminal often have Harlequin Duck, Black-bellied Plover, Greater Yellowlegs, and Black Turnstone and occasionally Sanderling in winter. A lucky observer may see a Parasitic Jaeger harrassing a flock of Common Tern in the fall. A Lapland Longspur or Snow Bunting may frequent the weedy patches between the drift-logs on the beaches along the causeway in the late fall.

Tsawwassen Ferry Terminal to Point Roberts, Wash.

Set your trip odometer to (00.0 km.). After the long man-made causeway, turn right at the second set of traffic lights (6.2 km.) off Highway 1 7 onto 56th Street (Point Roberts Road) towards the communities of Tsawwassen, B.C. and Point Roberts, Washington.

Along the drive you could turn left at the first set of lights at (5.2km.) for Reifel Refuge.

Continue south on Point Roberts Road, through the community of Tsawwassen to the border crossing, passing the Best Western Tsawwassen Inn en route (0.9 km.) (7.1 km.). After an additional (3.4 km.) (10.5 km.), show your identification to the U.S.A. Immigration Officer and continue onto the small isolated peninsula of Washington State and the town of Point Roberts. At the border crossing, Point Roberts Road becomes Tyee Drive.

POINT ROBERTS

Surrounded by the sea on three sides and Canada on the fourth, Point Roberts, while outside of Canada, is within the Vancouver checklist area. Birds seen at the point are, of course, not countable on your British Columbia or Canada lists. The U.S.A. portion of the peninsula provides excellent birding opportunities, and is especially noted for pelagic species and for wintering Yellow-billed Loon.

After the border crossing, turn right off Tyee Drive at Ben's Store onto Gulf Road (1.7 km.) (12.5 km.), keeping left at the jog and passing Marine Drive to the Strait of Georgia (0.9 km.) (13.4 km.). Scrutinize the many Double-crested Cormorant and Pelagic Cormorant roosting on the old pier at the end of this road for Brandt's Cormorant during the winter months. As you drive along all of the residential streets keep an eye open for California Quail, as Point Roberts is the only area on the lower mainland where these introduced resident gamebirds are common.

LIGHTHOUSE MARINE PARK

Return to Marine Drive, turning right (south) to where Marine Drive curves east and becomes Edwards Drive (1.2 km.) (14.8 km.). (Edwards Drive again becomes Marine Drive after 0.8 km.). Lighthouse Marine Park is to the right which is the access to the extreme southwest tip of Point Roberts. The point juts out into the straits, an advantage when trying to locate those wayward pelagics in the fall.

Sooty Shearwater (there is a record for Short-tailed Shearwater), Red Phalarope, Black-legged Kittiwake, and Sabine's Gull are possible in those years when pelagics invade the inner straits (see Iona South Jetty). Common Loon, Pacific Loon, and Red-throated Loon are all fairly common, while the rare Yellow-billed Loon is almost an annual event at this, the lower mainland's best site for this species. Oldsquaw, Common Murre, Pigeon Guillemot, and Marbled Murrelet are regular at the tip during winter. Rhinoceros Auklet and Ancient Murrelet, though very uncommon, are possible. Heermann's Gull, those distinctive post-breeding wanderers from the Gulf of California, disperse northwards each summer arriving around the point, their only regular site near Vancouver, in late June: maximum concentrations occur in October before returning southward in early November. Common Tern are often harrased by Parasitic Jaeger in the fall, while Pomarine Jaeger and Long-tailed Jaeger, though rare, could make an appearance. Look around the rocks for Harlequin Duck.

Continue east on Edwards Drive, veering left onto Marine Drive (1.0 km.) (15.8 km.), then immediately left onto Tyee Drive, and then right onto Apa Road (0.8 km.) (16.6 km.). Follow Apa Road to Larguad Drive, turning right (0.8 km.) (17.4 km.) to Edwards Drive (once again!) (0.5 km.) (17.9 km.). Turn right to its termination with the breakwater at the entrance of the Point Roberts Marina (0.4 km.) (18.3 km.). Black Turnstone are uncommon and Rock Sandpiper are very rare. The rocky breakwall is also an excellent site for those "clowns of the sea", the exquisitely decorative Harlequin Duck. The vacant lot is private property; birders are tolerated.

Return to Apa Road, turning right and continue along Apa Road, turning right onto South Beach Road (1.4 km.) (19.7 km.) to its termination with the sea (0.5 km.) (20.2 km.). Walk to the left at low tide to Lily Point, about (1.8 km.) away. Stay below the high tideline as many of the beach fronts have been posted. Waterfowl often concentrate at Lily Point in late winter and early spring before migration on this, the extreme southeastern corner of the peninsula.

Point Roberts to Beach Grove Regional Park

(00.0km.) From the foot of South Beach Road, return to Apa Road, turn right and continue to Boundary Bay Road, turning left (1.5 km.). The mixed, moist woods containing alder, cedar, and Douglas-fir along the drive are habitat for the uncommon resident Hutton's Vireo. After (1.9 km.) (3.4 km.), continue north on North and Goodman Roads, hence Elm Street which end as a "T" junction with Bayview Drive (0.3 km.) (3.7 km.). Turn left on Bayview Drive, veering left onto Roosevelt Way (0.3 km.) (4.0 km.) following Roosevelt Way west, back to to the border crossing at Tyee Drive (2.4 km.) (6.4 km.). After passing through Customs, continue on Point Roberts Road (56th Street) north to 12th Avenue, turning right (2.5 km.) (8.9 km.). Continue to the "T" intersection of 12th Avenue and Boundary Bay Road and park in the parking lot opposite the golf course (0.7 km.) (9.6 km.). Walk east from the parking lot along the dike to view the fields to the south, and Boundary Bay. (if you are doing this route from Highway 1 7, turn left at the third set of traffic lights 2.2 km. from the highway, proceeding along 1 2th Ave. to where the golf course seems to end at Boundary Bay Road).

BEACH GROVE REGIONAL PARK

During the winter months Short-eared Owl frequent the remaining fallow grassy areas in Beach Grove, one of the few remaining areas near Vancouver where these beautiful raptors can be seen. Unfortunately, residential development has depleted their former numbers. The intertidal basin along the north side of the dike supports migrant shorebirds that can often be viewed closely. Further out on the dike, scan the extensive mudflats for shorebirds and check the large flocks of American Wigeon for an occasional Eurasian Wigeon. Brant often feed on the eel-grass during their spring migration. Frequenting the neighbouring fields and tangles during the winter are mixed flocks of sparrows and finches: Song Sparrow, Dark-eyed Junco, White-crowned Sparrow, Golden-crowned Sparrow, Fox Sparrow, and House Finch. American Tree Sparrow and Common Redpoll occur occasionally.

Beach Grove to Boundary Bay Regional Park

(00.0km.) Return to Boundary Bay Road, turning left. Follow this windy road through rural farms and the ever growing residential areas. At (2.3 km.), turn left onto 3rd Avenue. Proceed along 3rd Avenue for (0.6 km.) (2.9 km.), then left onto Centennial Parkway (1.0 km.) (3.9 km.) to the park.

BOUNDARY BAY REGIONAL PARK

Boundary Bay Regional Park has sparrows and finches frequenting the fields in winter and,if ample fallow grassy areas remain, Short-eared Owl will be found. The intertidal mudflats support migrating shorebirds and in spring, Brant. Return to Beach Grove Regional Park

Beach Grove to Beach Grove Park

Return to the end of both 12th Avenue and Boundary Bay Roads, turning right (north) onto Beach Grove Road (00.0 km.). At the termination of Beach Grove Road at a "T" junction with 17 A Avenue, turn left (1.2 km.). After an additional (0.2 km.) (1.4 km.), park in the parking lot on the right at the tennis court. The small woodlot to the east with the towering cottonwoods is Beach Grove Park.

BEACH GROVE PARK

Both Red-tailed Hawk and Great Horned Owl have nested in the cottonwoods, and Barn Owl are occasionally found roosting in these tree's cavities. The park can be an excellent site for migrating passerines, especially warblers and sparrows.

At the east end of 17A Avenue is a path that leads to and follows the Boundary Bay shoreline, meeting with the extreme western end of the Boundary Bay dike road. The entire length of the dike is walkable from here to 112th Street.

Beach Grove Park to Boundary and Mud Bays

A number of excellent birding sites are accessible from the ends of 64th, 72nd, 88th, 96th, 104th, and 112th Streets leading south off Highway 10 (also known as Ladner Trunk Road), terminating at Boundary and Mud Bays (00.0km.) From Beach Grove Park turn right onto 17A Avenue, turning left onto 58th Street (0.2 km.), then right onto 17A Avenue. Turn left onto 57th Street (0.4 km.) (0.6 km.), then right onto 16th Avenue (0.3 km.) (0.9 km.). At 56th Street (Point Roberts Road) turn right (0.2 km.) (1.1 km.), continue along 56th Street, turning right onto Highway 17 at the traffic lights (1.2 km.) (2.3 km.). Turn right off Highway 17 onto 28th Avenue (1.6 km.) (3.9 km.), then right onto 64th Street (0.8 km.) (4.7 km.). Follow 64th Street to its termination with the Boundary Bay foreshore (0.5 km.) (5.2 km.).

After birding this site, return north along 64th Street, turning right onto 36th Avenue (2.0 km.) (7.2 km.), then right again onto 72nd Street (1.6 km.) (8.8 km.). Park at the foot of 72nd Street (0.9 km.) (9.7 km.).

After birding this site, return north along 72nd Street, turning right onto Highway 10 (3.1 km.) (12.8 km.), turning right onto 88th Street (3.3 km.) (1 6.1 km.). Park at the foot of 88th Street (2.4 km.) (1 8.5 km.).

Return north along 88th Street, turning right onto Highway 10 (2.4km.) (20.9 km.), turning right at the lights onto Hornby Drive (1.2 km.) (22.1 km.), then right onto 96th Street (0.4 km.) (22.5 km.). Park at the foot of 96th Street (2.1 km.) (24.6 km.).

After birding this site, return north along 96th Street, turning right onto Hornby Drive, which bends back and parallels Highway 99 (2.1 km.) (26.8 km.), then right onto 104th Street (1.7 km.) (28.5 km.). Park at the foot of 104th Street (1.4 km.) (29.9 km.).

After birding this site, return north along 104th Street, turning right onto Hornby Drive (1.4 km.) (31.3 km.). Continue east along Hornby Drive, passing under the railway overpass to the "T" junction with 112th Street, turning right (1.7 km.) (33.0 km.). Park at the foot of 112th Street at the dike gate (0.6 km.) (33.6 km.). For those birders comming directly from the Tsawwassen Ferry Terminal to this, the best of the Boundary-Mud Bay sites, use the following directions. After getting off the ferry set your trip odometer to (00.0 km.). Follow Highway 17 to the traffic lights at the junction of Highway 10 just outside of Ladner (12.0 km.). Turn right onto Highway 10 (also known as Ladner Trunk Road) after 1.2 kilometers you will see the recommended Tsawwassen Motel on your right; if you turn left at the Highway 10 and 17 junction onto 48th Avenue you will see the Primrose Hill Guest House after driving into Ladner (approx. 2.4 kilometers). Continue along Highway 10, turning right at the traffic lights onto Hornby Drive (5.8 km.) (1 7.8 km.). Continue east on Hornby Drive which bends back and parallels Highway 99 and turn right onto 112th Street at the "T" junction (4.0 km.) (21.8 km.). Park at the foot of 112th Street at the dike gate at Mud Bay (0.6 km.) (22.4 km.).

BOUNDARY BAY

Boundary and Mud Bays cover an extensive area from White Rock and Crescent Beach situated on the south and east side of the Bay, around to Beach Grove and Centennial Park along the north and west parameters. Boundary and Mud Bays are important staging areas andr winter home to huge concentrations of waterfowl.

Diving ducks prefer the offshore waters and at high tide you can observe, close to shore, Greater Scaup, Lesser Scaup, White-winged Scoter, Surf Scoter, Harlequin Duck, Oldsquaw, Common Merganser, and Hooded Merganser. The antics of courting Common Goldeneye are amusing to watch in early spring. Large flocks of Brant feed on the available eel-grass during spring migration and small numbers are occasionally found in winter in increasing numbers; rare non-breeders are sometimes present during the summer. During migrations the extensive tidal mudflats support thousands of shorebirds (the turf farm fields south of the railway tracks along 72nd Street should also be checked in the fall), while in winter the flats support huge flocks of Dunlin. As you drive along the numerous rural sideroads many raptors will be in evidence, particularly during the winter months; Northern Harrier, Red-tailed Hawk, and Rough-legged Hawk are common. An occasional Snowy Owl is often present in winter, especially in invasion years, resting atop the shoreline driftwood. Look among the cattle in any of the fields for Cattle Egret during November and December. There is only a single record of Red-throated Pipit.

The dike road along the bay extends for miles, an easy walk and a perfect vantage point from which to view the great expanse of tidal mudflats. Be sure to time your visit to coincide with a flooding tide, which forces the shorebirds into concentrations closer to shore. Tides of 3.6 meters or higher are best; local newspapers list tidal information with times and height information.

112th Street

The foot of 112th Street is known for its shorebirding, particularly for the larger species.

 Whimbrel are found in small flocks during migration; although rare this far north on the Pacific Coast, the occasional Long-billed Curlew, Marbled Godwit, and Willet could be found associating with them annually. The single record of Far Eastern Curlew (the only record south of Alaska) is of one photographed here in September. Among the other larger much rarer shorebirds are Bartailed Godwit and Hudsonian Godwit. Black-bellied Plover occur in flocks of thousands during fall migration, with smaller numbers of Red Knot. This is possibly the best site to find the Pacific Golden-Plover, although the American Golden-Plover will far outnumber the latter. Stints should be looked for among the huge concentrations of Western Sandpipers; Red-necked Stint and Little Stint have been positively identified. Greater Yellowlegs, Least Sandpiper, Baird's Sandpiper, and Pectoral Sandpiper frequent the various coastal shorebird habitats during migrations. The flocks of shorebirds and ducks regularly attract hunting Merlin and Peregrine Falcon, and in winter, Gyrfalcon, and rarely Prairie Falcon, are recorded.

The surrounding fields and hedgerows along the dike road are good for Golden-crowned Sparrow.

Boundary Bay to Serpentine Fen

(00.0km.) Return north from the foot of 1 1 2th Street, turning left onto Hornby Drive (0.6 km.). After (3.8 km.) (4.4 km.), turn right onto

Highway 10 and take the Highway 99 exit for White Rock and Blaine (east and south) (0.2 km.) (4.6 km.). Continue on Highway 99 to the Highway 99A (King George Highway) exit (10.7 km.) (1 5.3 km.). Proceed (0.8 km.) (1 6.1 km.), turning left onto Nicomekl Road for (0.1 km.) (1 6.2 km.) to the "T" intersection with Highway 99A. From here you have a choice of turning left on Highway 99 North for Serpentine Fen, or turning right on Highway 99A South toward White Rock, Blaine, Crescent Beach, and Blackie Spit. We will continue our loop first to Serpentine Fen, then Blackie Spit. Turn left onto Highway 99A, crossing over Highway 99 on the overpass, turning left onto 44th Avenue, the first road after the freeway (1.4 km.) (1 7.6 km.). Continue along the gravel road to the Ducks Unlimited visitors parking area on the left (0.4 km.) (1 8.0 km.).

SERPENTINE FEN

Serpentine Fen is maintained by Ducks Unlimited, please keep out of the posted areas to insure that birders will continue to be allowed to bird the area. Hundreds of ducks use the refuge during winter and migration, and also for nesting and disturbance at these times is controlled to minimize impact. Leading from the parking area are several trails that cover the entire area, observation towers are strategically placed from which the ponds can be viewed. Serpentine Fen is an excellent site for the widespread marsh species.

At high tide, the extensive mudflats at nearby Boundary and Mud Bays become completely covered forcing the shorebirds to find alternative resting sites. Serpentine Fen is one of these. Concentrations of shorebirds of several species fly into "the Fen" at high tides where they can be observed close-at-hand.

Black-bellied Plover, Greater Yellowlegs, Lesser Yellowlegs, Short-billed Dowitcher, Long-billed Dowitcher, Dunlin, Western Sandpiper, Least Sandpiper, Baird's Sandpiper, and Pectoral Sandpiper are regulars in migration. American and Pacific Golden-Plover, Red Knot, and the rare Sharp-tailed Sandpiper are occasionally recorded in the fall. A single record of Spotted Redshank, and records of such rarities as Ruff and Buff-breasted Sandpiper show the possibilities of finding "good" shorebirds.

The surrounding hedgerows and fields in winter harbour several species of sparrows: Spotted Towhee, Song Sparrow, Dark-eyed Junco, White-crowned Sparrow, Golden-crowned Sparrow, Fox Sparrow, and Lincoln's Sparrow are expected with the odd record of American Tree Sparrow and Harris' Sparrow.

Serpentine Fen to Blackie Spit

 Return to Highway 99A, turning right (00.0 km.). After crossing the overpass over Highway 99, veer left staying on Highway 99A South following the signs for Crescent Beach. Turn right off Highway 99A onto Crescent Road at the first set of traffic lights past the freeway (1.8 km.) (0.4 km. south of the Nicomekl Road and Highway 99A junction where you exited Highway 99). Continue along Crescent Road, down a hill, and soon after crossing the railway tracks, veer right onto Sullivan Street at the "V" intersection (5.0 km.) (6.8 km.). Turn right on McBride Street (0.5 km.) (7.3 km.), proceeding to the parking area at the spit, which is located at the mouth of the Nicomeki River (0.4 km.) (7.7 km.). The parking area is only open from 8:00 a.m. to dusk, if you arrive at other times just park on McBride, or Dunsmuir Road of Sullivan Street the closest access to "Farm Slough".

BLACKIE SPIT

Blackie Spit is a sandspit that juts out into Mud Bay, the shallow northeastern sector of Boundary Bay. Various grasses, shrubs small trees, and Himalayan blackberry form cover for open-country passerines, while salicornia is the main vegetation on the flats along the edges of the surrounding salt marshes and tidal inlets. A jogging trail branches out from the parking lot, follows the shoreline passing "Tidal Pond" and "Farm Slough", and ends after (0.8 km.) at an unnamed road which joins with Sullivan Street. Washrooms are located at the foot of Beecher Street, which branches off the corners of Sullivan Street and Crescent Road. The White Rock and Surrey Naturalists operate an information centre which is located next to the washrooms, open only on weekends from 1:00 to 5:00 p.m.. Drop-in and purchase a copy of the Blackie Spit checklist.

After parking your vehicle, scan offshore in the deeper channel northwest of the spit (higher tides best) for Common Loon, Pacific Loon, Red-throated Loon, grebes, cormorants, gulls, Black Scoter, White-winged Scoter, Surf Scoter, Oldsquaw, and other waterfowl. Brant are occasionally seen feeding nearshore during the spring migration period. The shallow, sheltered bays surrounding the spit attract numerous dabbling ducks during the winter with large flocks of American Wigeon; the uncommon Eurasian Wigeon is often recorded. As you walk through the low vegetation in the centre of the spit you may encounter migrant Lapland Longspur or Snow Bunting in the late fall or winter.

Walking south from the parking lot you will first come to a tidal inlet which is almost completely enclosed by land. "Tidal Pond", as it is known, has many small trees surrounding it which attract migrant passerines, and sparrows and finches during the winter months. After walking further south to the southeast corner of Blackie Spit you will arrive at another larger tidal inlet known as "Farm Slough", a backwater of the Nicomeki River. From the north side of Farm Slough scan both the slough and the adjacent Nicomekl estuary, which are often filled with shorebirds at higher tides; they are best viewed from this point using the dense broom as a screen. On the south side of "Farm Slough" is a path leading along the top of a wooded dike bordering the slough, the brush along the dike harbouring passerines. This path rejoins the jogging trail on another parallel dike at the slough's mouth; the slough's mouth marked by a row of rotting pilings and often by large congregations of Great Blue Heron.

Following the jogging trail past Farm Slough will bring you to an unnamed road which parallels the railway tracks and from here you could use the tracks and trestle to cross over the Nicomeki River ... use caution! While walking along the unnamed road watch the Lombardy poplars lining the road for Bullock's Oriole in summer; in winter the neighbouring fields hold the odd Northern Shrike.

Blackie Spit is an excellent site to observe shorebirds. The salt marsh on the opposite side of the Nicomekl River estuary from Blackie Spit may teem with shorebirds at higher tides. If scoping seems futile from Blackie Spit, cross over the river using the railway trestle. The rising and falling of the tides are imperative for viewing the shorebird congregations closely, thus making identification easier, be sure to check the tide tables in a local newspaper before arrival. During lower tides of three meters or so there are great expanses of tidal flats, the shorebirds at this time range over an enormous area.

The best tactic is to arrive one hour before high tide, waiting for the tide to push the shorebirds into concentrations closer to shore where they are more easily scrutinized. Maximum tides of 4 1/2 m, however, force the shorebirds to the inaccessible east shore of Mud Bay. Whimbrel are often seen in late spring and fall, with Red Knot possible in late fall and winter, Blackie Spit being the most reliable site on the lower mainland for these two species. A few non-breeding Whimbrel may linger through the summer months. Flocks of hundreds or thousands of shorebirds are associated with the nutrient-rich shores: Black-bellied Plover, Greater Yellowlegs, Long-billed Dowitcher, Dunlin, and Sanderling winter, with migrant Semipalmated Plover, American and Pacific Golden-Plover (both species; American far outnumbering Pacific), Lesser Yellowlegs, Semipalmated Sandpiper (uncommon), Western Sandpiper, Least Sandpiper, and Baird's Sandpiper (uncommon). During the past few years "The Gang of Four", a Marbled Godwit, Whimbrel, Long-billed Curlew, and Willet, all fairly rare, have spent the winter together on the spit. The locally-rare Hudsonian Godwit is recorded on occasion.

Resting in the salt marshes and tidal inlets are Ring-billed Gull (summer), Mew Gull (winter), Herring Gull (uncommon-winter), California Gull (mainly migrant), Thayer's Gull (winter), and Glaucous-winged Gull (resident). During the late summer and fall the flocks of Bonaparte's Gull should be checked closely for the rare Franklin's Gull and Little Gull, both of which have been recorded. Although unrecorded the Black-headed Gull is a possibility. Caspian Tern and Common Tern are reliable in season, check the nearby sandy beaches of Crescent Beach where resting terns are common; Elegant Tern has been recorded during El Nino years.

Blackie Spit to Campbell Valley Park

Retrace your route back to the intersection of Crescent Road and Highway 99A (King George Highway), turning right (00.0 km.). After driving (7.4 km.), turn left at the traffic lights at the "T" junction with 8th Avenue (Campbell River Road). Proceed east over the Highway 99 overpass along 8th Avenue to 200th Street (7.0 km.) (1 4.4 km.). Turn left onto 200th Street for (1.6 km.) (1 6.0 km.) to 16th Avenue, turning right (the park can also be accessed off of 8th Avenue). After driving (0.6 km.) (16.6 km.) along 16th Ave. turn into the large Campbell Valley Regional Park's parking lot on the right.

CAMPBELL VALLEY REGIONAL PARK

From the large parking lot, walk the main nature trail which allows access to a good cross-section of the forest habitats to be found in the Georgia Depression. A sample of mixed coniferous and deciduous woods, old fields, and marshes (that have harboured as many as 120 species) can be birded within a half-day.

Common species such as Northern Flicker, Downy Woodpecker, Pacific-slope Flycatcher, Swainson's Thrush, Red-eyed Vireo, Cassin's Vireo, Warbling Vireo, and Black-throated Gray Warbler announce their presence, singing and calling in spring and summer from the deciduous or mixed stands of forest. Townsend's Warbler breed commonly in the park's conifers, difficult to see in the branches high overhead. Orange-crowned Warbler sing their hammering trills from the deciduous scrub. The rarer Hutton's Vireo is resident as they prefer the cooler, mixed stands of forest that contain alder, cedar, and Douglas-fir. The marshes harbour breeding Mallard, American Wigeon, Wood Duck, Virginia Rail, Sora, Marsh Wren, and Common Yellowthroat.

Sharp-shinned Hawk are seen migrating commonly through the park with the great autumn movements; rare individuals are occasionally present throughout the year. Both resident Cooper's Hawk (uncommon) and Red-tailed Hawk (common) have nested within the parks boundaries. Northern Goshawk are rare winter visitants and certainly a prized species. Pileated Woodpecker, Chestnut-backed Chickadee, Brown Creeper, Red-breasted Nuthatch, Winter Wren, and Golden-crowned Kinglet are common characteristic residents of the deeper forests. A Dusky Thrush (the only record south of Alaska) was seen from January to March of 1993 just north of the park.

Campbell Valley Park is one of the better sites for "owling" in the lower mainland. Permission to enter the park after dark must be obtained in advance from the park superintendent. Great Horned Owl and Western Screech-Owl are common residents, with Long-eared Owl, Nothern Pygmy-Owl, and Northern Saw-whet Owl also occurring.

Campbell Valley Park to Ladner Sewage Lagoons

Retrace your route back to Highway 99 North, turning right onto the highway on-ramp toward Vancouver (00.0 km.). After driving 26.5 kilometers, take the River Road exit, turning left over the overpass toward the community of Ladner. After driving (0.5 km.) (27.0 km.), turn left at the traffic lights onto Highway 17 South towards the Tsawwassen Ferry Terminal. At (2.3 km.) (29.3 km.) turn right onto Ladner Trunk Road (48th Avenue) towards Ladner. At the traffic lights in downtown Ladner, turn right onto Elliott Street (1.8 km.) (31.1 km.). Follow Elliott Street for (0.4 km.) (31.5 km.), turning right onto River Road. After driving (0.4 km.) (31.9 km.) along River Road turn left at the Ladner Harbour Park sign onto a paved road, crossing a wooden bridge over a tidal lagoon. Park immediately past the bridge walking north along the overgrown trail through the old sewage lagoons.

LADNER SEWAGE LAGOONS

The Ladner Sewage Lagoons are principally an alternative site for finding the odd Franklin's Gull in the late summer and fall. Other gull species are numerous with Bonaparte's Gull, Mew Gull, Thayer's Gull, and Glaucous-winged Gull present in season. Red-necked Phalarope are possible in the fall months. The widespread marsh species are prolific.

Ladner Sewage Lagoons to Reifel Refuge

Retrace your route back to 48th Avenue in delightful downtown Ladner, turning right (00.0 km.), then left onto 47A Street (0.7 km.). From 47A Street, turn right onto West River Road (0.1 km.) (0.8 km.), following West River Road for (3.3 km.) (4.1 km.). Turn right onto Westham Island Road and cross over the bridge onto Westham Island.

or

Tsawwassen Ferry Terminal to Reifel Refuge

Driving off the ferry set your trip odometer to (00.0 km.). After the long causeway, turn left at the first set of traffic lights (5.2 km.) off Highway 17 onto 52 Street. At (7.1 km.) turn left onto 28th Avenue, then right onto 41B Street (9.4 km.). At (13.0 km.) turn left onto West River Road, then right onto Westham Island Road and cross over the bridge onto Westham

Island (14.7 km.). At (1 7.5 km.) keep left, at (18.2 km.) keep right; the fields at this corner may be filled with thousands of Snow Geese, as an occasional Ross' Goose has shown in these flocks, scan them carefully!. The "George C. Reifel Migratory Bird Sanctuary" sign will be seen at (20.0 km.) so keep left along the short-stretch of road into the Reifel Refuge, as it is more commonly called. If you continue straight ahead at the "Alaksen National Wildlife Area" sign at (20.0 km.) and proceed to the Administrative Offices (open only on weekdays!) you will find a double row of cedars in which Barn Owl often roost.

Along your drive through the flat, diked farmlands and fallow agricultural fields watch the isolated trees for a variety of raptors especially during the winter months when Bald Eagle, Northern Harrier, Red-tailed Hawk, Rough-legged Hawk, American Kestrel, and Peregrine Falcon are very likely to be encountered. Gyrfalcon, although rare, does occur annually in the Delta area. Most recently a Gyrfalcon spent the entire winter atop one of the high metal powerline towers (0.9 km.) along 27B Avenue past 41B Street near the base of the Roberts Bank Coal Port. Along the drive, large white shapes contrasting sharply with the black, wet earth materialize into flocks of Trumpeter Swan. Scan these flocks, as they feed on vegetable matter leftover from the fall harvest, for the few Tundra Swan that may be present. Great Blue Heron, from some nearby rookery, are a common sight - reptilean-like - as they hunt rodents in the fields. As thirty-eight barns on Westham Island are used by Barn Owl, a visit to one of the older, wooden buildings could produce a pair. Always stop at the farmhouse asking permission to enter the structures: this is not only common courtesy, but saves time, as the owners always know if there are owls present.

GEORGE C. REIFEL MIGRATORY BIRD SANCTUARY

The British Columbia Waterfowl Society operate the public area within the refuge. After parking, proceed to the gate where an admission fee is charged to enter the diked 400 hectare refuge, which is open from May through October at 9:00 a.m. to 5:00 p.m., and from November through April at 9:00 a.m. to 4:00 p.m.

The staff at the refuge feed grain to the waterfowl, which also attracts passerines, making this site quite active during the winter months; Spotted Towhee, Song Sparrow, Dark-eyed Junco, White-crowned Sparrow, Golden-crowned Sparrow, and Fox Sparrow take advantage of the scattered seed. American Coot are abundant through the winter at the waterfowl feeding station behind the entrance gate. After paying the fee, walk a short way down the path to the pond surrounded by willows and other dense brush on the right. Black-crowned Night-Heron are found roosting at the far end of the pond on occasion. From here there are numerous gravel-based walking trails on the tops of the dikes.

The Fraser Estuary provides the most important waterfowl habitat in the Georgia Depression and the area supports the largest concentrations of wintering waterfowl in Canada. The George C. Reifel Migratory Bird Sanctuary is winter home to 20,000 Snow Geese. These geese arrive in late October, departing in March and April on their way back to the breeding grounds on Wrangle Island off the coast of northeastern Siberia.

The outer dike is one of the better places to observe the vast flocks of Snow Geese and other waterfowl. Canada Geese are abundant with close to 6,000 resident in the Fraser Estuary. A few Greater White-fronted Geese are seen in mixed flocks with the Canada's during migrations. Those beautiful small, dark sea geese, formerly known as "Black" Brant, feed on the eel-grass beds along the shoreline during their spring migration in April in numbers that attain 30,000 individuals.

During the fall migration Brant are seldom seen, passing far offshore along the outer coast - directly to staging areas further south, very few stay to winter. Among the hundreds of wintering dabbling ducks attracted to the tidal marshes along the nutrient rich shores are Mallard, Green-winged Teal, American Wigeon, Northern Pintail, and Northern Shoveler are the most abundant. The refuge is used primarily as a haven to escape the hunting areas of the estuary; at dusk the ducks fly inland to feed on the unharvested crops in the flooded agricultural fields. Mallard, American Black Duck (introduced and are countable), Gadwall, Wood Duck, Blue-winged Teal and Cinnamon Teal breed at the refuge.

Scan the large grazing flocks of American Wigeon, the refuge is the best site in the Vancouver area to find the Eurasian Wigeon, look for the rusty-orange head and greyer plumage of the adult males. A few Redhead are expected in the ponds in winter. Such rare vagrants as Emperor Goose and Smew have been recorded.

The extensive tidal mudflats support an estimated five million migrating shorebirds of thirty-eight species each spring and fall; tens of thousands of Dunlin wintering. Along the shoreline among the mosaic of grass-lined pools, tidal inlets, and backwaters within the refuge are Greater Yellowlegs, Lesser Yellowlegs, Spotted Sandpiper, Short-billed Dowitcher, hundreds of Long-billed Dowitcher, Common Snipe, Western Sandpiper, Least Sandpiper, and Pectoral Sandpiper. Solitary Sandpiper and Baird's Sandpiper are uncommon. As the rare Sharp-tailed Sandpiper are recorded annually during mid-September through to late October, scrutinize each Pectoral Sandpiper looking carefully for one with a bright rusty cap. The refuge boasts to be North America's mecca (south of Alaska) for Spotted Redshank, with three records. The ditches lining the entrance road to the refuge are good for shorebirds, the only Canadian record of Temminck's Stint was made here!

Some 250 species have been recorded to date from the vicinity of the refuge. The large areas of bullrushes, reeds, and sedges support nesting

American Bittern, one of the best sites in the "Lower Mainland" for this secretive species, as well as Virginia Rail, Sora, and Marsh Wren. Common Redpolls visit the refuge during most winters feeding in the alders. The conifers along the entrance road, or anywhere along the dikes, should be checked for roosting Barn Owl, Long-eared Owl, Great Horned Owl, and Northern Saw-whet Owl. Snowy Owl are found most winters perched on the drift-logs along the outer dikes. Peregrines are resident, feeding upon the abundant prey; at least one Gyrfalcon is reported every year.

NOTE:The refuge has a few pinioned captives for display purposes; one Sandhill Crane, Tundra and Trumpeter Swans, Ross' Goose, and a few American Black Duck, so be wary!

Reifel Refuge to Brunswick Point

 Return along Westham Island Road, crossing the bridge and turn right along West River Road (00.0 km.). After driving (2.4 km.) park on the shoulder of the road at its termination. Check the fields en route for Tundra Swan and Trumpeter Swan, a few hundred winter in the area.

BRUNSWICK POINT

Walk the wide gravel-based trail found on top of the dike to the right. The trail parallels the straits of Georgia passing tidal mudflats and adjacent coastal marshes. Many species of shorebirds are possible, with thousands of Dunlin present during the winter months. Snowy Owl are seen virtually every winter sitting on the drift-logs. A small group of American Tree Sparrow are often found wintering in the available cover along the dike. Walk the dike west and south for approximately (1.8 km.) towards the line of trees and farm house. The line of trees holds a huge active Bald Eagle nest. A Prairie Falcon has wintered in the area for a number of years, roosting in this line of trees or atop the triangular cable marker sign. The falcon can be very difficult to see among the maze of bare branches, so scope them very carefully. Peregrine Falcon are also seen repeatedly in the area.

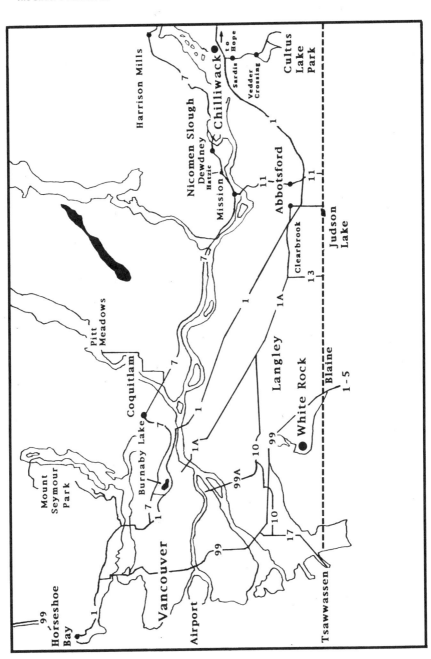

MAP 5   LOOP 4   HORSESHOE BAY TO HOPE

LOOP 2 VANCOUVER

Brunswick Point to Iona Island and Sea Island

Return along West River Road, through Ladner to Highway 17, turning left (00.0 km.). Drive (2.1 km.), keeping right onto the Highway 99 on-ramp (following signs for Highway 99 North toward Vancouver), crossing over the overpass and merging onto Highway 99 North. Soon you will pass through the George Massey Tunnel (2.0 km.) (4.1 km.) and after driving an additional (1 0.6 km.) (14.7 km.) take the exit signed for the Vancouver International Airport (00.0 km.).

After leaving Highway 99 continue along the exit road, turning left onto Bridgeport Road at the "T" junction and traffic lights (0.5 km.). Turn left onto No. 3 Road following signs for the airport (1.2 km.) (1.7 km.), then right onto Sea Island Way (0.2 km.) (1.9 km.). Sea Island Way has a very small number of Crested Myna in the area. After (0.6 km.) (2.5 km.) you will reach the bridge over the Moray Channel, the middle arm of the Fraser River, onto Sea Island. The introduced Crested Myna are occasionally found in the vicinity just past the bridge, check around the Delta River Inn and the roadsides. Take the first right onto Airport Road (0.2 km.) (2.7 km.) after crossing the bridge and then drive beside, and then under, the Arthur Laing Bridge where Airport Road becomes Grauer Road (0.6 km.) (3.3 km.).

IONA ISLAND AND SEA ISLAND

Located along the coastal flyway, Iona and Sea Islands are located at one of the prime geographical positions in the world for viewing the migration of birds going to-and-from their Arctic breeding grounds. The islands and surrounding seas act not only as staging sites for teeming hords of shorebirds and huge rafts of waterfowl, but also as a migratory conduit for avifauna crossing the Coast and Cascade Mountain Ranges. The location also serves as a migrant trap for vagrants from any point on the compass. Accompanying the stretches of abandoned fallow agricultural fields on the islands are high populations of rodents which, especially in winter, attract a wealth of raptors. Relevant is the position of the rising and falling tides on the birding success on these islands. A rising tide or high tide is best along the Iona South Jetty, while a very high tide is optimum for viewing shorebirds in the sewage ponds. Plan your schedule to arrive on a rising tide, first birding the jetty, then at high tide, the sewage ponds.

Continue along Grauer Road paralleling the adjacent airport property for an additional 3.3 km. (6.6 km.) looking for Bald Eagle, Northern Harrier, Red-tailed Hawk, Rough-legged Hawk, Common Pheasant, Short-eared Owl, and Northern Shrike in winter months. Park and walk to the right for (0.5 km.) to an derelict subdivision where the available cover, and subsequent rodents, attracts a substantial population of owls. Barn Owl, Long-eared Owl, and Northern Saw-whet Owl, along with the occasional Great Horned Owl, roost in the rows of conifers that await the buildozer's blade. If you arrive at dusk, the resident Barn Owl are often seen hunting over the old weedy yards like giant white moths or sitting on the overhead wires. Short-eared Owl can be quite common during the fall and winter, and are often seen hunting in daylight. Three southern vagrants, Tropical Kingbird, Ash-throated Flycatcher, and Northern Mockingbird have been recorded, so the potential for rarities is high.

After an additional (2.5 km.) (9.1 km.) Graver Road makes a right along the ocean where the name of the road changes to Iona Island Causeway. Once two islands, Sea Island and Iona Island are now linked by this made-made causeway. Hudsonian Godwit and Little Gull are among the rarities recorded on the vast mudflats, among the drift-logs, or on the neighbouring log booms. Once crossing the narrow causeway, you are on Iona Island.

IONA SEWAGE TREATMENT PLANT

After an additional (0.9 km.) (10.0 km.) you will arrive at the Iona Sewage Treatment Plant. You may gain entry as special arrangements have been made to accommodate birders. A key is available to open a walk-through gate a few yards to the west; information for entry can be obtained by phoning the Vancouver Rare Bird Alert at 737-3074. Birders are encouraged to use the birders-log at the gate and sign-in; this registers the names of those using the facility and also serves as a guide to alert newcomers as to the latest rarities. Follow the sweet aromatic breezes to the ponds, located just west of the buildings.

The Iona Sewage Treatment Plant has become a legion for the quality of shorebirds that have been recorded, and may be the best site for shorebirds in North America: Snowy Plover, Rufous-necked Stint, Little Stint, White-rumped Sandpiper, Curlew Sandpiper, Spoonbill Sandpiper, Ruff, Upland Sandpiper, and Buff-breasted Sandpiper have all occurred. Other exciting finds are made with records of Garganey, Common Moorhen, Tropical Kingbird, Alder Flycatcher, and a wagtail species. Sharp-tailed Sandpiper are found annually (usually in mid-September through late October), the only site in North America where this beautiful Siberian shorebird sometimes occurs in numbers outside of Alaska. The Rufous-necked Stint has also been recorded several times, usually in late June or very early in July when still in distinctive alternate plumage.

The best season to find rare shorebirds is during the fall migration, beginning in late June and continuing through October. Spring migration rarely brings rarities, and is much shorter, lasting from late April to late May.

 The sewage lagoons serve as a roosting site for shorebirds at high tides, spectacular flocks of thousands of Western Sandpiper converge twice daily when the neighbouring extensive mudflats are completely flooded. As these high tides are imperative for viewing the shorebird congregations closely thereby making identification easier, be sure to check tide tables in the local newspapers before arrival. Least Sandpiper are the second-most common "peep", while Semipalmated Sandpiper gather in the settling ponds in surprising numbers for the west coast of North America where they are generally uncommon or rare. Greater Yellowlegs, Lesser Yellowlegs, Solitary Sandpiper, Spotted Sandpiper, Wilson's Phalarope (migrations and summer), Red-necked Phalarope, Red Phalarope (rare), Short-billed Dowitcher (less common than the Long-billed except in spring), Long-billed Dowitcher, Stilt Sandpiper, Common Snipe, (Rock Sandpiper has even occurred!), Red Knot (rare), Baird's Sandpiper, and Pectoral Sandpiper occur. Tens of thousands of Dunlin and lesser numbers of Sanderling begin their arrival in October on the vast tidal mudflats and remain through the winter.

As you scan the migrating flocks of shorebirds, others are doing the same. Resident Merlin and Peregrine Falcon are regular, skimming over the ponds at tremendous speed, scattering the hundreds of shorebirds you checked laboriously moments ago into new locations of the ponds! An occasional Gyrfalcon may make a late fall or winter appearance.

The sewage lagoons and adjacent jetty and mudflats also draw thousands of gulls; Ring-billed Gull, California Gull, and Glaucous-winged Gull are common residents. Scrutinize the abundant Bonaparte's Gull on the outflow pond across the road, south of the sewage plant's entrance gate. Franklin's Gull occur annually in September and there is a record of Little Gull; the accidental Black-headed Gull is always a possibility. Check through the common Thayer's Gull and Mew Gull as there are records of Iceland Gull (now considered a pale race of Thayer's Gull). In winter, a few Herring Gull, Western Gull (rare), and Glaucous Gull (rare) should be looked for.

This area is the most westerly nesting of the Yellow-headed Blackbird in British Columbia. A colony existed at a small marsh at the edge of the airport runway until recently and has now re-established at the lagoons. Bank Swallow are rare to uncommon migrants, usually in August and September.

IONA SOUTH JETTY

Return to your vehicle, and continue ahead towards the sea. A second parking area is found at the end of the paved road (0.9 km.). On the large "outer pond", lying east of the parking lot and west of the fenced settling ponds, there is usually a selection of ducks. Mallard, Gadwall, Green-winged Teal, American Wigeon, an occasional Eurasian Wigeon, Northern Pintail, Northern Shoveler, Blue-winged Teal and Cinnamon Teal (spring and summer), and Ruddy Duck. Among the scaup one could find a Tufted Duck, which is found almost annually in winter.

The parking lot is situated at the base of the Iona South Jetty, a four kilometer long made-made causeway projecting northwest out to sea which serves to divert the flow of effluent into the Strait of Georgia. At the base of the spit, in the available grassy habitat, are large flocks of migrant and/or wintering sparrows. Interior sparrows, Grasshopper Sparrow, Vesper Sparrow, Lark Sparrow, and Brewer's Sparrow have all occurred, but are extremely rare. In the fall the large mixed flocks are dominated by Savannah Sparrow with smaller numbers of White-crowned Sparrow, Golden-crowned Sparrow, Fox Sparrow, and Lincoln's Sparrow. Later in the fall, and through the winter months, the Dark-eyed Junco flocks are joined by an occasional American Tree Sparrow, Harris' Sparrow, or White-throated Sparrow.

There is a gravel road that runs the full length of the four kilometer long jetty. You must walk or ride a bike to reach the tip of the jetty as cars are prohibited, and the road is gated. Allow at least two hours. In the fall as you reach the pumphouse, about (0.9 km.) into the walk, begin looking for Horned Lark, American Pipit, Lapland Longspur, and Snow Bunting, all of which could occur into the winter months. They can be found from here to the tip where they sometimes congregate. The Burrowing Owl occurs on the jetty as a rare vagrant from the interior every few years and may be found anywhere along its length.

The jetty offers a better chance of seeing another group of shorebirds that seldom visit the settling ponds. The rocky shoreline has Black Oystercatcher (rare), Wandering Tattler, Black Turnstone, Surfbird (occasional), and Rock Sandpiper (rare). The South Iona Jetty is one of the few places in Vancouver for rock shorebirds, and a fairly reliable site for Wandering Tattler. In late July through late September a rapid, ringing series of "tu-tu-tu-tu-tu" whistles will announce their presence as they take flight. On landing, their characteristic teetering and bobbing will commence again on some distant black and white barnacle-encrusted rock. American and Pacific Golden-Plover (the American far-outnumbering the Pacific) and Black-bellied Plover are found resting on the jetty. The jetty also has served as the most southerly record for the nesting of the Semipalmated Plover.

Common Loon, Yellow-billed Loon (R), Pacific Loon (uncommon), Red-throated Loon, Western Grebe, Clark's Grebe (Acc), Red-necked Grebe, Horned Grebe, Eared Grebe (R), Snow Goose, Greater White-fronted Goose (uncommon), Brant, Canvasback (uncommon), Redhead (fairly rare), Black Scoter, White-winged Scoter, Surf Scoter, Barrow's Goldeneye, Common Goldeneye, Red-breasted Merganser, Common Murre, Pigeon Guillemot, Marbled Murrelet, and Rhinoceros Auklet (uncommon) all occur on the salt waters surrounding the jetty. Scan the huge rafts containing both Greater Scaup and Lesser Scaup for the rare Tufted Duck and Ring-necked Duck. The odd vagrant King Eider occurs when scoter numbers are higher.

Scope the old lighthouse off the tip of the jetty for Double-crested Cormorant, Pelagic Cormorant, and Brandt's Cormorant, which is less common than the other two.

During south-easterly winds in late May and early June, and again in late August to mid-October, there is an increased chance of observing a wayward pelagic from the tip of the jetty, its origin possibly from the inner Juan de Fuca Strait or from the northern Johnston Strait. Most pelagic species are seen during the fall migration period and their occurrence this far up the straits may be weather related, the birds being blown in during storms or lost in heavy fogs. Fluctuating food resources and conditions such as El Nino are certainly factors contributing to "invasions".

The sudden influx of large numbers of pelagics into the Juan de Fuca Straits such as Sooty Shearwater, Short-tailed Shearwater, Northern Fulmar, and hundreds of Fork-tailed Storm-Petrel, and thousands of Red Phalarope in various years contribute to the individuals occurring even further into the Georgia Straits. Sooty Shearwater, Fork-tailed Storm-Petrel, Red Phalarope, Pomarine Jaeger, Long-tailed Jaeger, Black-legged Kittiwake, Sabine's Gull, and Tufted Puffin have all been seen from the jetty on rare occasions. Parasitic Jaeger are regular in the fall, their appearance coinciding with that of the Common Tern which they parasitize. When the silence is broken by screaming, wheeling terns, one or more are in the vicinity. Scan the large flocks of Common Terns in the fall carefully for two tern rarities, Arctic Tern and Forster's Tern. Caspian Tern are common summer residents often found in tight flocks resting on neighbouring bars.

Iona and Sea Islands to Crested Myna sites

Retrace your route back to Sea Island Way and Airport Road, turning left (00.0 km.). Proceed east for (1.5 km.), keeping left and passing under the highway overpass to the on-ramp for Highway 99 North towards Vancouver (1.0 km.) (2.5 km.). Soon you will cross over the North Arm of the Fraser River using the Oak Street Bridge, after which this freeway ends, becoming a nightmare during rush-hours!

CRESTED MYNA

The city of Vancouvef is home to North America's only population of Crcsted Myna. Accidently introduced in the 1890's the residential population now of approximately 100 pairs, is confined to the city in an area bordered by Granville Street on the west, Boundary Road on the east, South West Marine Drive on the south, and anywhere north to False Crcek. The optimum range covers an area from downtown North Vancouver, south through Richmond and rarely Ladner. The myna is local and thinly distributed in Vancouver and although declining, they are still countable by A.B.A. standards; those remaining pairs should be found at their limited sites with persislence. The Vancouver Rare Bird Alerl of ten has rccrni sightings of mynas noted on their tape.

Crested Myna are most easily seen as they feed on lawns, around fast food restaurants, grocery stores, and garbage cans in early morning and again in the late afternoon. The mynas often mix in with flocks of European Starlings, which they resemble both in dark plumage and habits. Watch for the larger size, bushy crest, and wings emblazoned with striking white flashes when they take flight. At anytime of the day they are often viewed as they perch on overhead wires, on telephone poles, roof tops, or on chimneys along laneways and side streets.

After crossing the Oak Street Bridge (1.9 km.) (4 4 km.) you can turn right onto South West Drive if you are seeking the Crested Myna. Proceed to Fraser Street (3.1 km) (7.5 km.) Where they are found or anywhere along the four kilometer stretch of South West Marlne Drive to the Knight Street Bridge. Recent sites along South West Marine Drive include the junction with Hudson Street and the Oak Street Bridge and Manitoba Street and 70th Avenue. If you do not find any here, check the area around the False Creek warehouse district where they have been recorded most often recently - especially Wylie Strect off 2nd Avenue, 7th Avenue and Yukon Street, and just west of the False Creek area at # 191 Broadway between St. Catherines and Carolina Slreets, (Also see Oak Street Bndge to Queen Elizabeth Park below).

The myna's optimum range covers an area from downtown North Vancouver, south through Richmond and rarely Ladner, mainly west to Granville Street, and east to New Westminister.

After crossing the Oak Street Bridge (1.9 km.) (4.4 km.) you can turn right onto South West Marine Drive if you are seeking the Crested Myna. Proceed to Fraser Street (3.1 km.) (7.5 km.) where they should be found quickly, or anywhere along the four kilometer stretch of South West Marine Drive to the Knight Street Bridge. If you do not locate any here, check north as far as 41st Avenue, (3.5 km.) from South West Marine Drive, along both Cambie and Main Streets (1.2 km. and 2.4 km. respectively from the Oak Street Bridge) (i.e. anywhere in the city in an area bordered by Granville Street on the west, Boundary Road on the east, South West Marine Drive on the south, and anywhere north to 4th Avenue).

Other sites that mynas can be located include: New Westminister and East Burnaby region along 6th Street from the Fraser River to Edmonds Street, along Edmonds from 6th Street to Kingston, or near the Middlegate Shopping Centre. (Also see Oak Street Bridge to Queen Elizabeth Park below).

Oak Street Bridge to Queen Elizabeth Park

(00.0km.) After crossing the Oak Street bridge, follow the Highway 99 signs along Oak Street. Oak Street (Highway 99) is the main route through downtown Vancouver and is a fair site for Crested Myna: scrutinize the holes near the tops of the metal telephone poles lining the street, the mynas have used them for nesting. At (3.5 km.) you could turn right for a 6.5 kilometer drive along 41st Avenue between Oak Street and Highway 1A -99A for an additional search for Crested Myna. Check especially at the McDonald's Restaurant at #2095 West 41st Avenue, reached by turning left from Oak Street for (2.0 km.).

Continuing our loop along Oak Street, turn right off Oak Street at 33rd Avenue West (0.9 km. past 41st Avenue) (4.4 km.). Proceed along 33rd Avenue West passing Cambie Street to the entrance of Queen Elizabeth Park (0.8 km.) (5.2 km.). The road traverses a hill branching to the right at the edge of the golf course to the west parking lot and the washrooms. Another smaller parking lot is located by driving straight ahead.

QUEEN ELIZABETH PARK

Queen Elizabeth Park, the remains of an extinct volcano, is elevated above the surrounding metropolis of Vancouver. Upwellings of lava everywhere in the park are evidence of its origin. As migrant passerines are confronted by southerly low pressure systems bringing adverse weather, "fall-outs" occur. When these ideal conditions exist the park then becomes attractive to these migrants, the small navigators often seeking the highest point of land. The prime season for weather systems and migrants to coincide creating these Òfall-outsÓ is during the months of May and early June: at other times, especially during sunny weather, there will be few birds. For visiting birders the park has a fair selection of western specialities. For locals it provides the opportunity of experiencing passerine fall-outs and the chance of locating some wayward vagrant from the east or south.

Starting from the smaller parking lot at the end of West 33rd Avenue, follow the south trail past a large stand of trees to an opening where there is a dump of vegetation clippings and a tall red-and-white radio tower. Red-naped Sapsucker, rare along the coast, occurs in this region of the park each spring. Hammond's Flycatcher, Pacific-slope Flycatcher, Golden-crowned Kinglet, Ruby-crowned Kinglet, Swainson's Thrush, Hermit Thrush, Varied Thrush, Orange-crowned Warbler, Nashville Warbler (rare-regular), Yellow-rumped Warbler, Yellow Warbler, MacGillivray's Warbler, Wilson's Warbler, White-crowned Sparrow, and Golden-crowned Sparrow are regulars in the available shrubbery.

After checking through the large number of migrants in the shrubbery, walk towards the parkÕs golf course trees next to the lawn bowling club which are often productive for various flycatchers. Walking to the east side of the park, watch the open skies for aerial feeders such as flocks of swallows, both Black Swift and Vaux's Swift cut across the spectacular vistas on sickle wings at unimaginable speeds. Proceed past the east parking lot and beyond East 33rd Avenue to the east look-out.

The habitat on the east side of the park is quite varied with coniferous woods, deciduous woods, shrubs, mixed woods, a small stream, and small ponds. During fall-outs vagrants occur regularly in this area of the park with such records as Dusky Flycatcher, Northern Waterthrush, and Tennessee Warbler. The conifers in this corner of the park are paramount for finding the Hermit Warbler in Canada, with three sightings. The songs of the two species can sound quite similar and hybrids of Hermit x Townsend's Warbler have occurred, so scrutinize each Townsend's Warbler carefully!

 In the tall conifers look for Olive-sided Flycatcher, Hammond's Flycatcher, the odd Steller's Jay, Chestnut-backed Chickadee, Red-breasted Nuthatch, Townsend's Warbler, and Western Tanager.

In the more deciduous tracts are Western Wood-Pewee, Black-throated Gray Warbler, and Black-headed Grosbeak. The vine maple trees harbour Townsend's Solitaire, Willow Flycatcher, CassinŌs Vireo, and in late May, but usually in early June, Red-eyed Vireo. Lucky observers could find a flock of Band-tailed Pigeon.

On the northwestern side of the park is an old quarry pit, famous for its variety of wild flowers. Walking to the look-out above the pit will bring you at eye level with the tops of the conifers, resulting in excellent views of tree-top dwellers such as Townsend's Warbler. Each April, Townsend's Solitaire migrate along the coast and this could possibly be the best site to view them in the Vancouver area. In May of 1993, the second record of Green-tailed Towhee for the province was made at the quarry.

On the west side of the park is a clearing that is surrounded by a thickly wooded area full of dense shrubs which support migrant flycatchers with Western Wood-Pewee, Willow Flycatcher, and Pacific-slope Flycatcher expected. An unexpected visitor was an accidental Eastern Phoebe in 1989. When the flowering trees and bushes are in bloom they attract numerous hummingbirds. Rufous Hummingbird are abundant, Anna's Hummingbird and Calliope Hummingbird are casual, and an accidental Ruby-throated Hummingbird has been recorded once.

Queen Elizabeth Park to Stanley Park

Retrace your route back to Oak Street, turning right (00.0 km.). At (1.5 km.), turn left onto West 19th Street following the signs for the Granville Bridge. After (0.9 km.) (2.4 km.) proceed straight through the multi-intersection, and downhill on 19th for (0.1 km.) (2.5 km.) to Granville Street. Turn right on Granville Street to the Granville Bridge (1.0 km.) (3.5 km.); after crossing the bridge you will arrive in downtown Vancouver. From the bridge, proceed onto Granville Street to Smithe Street, turning left (2.0 km.) (5.5 km.). Proceed on Smithe Street for (0.2 km.) (5.7 km.), turning right onto Hornby Street. Proceed along Hornby for (0.3 km.) (6.0 km.), turning left onto Georgia Street. Follow Georgia Street turning right (1.8 km.) (7.8

km.) onto one-way (anti-clockwise) Park Drive at the south, and main entrance, to Stanley Park. Keep right passing under the small stone bridge.

NOTE:Be careful that you exit the park near this same entrance if you do not wish to get onto the causeway (Highway 99-1). Once on the causeway there are no exits until you cross over the Lion's Gate Bridge. For those proceeding over the Lion's Gate Bridge do a full-loop of the park, exiting the park just east of Prospect Point, the most convenient entrance for the bridge from the park. If you continue along Georgia Street (Highway 99-1) it is an additional (4.3 km.) through the park and over the Lion's Gate Bridge to Marine Drive for the (00.0 km.) starting point for the Vancouver to Horseshoe Bay Loop.

STANLEY PARK

Stanley Park, with a total area of 2,470 hectares, is situated on a peninsula at the mouth of Burrard Inlet adjacent to Vancouver, an easy access for motorists, or only a half-hour walk from the downtown core. The best way of birding the park (where 230 species have been recorded) is to drive making periodic stops, but a two-to-three hour hike will also take you thirteen kilometers around the perimeter of the park.

Three hikes are suggested.

1) From the bus loop at the park entrance, walk along the south side of Lost Lagoon, over the stone arch bridge, then to the sea wall along the edge of Burrard Inlet. Proceed along the sea wall north, about halfway to the tip of the peninsula to Ferguson Point, and then cut east via a forest trail, back to Lost Lagoon and the park entrance.

2) If you have the energy, proceed beyond Ferguson Point, around the tip to Lumberman's Arch on the east side (a total of 13 km.), and back through the zoo to the park entrance.

3) A much shorter hike is to walk east from the main entrance along the shore to Brockton Point, then northwest to Lumberman's Arch and through the zoo and again back to the main entrance. Driving along Park Drive around the periphery of the park, which basically follows the shoreline, and stopping for short strolls is faster and more productive.

At the edges of the selectively logged, mature Douglas-fir coastal forest within the park are forest edge habitats. Extensive areas have been cleared for gardens, which attract urban avifauna such as the resident Bewick's Wren. Other habitats include deciduous treed areas, shrubbery, rocky shorelines, sandy beaches, littoral waters, and two lakes, Beaver Lake and Lost Lagoon. A walk will usually produce 60 to 70 species. Species diversity is best during migrations, good from mid-November through mid-March, and poor during the breeding season.

Over the years an astonishing selection of vagrants have appeared within the park's boundaries. In spring Calliope Hummingbird, Red-naped Sapsucker, Black Phoebe, Say's Phoebe, House Wren, Mountain Bluebird, and Yellow-headed Blackbird have occured. In fall Ash-throated Flycatcher, Clark's Nutcracker, Philadelphia Vireo, Black-and-white Warbler, Palm Warbler, Northern Waterthrush, American Redstart, Grasshopper Sparrow, Rusty Blackbird, and White-winged Crossbill have occured.

After entering the park, drive along Park Drive keeping right at junctions to the Yacht Club and adjacent Deadman's Island in Coal Harbour (1.1 km.). At low tides, the mudflats from upper Coal Harbour around to Ferguson Point should be checked for shorebirds. Be sure to arrive early before human disturbance. Black-bellied Plover, Greater Yellowlegs, Lesser Yellowlegs, Spotted Sandpiper, Western Sandpiper, and Least Sandpiper are among the most common species expected. Offshore during winter are large rafts of Greater Scaup.

Proceed along Park Drive to the lighthouse at Brockton Point (0.7 km.) (1.8 km.). From the point it is possible to walk the seawall around the park. This site is one of the better areas for wintering waterfowl on the lower mainland.

Offshore in Burrard Inlet, the world's largest concentration of Barrow's Goldeneye, and Surf Scoter ride the waves. Over 4,000 Western Grebe also call Burrard Inlet winter home. Common Loon, Red-throated Loon, Red-necked Grebe, Horned Grebe, American Wigeon, Greater Scaup, Oldsquaw, Common Goldeneye, Bufflehead, and Red-breasted Merganser are common winter visitants. Double-crested Cormorant, Pelagic Cormorant, Pigeon Guillemot and Marbled Murrelet are common residents, while well-offshore Common Murre are occasionally seen outside the summer months. Wintering Black Turnstone feed amongst the seaweed-covered rocks and diligent examination of the Glaucous-winged Gull and Mew Gull flocks should produce a rarity; Heermann's Gull and Sabine's Gull have been recorded on occasion. Franklin's Gull are rare but regular migrants, travelling with groups of the common Bonaparte's Gull during late summer and fall.

Scan the Common Tern flocks that are regular in autumn as Arctic Tern, Forster's Tern, and Caspian Tern have all been recorded. Great Blue Heron have a rookery adjacent to the zoo, numbers are seen feeding on the tidal flats during lower tides. Check the flowering broadleaf maples at Brockton Point in spring; the flowers peak in April and are riddled with insects thus attracting throngs of insect-eating migrants, especially vireos and warblers.

Proceed along Park Drive to the "Figurehead', the sculpture of a female skin diver on a rock (0.9 km.) (2.7 km.). Yellow-billed Loon have been recorded offshore. These loons are winter visitors, most often recorded in the month of February as they again move northward.

 Several other trails criss-cross through the forest. A side trip to Beaver Lake, with the only real marsh in the park, is recommended.

After passing the saltwater swimming pool at "Lumberman's Arch", watch for a stone bridge over a small creek (0.9 km.) (3.6 km.). Park, and walk up the pathway along the stream. This inland trail passes Beaver Lake and then follows the lake's shore.

A pair of Bald Eagle have an active nest in a large snag between the lake and the minature railway. Wood Duck nest in the man-made nest boxes around the lake, and, with Pied-billed Grebe, Mallard, and Hooded Merganser (uncommon), are often viewed on the lily-choked lake's surface. The Trumpeter Swan and Tundra Swan here are pinioned: the Mute Swan and Black Swan within the park are also for display. Virginia Rail and Sora, although sometimes seen emerging into open areas, are typically viewed as cryptic shapes lurking amongst the waterside vegetation.

The denser forest stands within the park are found around Beaver Lake. Nearby forests contain Northern Pygmy-Owl and Red-breasted Sapsucker (rare; mainly winter), Hairy Woodpecker, Olive-sided Flycatcher, Hammond's Flycatcher, Pacific-slope Flycatcher, Chestnut-backed Chickadee, Brown Creeper, Red-breasted Nuthatch, Winter Wren, Golden-crowned Kinglet, Swainson's Thrush, CassinŌs Vireo, Orange-crowned Warbler, Black-throated Gray Warbler, Townsend's Warbler, Wilson's Warbler, and Western Tanager.

The shrubbery around the lake's perimeter have Downy Woodpecker, Willow Flycatcher, Yellow Warbler, Song Sparrow, Black-headed Grosbeak, and Red-winged Blackbird. Quiet in winter, long periods of time may pass before a mixed-species feeding flock is encountered in these deep woods. At this time a Northern Goshawk is possible, sitting hunched in the chilly dawn waiting for the sun's ray's to warm its plumage before starting on another day's hunting.

Return to Park Drive and proceed westward towards the Lion's Gate Bridge, looking under the bridge for Pigeon Guillemot and Marbled Murrelet. After driving (0.9 km.) (4.5 km.) Park Drive turns sharply back on itself, and after a series of right turns passes over Highway 99 after an additional (0.7 km.) (5.2 km.). At this point you can enter Highway 99-1 for the Lion's Gate Bridge (see page 84). NOTE: This exit is closed between 3:30 p.m. and 6:30 p.m. Monday to Friday. Just past the highway overpass (0.3 km.) (5.5 km.), pull over at the lookout at Prospect Point, the highest elevation in the park.

Pigeon Guillemot nest on the cliff-face, while in winter, Harlequin Duck forage around the rocks below. On fair days, during north-west winds, the lookout serves as a good vantage point to look for migrating raptors.). A few Turkey Vulture and Osprey are found among the more common birds in the great southward movement: Sharp-shinned Hawk, Cooper's Hawk and Red-tailed Hawk.

One kilometer past Prospect Point, watch for the signs on the right designating the trailhead for Siwash Rock (6.5 km.). Pelagic

Cormorant and Glaucous-winged Gull always decorate this seastack. In winter, the rocks exposed at low tide along this stretch of coastline, around to Ferguson Point, are foraged by Black Turnstone and Sanderling (rarely Wandering Tattler, Ruddy Turnstone, and Red-necked Phalarope). Harlequin Duck frolic in the torrents among the rocks just offshore in winter, while Common Merganser nest in the vicinity. There has been at least four records of King Eider wintering in company with the large rafts of Surf Scoter and a common Eider through 1997-98. The odd Eurasian Wigeon is seen in accompaniment with the flocks of American Wigeon. Parasitic Jaegers are seen parasitizing the Common Tern during autumn. Although single jaegers are the norm, groups of three or four jaegers are often seen. The odd wayward pelagic species is recorded with such species as Black-legged Kittiwake.

Continue southwest past Third Beach toward Ferguson Point, an additional kilometer (7.5 km.). Check the point for a range of similar species noted above. Third Beach also has many broadleaf maples which attract migrants in April when the trees are in bloom.

Continue along Park Drive for an additional kilometer (8.3 km.), bearing left after the road divides, parking at the first opportunity near the lake (0.4 km.) (8.7 km.). Lost Lagoon, as the lake is named, contains a variety of wintering waterfowl with Canada Goose, Mallard, American Wigeon, Wood Duck, Canvasback, Tufted Duck (rare; recorded almost annually), Greater Scaup, Lesser Scaup, Common Merganser, Red-breasted Merganser, Hooded Merganser (rare), and American Coot. A few Redhead and Ring-necked Duck winter regularly, one of the better sites for these locally rare ducks in the Vancouver area. Barrow's Goldeneye and Common Goldeneye use the lake as a night roost, leaving to feed elsewhere during the day. The accidental Smew has occured, associating one winter with the roosting goldeneye. The flock of Mute Swan on the lake are not "countable". Double-crested Cormorant often rest on the fountain. Bonaparte's Gull, Ring-billed Gull, Mew Gull, Herring Gull (uncommon), California Gull, Thayer's Gull (uncommon), Western Gull (rare), and Glaucous-winged Gull occur in season. Virginia Rail breed around the lake and remain through the winter some years, albeit in small numbers.

The bridge west of Lost Lagoon is a mandatory site for anyone with a keen interest in finding a plethora of migrants and the everpresent possibility of vagrants. The single record of Black Phoebe for the province was made at Lost Lagoon, as was the only coastal British Columbia record of Philadelphia Vireo (Nov. 1973). The unobstrusive vireo feed in the sycamore trees lining the road for almost three weeks.

The ornamental plantings and woods around Lost Lagoon are excellent for finding migrants: Vaux's Swift, Rufous Hummingbird, Western Wood-Pewee, Ruby-crowned Kinglet, Swainson's Thrush, Hermit Thrush, American Robin, American Pipit, Cassin's Vireo, Warbling Vireo,

Orange-crowned Warbler, Yellow-rumped Warbler, Black-throated Gray
Warbler, Townsend's Warbler, Yellow Warbler, Wilson's Warbler, Savannah
Sparrow, White-crowned Sparrow, Golden-crowned Sparrow, Lincoln's
Sparrow, and Western Tanager are commonly found. Townsend's Solitaire
and Nashville Warbler are rare to uncommon migrants, regularly found in
spring. The ubiquitous House Finch and belligerent Bewick's Wren are
resident, singing unremittingly throughout the spring

   The tangle of shrubbery east of the bridge contains several feeders. Black-
capped Chickadee, Chestnut-backed Chickadee, Spotted Towhee, Song
Sparrow, Dark-eyed Junco, White-throated Sparrow (rare; regular),
occasionally Golden-crowned Sparrow, Fox Sparrow, Red-winged Blackbird,
and occasionally Brown-headed Cowbird use the feeders in season. American
Tree Sparrow and Harris' Sparrow have been recorded in winter. On the
stream beneath the bridge are Wood Duck and a small introduced (and
"uncountableÓ) population of Mandarin Duck.

   Retrace your route back to Park Drive and proceed to the
southwestern boundary of the park along Beach Avenue, an
additional kilometer (9.3 km.). The offshore waters are known as English Bay.
On the bay are Marbled Murrelet and Pigeon Guillemot with the oddt
Rhinoceros Auklet appearing during summer. You may return to the one-way
circular drive of Park Drive, continuing your loop around Stanley Park, as the
road from Lost Lagoon to English Bay is two-way.

NOTES & OBSERVATIONS

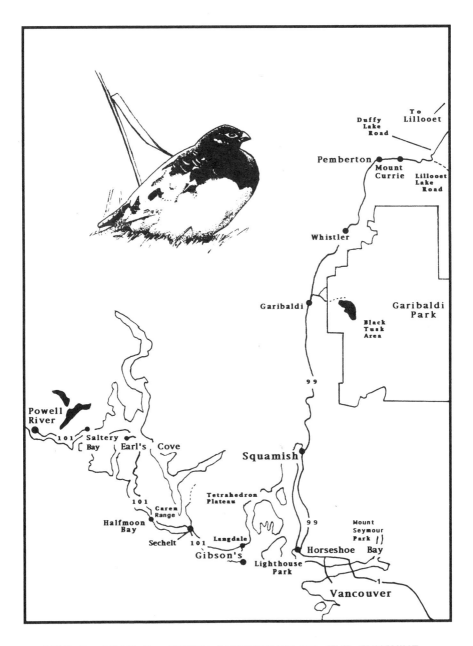

MAP 3 LOOP 3 NORTH VANCOUVER TO THE SUNSHINE COAST AND LILLOOET

LOOP 3 NORTH VANCOUVER TO THE SUNSHINE COAST AND LILLOOET

VANCOUVER to HORSESHOE BAY

Horseshoe Bay is only a twenty minute (I 7.9 kilometer) drive north and west from the junctions of Seymour and Georgia Streets in downtown Vancouver along Highway 99 and 99-1. Follow the Highway 99 signs through Stanley Park, north across the Lion's Gate Bridge to West Vancouver. Soon after crossing the bridge, a traffic circle will bring you down and under the overpass onto Marine Drive (00.0 km.). Heading west on Marine Drive for (0.5 km.), you will then veer north on Taylor Way for an additional (1.3 km.) where you will drive under the Highway 99-1 overpass, hence using the on-ramp for Highway 99-1 West. It is an additional 11.7 kilometers (1 3.6 km.) to the Horseshoe Ferry Terminal from this point.

(NOTE:If you are heading for Mount Seymour use the on-ramp for Highway 99-1 East (actually Highway 1) and follow the signs for Mount Seymour.)

Proceed along Highway 99-1 West to the ferry terminal. The Horseshoe Bay Ferry Terminal is accessible from the highway, immediately off to the left; an off-ramp directs traffic to the tollbooths and traffic lanes. Several signs warn well in advance of your approach to the ferry terminal. Whyte Cliff Park, two kilometers distant, is attainable from Exit 1 for the town of Horseshoe Bay along meandering Marine Drive; "rock shorebirds" are seen here on occasion.

LIGHTHOUSE PARK

Along the way to Horseshoe Bay you may consider a short side-trip to Lighthouse Park where 151 species have been recorded. Lighthouse Park provides access to old-growth forest and is one the few sites in Vancouver for shorebirds that inhabit rocky shores. Rock shorebirds are, however, more reliable at sites on the Sunshine Coast or on Vancouver Island!

Follow the above directions towards the ferry terminal. At the on-ramp for Highway 99-1 West at Taylor Way start at (00.0 km.). At (5.9km.) take the Hollyburn Heights exit, turn left at the overpass and over to the south side of Highway 99-1 onto Westridge Ave. (0.4 km.)(6.3km.). Turn right onto Southridge Ave., then immediately left onto Bayridge Avenue for (0.2 km.) (6.5 km.), jogging right (0.2 km.) (6.7 km.), then left (0.4 km.) (7.1 km.), and again right to Sharon Street (0.1km.) (7.2 km.). Follow Sharon Street (left) to Marine Drive (0.3km.)(7.5 km.). At Marine Drive turn right and continue an additional (3.0km.) (10.5 km.), watching on the left for a small "LighthousePark" sign. Turn left at the sign onto Beacon Lane, bearing left to the park entrance (0.2 km.) (I0.7 km.). It is an additional (0.8 km.) (I1.5 km.) to the turnaround within Lighthouse Park. Using the highway may save time, alternatively, continue west along Marine Way after crossing the Lion's Gate Bridge (1 1.5 km.) to the junction of Marine Way and Beacon Lane.

Indian Bluff, the isolated western sector of the park (which is mainly residential properties) is reached from Bear and Happy Valley Lanes (0.5 km.). Offshore is a group of islets, the small Grebe Islets, which are best scoped from Jack Pine Point at the end of Pitcairn Place off Marine Drive (continue on Marine Drive past the Beacon Lane turnoff for (0.5 km.) to Pitcairn Place, turning left to the termination (0.2 km.) (0.8 km.).

Black Oystercatcher frequent the tidewashed rocky shores of the Grebe Islets throughout the year, while migrant Wandering Tattler, and wintering Black Turnstone, Surfbird, and Rock Sandpiper occur here or at other rocky shores throughout the park on a fairly regular basis. Congregating on the "salt chuck" around the Grebe Islets are large rafts of wintering Western Grebe. Off the West Vancouver Yacht Club, (3.4 km.) further northwest along meandering Marine Drive, is Eagle Island and other islets and rocks lying in Fisherman's Cove where rock shorebirds are occasionally found.

From an infuriatingly high level among the Douglas-firs, a buzzy song drifts down to the ear. Glimpses of the active singer will reveal a vibrant chrome-yellow breast and bold patches of lamp-black; only these intense markings will enable the viewer to identify the Townsend's Warbler. Another song of similar quality, though of a more "weezy" tone, emits from the among the deciduous branches nearby, a striking male Black-throated Gray Warbler! The silence of the park's mature west coast conifer forest is broken by the "morse-code" drumming of the Red-breasted Sapsucker. Pileated Woodpecker, Hairy Woodpecker, Olive-sided Flycatcher, Hammond's Flycatcher, Pacific-slope Flycatcher, Chestnut-backed Chickadee, Red-breasted Nuthatch, Winter Wren, and Golden-crowned Kinglet will, on occasion, all add their own music to this moss-festooned forest.

In spring, a series of extremely low pitched hoots (just within range of the hearing ability of the human ear and "felt" more than heard) will reveal the presence of a male Blue Grouse. Exploration in the direction of the "booming" (somewhat difficult because of the ventriloquistic quality) may find the owner high on a branch above the ground. Soon you will have unobstructed views of the courting male's cadmium neck-sacs as they are repeatedly inflated to amplify each hoot; the sacs are surrounded by a beautiful fluffy ruff of white-based feathers which cover the bare patch when it is not in use. As the grouse may creep off on approach, you must stock the gamebird carefully, climbing to the top of a rocky knoll where the moss gives silent footing, and from which the birds often call.

NOTES & OBSERVATIONS

LOOP 3   HORSESHOE BAY to the SUNSHINE COAST

The Sunshine Coast has a long, deeply indented coastline with dramatic fjords and surf-swept headlands, constantly battered by the cold waters of the Straits of Georgia. Breathtaking mountains of almost perfect symmetry stand as sentinels over an inland waterway comprised of Salmon, Sechelt, Narrows and Jervis Inlets. The highest of these mountains, rising 3,000 m. from the sea, are crowned with vast icy peaks, glaciers, and alpine meadows of awesome magnificence. The spine of Vancouver Island's mountains tower into the blue heavens offshore, this sleeping giant, and numerous smaller islands punctuating the western skyline with untimely beauty.

Horseshoe Bay to Wilson Creek Estuary

Catch the ferry from Horseshoe Bay to Langdale. After landing at Langdale (00.0 km.), turn left onto Highway 101 towards Gibsons. After driving (5.0 km.) you will arrive at the community of Gibsons, turn left and check out the harbour for a variety of loons, grebes, cormorants, sea ducks, gulls, and alcids. Winter is the best season, although several species of marine birds will be present throughout the year.

WILSON CREEK ESTUARY

After driving (22.0 km.), turn left at the shopping mall onto Field Road and park at its termination at the Strait of Georgia. Walk a short distance towards the ocean, you will find a path that leads around to the northern side of the Wilson Creek Estuary and after walking some 250 meters you will arrive at the beach. This area (under threat of development) has been a migrant trap for rarities with recordings of Ash-throated Flycatcher, Say's Phoebe, Rock Wren, and Lesser Goldfinch. The small mudflats in the estuary at lower tides attract a restricted number of shorebirds, but there can be as many as sixteen species with Black Oystercatcher, Whimbrel, Stilt Sandpiper, Black Turnstone, Surfbird, and Rock Sandpiper topping the list.

Wilson Creek Estuary to Mission Point

Return to Highway 1 01 and turn left. After driving an additional (0.5 km.) (22.5 km.) park, walk down the street that parallels the gas station and you will come to an old log-booming ground. A visit at low tide in August could reward you with such uncommon birds as Green Heron, Franklin's Gull, and Whimbrel.

MISSION POINT

Continuing along Highway 101 towards Sechelt, Highway 101 will soon run alongside Davis Bay and the Strait of Georgia; pull over to the left and park (23.0 km.). A walk along the sandy beach in a southerly direction for 200 meters will bring you to Mission Point, a shingle spit at the mouth of Chapman Creek. Mission Point is the best site on the mainland for shorebirds that are associated with rocky shorelines. Black Oystercatcher, Black Turnstone, and Surfbird are found irregularly from mid-July to mid-April. Rock Sandpiper, often in flocks of 50, do not appear regularly until November. Mixed flocks of all four species are reliable at this site, occasionally with Black-bellied Plover, on lower tides from November through to mid-April.

 Mission Point provides a good viewing point to scan the adjacent straits for Common Loon, Pacific Loon, Red-throated Loon, Western Grebe, Red-necked Grebe, Horned Grebe, Double-crested Cormorant, Brandt's Cormorant, Pelagic Cormorant, Greater Scaup, White-winged Scoter, Surf Scoter, Common Goldeneye, Bufflehead, Red-breasted Merganser, Common Murre, Pigeon Guillemot, and Marbled Murrelet. Ancient Murrelet is present during the months of November and December and Rhinoceros Auklet in late summer. Large flocks of gulls rest on the beach in winter, worth checking through, as twelve species of gull have been recorded here.

For better access to the south side of Chapman Creek, return to Highway 101, turn right, pass over the Chapman Creek bridge and turn right at the first road (0.2 km.) and park at its termination. Walk down Chapman Creek for 50 meters to the spit.

SECHELT

Continue on Highway 101 to Sechelt for an additional (6.0 km.) (29.0 km.). If you wish to obtain a copy of a map of the access roads and trails of the Tetrahedron Plateau, one is available from the Ministry of Forests field office in Sechelt.

NOTE:Logging roads on the Sunshine Coast may have their access limited to weekends, always obey these and heed warning signs!

Turn right off Highway 101 at the only set of traffic lights in Sechelt onto Wharf Road. After driving (1.0 km.) (30.0 km.) you will reach the head of the tidal Sechelt Inlet. Porpoise Bay, as the inlet is known, is on your right, and Sechelt Marsh is on your left.

Porpoise Bay is rimmed with tidal mud-flats, which, at low tides, are favoured by migrant shorebirds. In winter there are many species of duck with rafts of American Wigeon, the odd Eurasian Wigeon among them. Peregrine Falcon feed regularly on these wintering waterfowl. Sechelt Marsh, a small pond, shelters such fresh water species as Mallard, Green-winged Teal, American Wigeon, Northern Pintail, Wood Duck, Canvasback, Redhead, Ring-necked Duck, Lesser Scaup, and Hooded Merganser on occasion. American Bittern, Sora, and Green Heron are among the rarer marsh specialists that have been recorded. Check the surrounding vegetation for various migrant passerines.

PORPOISE BAY PROVINCIAL PARK

Porpoise Bay Provincial Park, a mature coastal forest containing the usual species associated with these humid forests, can be reached from Porpoise Bay by bearing right from Wharf Road onto East Porpoise Bay Road for (7.0 km.) (37.0 km.), along the east side of Porpoise Bay (follow the Porpoise Bay Provincial Park signs).

After parking near the beach, check the forest trails for Hairy Woodpecker, Pileated Woodpecker, Chestnut-backed Chickadee, Red-breasted Nuthatch, Brown Creeper, Winter Wren, Golden-crowned Kinglet, Swainson's Thrush, Varied Thrush (mainly winter), Hutton's Vireo, CassinŌs Vireo, Warbling Vireo, Orange-crowned Warbler, Black-throated Gray Warbler, Townsend's Warbler, and MacGillivray's Warbler. The Western Tanager is heard, singing their "robin-like" songs from within the huge broadleaf maples. Virginia Rail and Common Yellowthroat inhabit the cattail marsh at the estuary of Angus Creek. Lapland Longspur occur in the estuary as an uncommon fall migrant, while only a single record for Swamp Sparrow exists. American Dipper can be found frolicking among the torrents along Angus Creek in winter and spring.

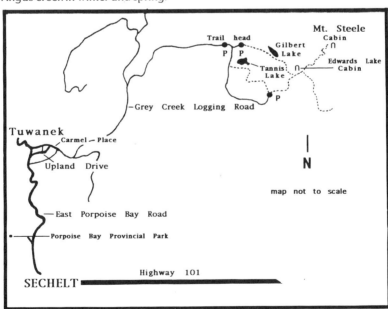

Map 4   TETRAHEDRON PLATEAU

TETRAHEDRON PLATEAU

Continue along East Porpoise Bay Road for an additional (2.5 km.) (39.5 km.) to Upland Drive - just past Jackson Brothers' Logging Road. (NOTE: the following kilometerages are from (00.0 km.) at the junction of East Porpoise Bay Road and Highway 101 in downtown Sechelt (East Porpoise Bay Road is just past Interfor Logging Road). From Sechelt, turn right onto East Porpoise Bay Road for 9.5 kilometers to Upland Drive in the community of Tuwanek. Turn right onto Upland Drive, go (0.5 km.) (1 0.0 km.), and turn right onto Carmel Place which becomes the Grey Creek Logging Road after an additional (0.4 km.) (1 0.4 km.). Keep to the left at the fork (0.4 km.) (1 0.8 km.), driving up the west main following the ski signs, and keeping right at the "Mile 7" marker (21.6 km.).

Continue to the parking area (26.3 km.), then continue on the left road past the forking of the logging roads and the trail head if the road is passable (27.3 km.). A second parking area is found at the logging roads termination at (27.5 km.) below the Tetrahedron Plateau where well-defined trails (these trails are cross-country ski trails in winter) lead to the peaks of Panther (1,866 m.), and Mt. Steele (1,800 m.). There are no trails to the highest peak of Tetrahedron (1,900 m.). A strenuous 8 km walk, climbing some 3,200 ft. in elevation, is required to reach the summit of the Tetrahedron Plateau. En route there are two strategically placed cabins available for free use, one at Edwards Lake, the other near the summit of Mt. Steele.

Rock Ptarmigan breed irregularly in the restricted rocky alpine slopes on Mt. Steele and are most easily found during the months of June, July and August. The best area to search is on the partially treed rocky-slope that lies just behind and above the Mt. Steele cabin. Northern Goshawk, the secretive Blue Grouse, Band-tailed Pigeon, Northern Pygmy-Owl, Gray Jay, Townsend's Solitaire (uncommon), Townsend's Warbler, the sedate Pine Grosbeak, and the beautiful Gray-crowned Rosy Finch may be encountered along the walk. Three-toed Woodpecker occur around Gilbert Lake which lies along the trail to Mt. Steele.

From the second parking area, walk the only trail which leads to Gilbert lake (2.4 km.), then on to Edwards Lake an additional (0.9 km.). At Edwards Lake there is a "T" junction in the trails, take the left trail that leads to the Edwards Lake Cabin an additional (1.6 km.). Keep left again at the trails forking, and on to the Mt. Steele Cabin after an additional (3.1 km.)

TETRAHEDRON PLATEAU

Sechet to Wakefield Creek

Return to Sechelt, turning right towards Halfmoon Bay (00.0 km.). After driving (3.0 km.) you will see the Wakefield Inn.

WAKEFIELD CREEK

After a brief repast, walk left and down the short cul-de-sac of Wakefield Creek to the shore where migrant Common Terns, in fall, are often harrased by Parasitic Jaeger. When the silence is broken by wheeling, screeming terns, one or more are in the area. The beach at the mouth of Wakefield Creek is an excellent viewpoint from which thousands of Ancient Murrelet can be seen moving southward on certain days during the winter months; numerous Common Murre, Pigeon Guillemot, Marbled Murrelet, and a few Rhinoceros Auklet are seen in season.

Wakefield Creek to Honeymoon Bay

Continuing along Highway 1 01 north towards Halfmoon Bay you will see Trout Lake on the right after driving (5.0 km.) (8.0 km.) where, in winter, there are Pied-billed Grebe, Mallard, Ring-necked Duck, Lesser Scaup, and Hooded Merganser.

CAREN RANGE

A well-maintained logging road leads off to the right at (9.5 km.) (500 m. before the left turn to Halfmoon Bay), which leads to the Caren Range. Continue along the main gravel road, ignoring all smaller sideroads, for twelve kilometers where the road forks.

Both roads offer spectacular vistas of the surrounding countryside. Alongside the right fork is Lyon Lake, around which is a remnant of old-growth forest, you can hear, at dawn, a strange and beautiful chorus of Varied Thrush and Hermit Thrush songs drift from the undergrowth of the ancient western hemlocks and yellow-cedars. Dark shapes against a blue sky materialize into flocks of Black Swift and Vaux's Swift hawking for insects at tremendous speeds high over the forests. Aerial Turkey Vulture float by on still dihedral wings. Species that will be found on the Caren Range are similar to those on the Tetrahedron Plateau including Northern Goshawk, Blue Grouse, Band-tailed Pigeon, Northern Pygmy-Owl, Three-toed Woodpecker, Gray Jay, Townsend's Solitaire (uncommon), and Townsend's Warbler.

At the community of Halfmoon Bay (10.0 km.) or 39.0 kms from Langdale, you could drive to the red government wharf for an additional opportunity to scope for marine birds.

SMUGGLERS COVE PROVINCIAL PARK

One kilometer past the town of Halfmoon Bay (12.0 km.), turn left onto Brooks Road at the Smugglers Cove Provincial Park sign. After driving an additional (3.0 km.) (15.0 km.) you will reach Smugglers Cove Provincial Park.

The park offers walks along a 800m long trail through old-growth and second-growth humid coast coniferous forest, through mixed deciduous forest, past two marshes, and on to a rocky, arbutus-covered headland. This sunny, dry setting, surrounded by a peaceful cove on Welcome Passage, will entice birders to linger awhile before returning to the cool, damp interior of the forests.

Around the rocky shoreline of the headland you could encounter Harlequin Duck, Black Oystercatcher, Black Turnstone, or Surfbird. Offshore are Common Murre, Pigeon Guillemot, and Marbled Murrelet. Virginia Rail (marshes), Ruffed Grouse, Hairy Woodpecker, Olive-sided Flycatcher, Western Wood-Pewee (uncommon), Hammond's Flycatcher, Willow Flycatcher (willow scrub), Pacific-slope Flycatcher, Chestnut-backed Chickadee, Red-breasted Nuthatch, Winter Wren, Golden-crowned Kinglet, Swainson's Thrush, Hutton's Vireo, Black-throated Gray Warbler (mixed forest), and Red Crossbill (irregular) are to be expected along the trail.

Return to Horseshoe Bay

LOOP 3. HORSESHOE BAY TO LILLOOET

Horseshoe Bay to Garibaldi Park

Horseshoe Bay (00.0 km.). After (60.0 kms.) you will pass through Squamish, another (35.0 kms.) (95.0 kms.) and you will pass through Garibaldi, after an additional (2.0 km.) (97.0 km.), take the paved road leading (3.0 kms.) to the Rubble Creek parking lot that is signed for Black Tusk Nature Conservancy Area and Garibaldi Provincial Park.

GARIBALDI PARK

A mere hundred kilometers from Vancouver, Garibaldi Provincial Park is a quick escape from the noise and traffic to a pristine alpine wilderness. Although a strenuous nine kilometer hike is involved, this is one of the closer areas to Vancouver for two alpine specialties, White tailed Ptarmigan and Gray-crowned Rosy Finch. For those in good shape, and walking at a very quick pace, a round-trip is possible in one day; others with more time and less energy will find camping at Garibaldi Lake or Taylor campgrounds. Main trails lead into Diamond Head, Black Tusk and Garibaldi Lake, Cheakamus Lake, and Singing Pass. The best season to visit is in July and August when most of the snow has melted and the parent ptarmigan are protecting chicks, thus making them easier to find.

A hike from the parking lot along the excellent trail to Garibaldi Lake in sub-alpine at 1,468 m. takes about three hours, traversing 9 kilometers and climbing 600 m. Around the lake's campground are the confiding Clark's Nutcracker and Gray Jay, which often raid the picnic tables, and are constant companions at this altitude. Three-toed Woodpecker are seen on occasion. Other birds associated with the lake are Common Loon, Spotted Sandpiper, occasionally California Gull, Bonaparte's Gull, and Mew Gull on the rocks near Battleship Islets, Osprey, and American Dipper.

When leaving the parking lot towards Garibaldi Lake, you will climb through wet forest dominated by Douglas-fir containing the characteristic avifauna: Red-breasted Sapsucker, Pacific-slope Flycatcher, Steller's Jay, Chestnut-backed Chickadee, Red-breasted Nuthatch, Winter Wren, Golden-crowned Kinglet, Ruby-crowned Kinglet, Hermit Thrush, Varied Thrush, Townsend's Warbler, and Pine Siskin.

As you pass Barrier Lake and Lesser Garibaldi Lake, about six kilometers into your hike, look for a possible Barrow's Goldeneye or Harlequin Duck. Yellow-rumped Warbler, Wilson's Warbler and White-crowned Sparrow inhabit the willows around the shoreline.

Trails lead from Garibaldi Lake to higher elevations, through sub-alpine meadows to Panorama Ridge, Black Tusk, Heim Lake, and Heim Glacier. In the sub-alpine are Blue Grouse, Mountain Chickadee and Red Crossbill. As you approach Black Tusk, or the other vand-swept ridges, search around the remaining patches of snow for feeding Gray-crowned Rosy Finch and then carefully investigate the talus slopes for White-tailed Ptarmigan; the pale rocks with their multi-patchwork of black lichens create the perfect camouflage for these mottled alpine grouse. A Golden Eagle may make an appearance overhead.

Garibaldi to Pemberton - Mount Currie - Lillooet

Those wishing to see Spotted Owl can continue on Highway 99 north along Howe Sound towards Squamish, Whistler and Pemberton. From Pemberton one can continue on a secondary paved road through to Lillooet, thence onwards to the Okanagan Valley or points north.

When you reach Pemberton (1 43.0 km.), follow the signs right for Mount Currie, an additional (6.0 km.) (149.0 km.). In Mount Currie watch for the Duffy Lake Road sign and continue right on this secondary paved road towards Lillooet Lake, Duffy Lake, and distant Lillooet. Soon after crossing the Joffre Creek bridge, an additional (1 1.5 km.) (1 60.5 km.), there is a fork. The left paved section continues on to Duffy Lake and Lillooet, the right well-maintained gravel section is the Lillooet Lake Road. Take the right fork towards Lillooet Lake, watching for the kilometer markers alongside the road.

When you reach kilometer 9, continue an additional (0.6 km.) (1 70.1 km.) and watch for a large snag on the rightside of the road. Directly across the road from here is a very large tree standing on a hill. This has been the most reliable site for Spotted Owl in British Columbia, check along the leftside of the road from here back to kilometer 8 or up to km. 13. If the forested-slope terminates, you have passed the site. During the first hours after sunset and again before dawn, from mid-April through July, the owls will respond to taped calls. June and July are the better months when they will sometimes respond during the daylight hours.

Continue onto Lillooet (80 km.) or return to Horseshoe Bay.

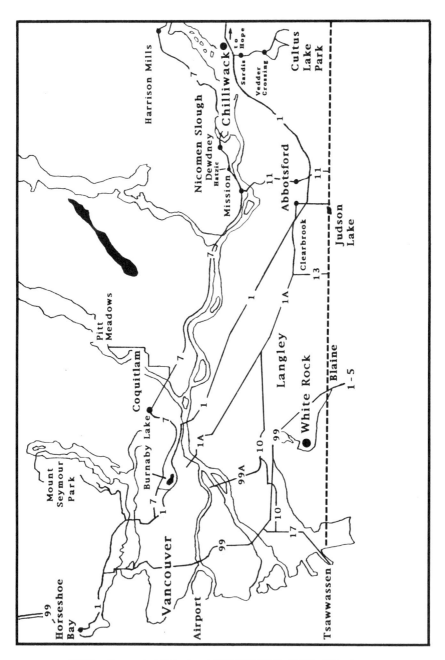

MAP 5   LOOP 4   HORSESHOE BAY TO HOPE

LOOP 4   HIGHWAY 1 - HORSESHOE BAY TO HOPE

For those wishing to drive straight through to Hope from Horseshoe Bay the total distance is (1 78.0 km.), a 2 1/2 hour drive.

Horseshoe Bay to Mount Seymour Park

 (00.0km.) We begin this loop from the on-ramp for Highway 99-1 East at Horseshoe Bay. Proceed on Highway 99-1 East, continuing straight ahead where Highway 99 splits off for Vancouver, following Highway 1. Take the Dollarton Highway exit ramp at (21.4 km.) (signed for Mount Seymour Park), just before crossing the Second Narrows Bridge. Turn left onto Main Street, turning right onto the Mount Seymour Parkway (0.4 km.) (21.8 km.). Continue to follow the Mount Seymour Park signs. Proceed along Mount Seymour Parkway for (4.4 km.) (26.2 km.), turning left at the traffic lights onto Mount Seymour Road.

MOUNT SEYMOUR PARK

Mount Seymour, with a paved road that climbs to a skiing area close to the summit, provides the best access to sub-alpine and alpine habitats adjacent to the city of Vancouver. Snow cover usually is present at the higher elevations until mid-June and chains or snowtires are often required on the park's roads after winter snowfalls. This 3,508 hectare park has a park office at the entrance which has a checklist of the park's birds and a brochure giving trail information. Elevation rises from 100 m. at the gate to 1000 m. at the base of the ski chair lift at the top. Lower slopes of the park (below 900 m.) are clothed in cedars and western hemlock where old-growth forests once stood. Mountain hemlock dominates the higher slopes.

(00.0km.) From the park entrance, at the corner of Mount Seymour Parkway and Mount Seymour Road, there are mileposts along twisting Indian River Drive which also give altitudes. The best time of year to bird the lower elevations is during spring Ð mid-April to early June. Typical denizens of these lower forests are Western Screech-Owl, the jewel-like Rufous Hummingbird, Brown Creeper, Red-breasted Nuthatch, the demure Winter Wren, Hutton's Vireo, CassinÕs Vireo, Black-throated Gray Warbler, Townsend's Warbler, Wilson's Warbler, and the beautiful Western Tanager. The secretive Blue Grouse are fairly common residents of the park. As you progress upwards towards the summit, make frequent stops listening for "hooting" during April through the month of June; lucky observers could see one alongside the road. Spotted Owl have been heard on rare occasions along the road. A night of owling, making similar stops between the park entrance and the summit listening for this rare owl's hesitant dog-like barks, is recommended.

At the Mile 1.6 marker (2.6 km.) look for a log arch crossing the road. The Baden-Powell trail leads off through western hemlock woods here. The exquisite and highly elusive Red-breasted Sapsucker is resident in these forests. Listen in spring for their "morse code" drumming. This is always a productive site for Hutton's Vireo, a monotonous "zu-weep, zu-weep, zu-weep" song drifting from the dense foliage above announcing their presence.

At the Mile 4 marker (6.4 km.) a road on the left leads to a large cleared area. A short walk past the willow and alder scrub (where Downy Woodpecker, Western Wood-Pewee, Willow Flycatcher, and MacGillivray's Warbler are found) will bring you to the clearing. Sharp-shinned Hawk, Cooper's Hawk, Northern Goshawk, and Red-tailed Hawk are seen from the clearing in season.

At the Mile 5.5 marker (8.8 km.), pull over at the Deep Cove roadside lookout. During summer, Black Swift and Vaux's Swift are seen flying past the lookout, crossing a spectacular backdrop. As the shadows lengthen in the late evening hours the golden rays of the sun illuminate the awesome vista. Scan the multi-hued skies for Common Nighthawk as they hawk for insects. The lookout also serves as the Perimeter Trail trailhead. Red-breasted Sapsucker are often found along the trail or in the vicinity.

At Mile 8 (12.9 km.) is the main parking lot. The picnic sites here often attract the confiding Gray Jay and Common Raven (which often raid the tables). Two trails that serve as cross-country ski trails during the winter lead from the parking lot (be sure to stay on these trails when snow-covered to prevent getting lost!).

The Goldie Lake Trail leads from the east side of the parking lot, an easy (2.6 km.) hike through sub-alpine forest. Typical residents of this habitat are Blue Grouse, Hairy Woodpecker, Mountain Chickadee, Chestnut-backed Chickadee, Hermit Thrush, Varied Thrush, Red Crossbill, the rare White-winged Crossbill and Pine Grosbeak (Oct and Nov are the best), and Purple Finch. Fox Sparrow are rare breeders in the area.

The second trail leads to the summit of Mount Seymour, a strenuous eight hour hike. Bald Eagle, Turkey Vulture, and a variety of hawks, especially during the fall, may be noted from the summit, quartering the weather-worn crags or drifting silently overhead. Northern Pygmy-Owl are permanent residents, investigate any scolding from the smaller passerines as one of these tiny diurnal predators could be the cause of their alarm. Although rare, both White-tailed Ptarmigan and Rock Ptarmigan have been found around the summit. Rock Ptarmigan are found here (at their ranges' southern terminus) along the crest of Mount Seymour. The ptarmigan are found irregularly during fall some years before deep snows prevent exploration. Check the trail under the ski chair lift or the trail leading to Mount Seymour and in the valleys between Mystery Peak and Pump Peak;

the best season is just before the snows in late November. The exhuberant songs of the American Pipit or the sight of a rare dazzling Gray-crowned Rosy Finch or uncommon Pine Grosbeak (Oct and Nov are the best times) make the harsh but beautiful tundra landscapes even more resplendent.

Mount Seymour Park to Burnaby Lake

Retrace your route back to Highway 1, proceed over the highway overpass turning left off Main Street onto the on-ramp for Highway 1 East (00.0 km.). Take the Sprott Street - Kensington Avenue exit to the right off the freeway (10.0 km.), turning left onto Sprott Street. Proceed over the highway overpass, crossing the intersection of Kensington Ave. to the "T" junction with Sperling Ave. (0.8 km.) (10.8 km.). Turn right (south) on Sperling Avenue. After driving (0.5 km.) (11.3 km.), turn left on Roberts Road for the Burnaby Rowing Pavillion. At (0.4 km.) (1 1.7 km.) you will reach the viewing stands.

BURNABY LAKE

Burnaby Lake is a fairly large lake surrounded by a regional park that is criss-crossed by nature trails leading to the adjacent marshes and second-growth woodlands. There is a nature house on the north side that is open in summer.

The Burnaby Rowing Pavillion's grandstand provides an excellent viewpoint of the lake and marshes. Scope the mouth of Deer Lake Creek and the float plane dock to the southeast.

 The private bird sanctuary there has large congregations of Canada Geese, American Coot, Mallard, Green-winged Teal, and American Wigeon. Among the less common waterfowl, which are often seen grazing on the lawns, are Greater White-fronted Geese, Snow Geese, (a single record of Ross' Goose), Northern Shoveler, and Wood Duck. Pied-billed Grebe are resident around the lake and several hundred Common Merganser and a few Hooded Merganser winter. All waterfowl stay on the lake through winter if the lake remains unfrozen.

Just southeast of the grandstand is a marsh that is enlivened by hovering Belted Kingfisher and Virginia Rail and Sora nervously creep along the water's edge and scurry away through the thick reeds. Marsh Wren and Common Yellowthroat are common breeders with the odd bird of either species wintering. Green Heron are occasionally seen around the lake's thick vegetation in late summer. Black-headed Grosbeak are common.

(00.0km.) From the pavillion, retrace your route back to Sprott Street, then right onto Kensington Ave. (00.0 km.). Proceed north on Kensington for (1.7 km.), turning right onto the Lougheed Highway

East exit, then right at the traffic lights onto Winston Road (0.2 km.) (1.9 km.). Crested Myna are occasionally found in the vicinity. Proceed east on Winston Street for (1.6 km.) (3.5 km.), turning right onto Phillips Avenue to its terminus with the lake (0.4 km.) (3.9 km.). Walk over the railway tracks to the lakeshore trail.

The large dead trees near shore on the raised point are perched upon by Bald Eagle (mainly in the winter) and Osprey in summer. Continue walking west along the nature trail for a few hundred meters to an access leading down to the marsh's edge. Virginia Rail and Sora will be heard at dawn or dusk and can be enticed to call at anytime of the day with taped calls. Other characteristic marsh birds such as Marsh Wren, Common Yellowthroat and Red-winged Blackbird will also be present.

Return to Winston Street (0.4 km.) (3.5 km.), turning right for an additional (1.0 km.) (4.5 km.), then right (south) onto Piper Avenue at the Burnaby Lake Nature House sign. The nature house is situated near the end of Piper Avenue (0.4 km.) (4.9 km.). There are nature trails leading east and west from the nature house.

You may view the lake from the end of Piper Avenue or from an observation tower a short distance to the west. Check the creek mouth for Mallard, Green-winged Teal, American Wigeon, Northern Pintail, and Wood Duck. Ring-necked Duck, a localized species in the Vancouver region, can be found outside of the summer months. In fall and winter Black-bellied Plover, Greater Yellowlegs, Long-billed Dowitcher, and Dunlin may feed close to the creek. Check the floating vegetation on the lake in the fall for migrating American Pipit; a single Red-throated Pipit and Yellow Wagtail were recorded in these flocks one year.

The nature trails around Burnaby Lake rank among the better sites on the lower mainland for finding the diminutive Bushtit. The air is sometimes filled with their soft pinging calls when a family group passes. The resident Bewick's Wren sing commonly from within the thickets, whilst Black-headed Grosbeak sing in summer from the deciduous brush surrounding the lake. The nature trails are productive in the evenings for Long-eared Owl, Great Horned Owl, and Western Screech-Owl.

Burnaby Lake to Pitt Meadows

Retrace your route back to Winston Road and the Lougheed Highway, proceeding straight across at the traffic lights onto the Kensington Ave. overpass. Proceed south along Kensington Ave., crossing the highway overpass and onto the on-ramp for Highway 1 East (00.0 km.). At (1 0.7 km.) take the #44 exit on the right for the Lougheed Highway (Highway 7) east and north towards Port Coquitiam. This is the last exit before crossing the Port Mann Bridge over the Fraser River. Following the signs of the complicated cloverleaf will take you over Highways 1 and 7 where you will eventually merge onto the lanes for Highway 7 East (1. 5 km.) (1 2.2 km.). (At this point you could also take the Pitt Meadows exit ramp). At (5.4 km.) (17.6 km.) veer right onto the Lougheed Highway East (Highway 7) on-ramp towards Port Coquitlam (the highway changes from a north/south direction at a "T" junction to an a east/west direction). Continue on Highway 7 East, crossing over the large Pitt River Bridge (along the drive you will see the Best Western Hotel on the left (3.5 km.) past Port Coquitlam). Take the first left onto Dewdney Trunk Road at the traffic lights just past the bridge (6.5 km.) (24.1 km.).

 In summer, turn left off of Dewdney Trunk Road onto Rippington Road (1.5 km.) (25.6 km.) if you wish to see Bullock's Oriole. The cottonwoods lining the road harbour a nesting pair. The hedgerows along Rippington Road (and other roads in this area) will have numerous sparrows and finches during the winter months with Spotted Towhee, Song Sparrow, Dark-eyed Junco, White-crowned Sparrow, a few Golden-crowned Sparrow, Fox Sparrow, Purple Finch, and House Finch. Harris' Sparrow and White-throated Sparrow are occasionally found. Proceed along Dewdney Trunk Road turning left at the ÒT" junction onto Harris Road (2.2 km.from Highway 7) (26.3 km.). After (3.1 km.) (29.4 km.), turn right onto McNeil Road, which twists around the base of Sheridan Hill.

PITT MEADOWS

 Pitt Meadows, an area of farmland and wetlands, is the only locality in the Georgia Depression where Sandhill Crane, Eastern Kingbird, American Redstart, and Gray Catbird are known to breed. Common Snipe may be heard to winnow in spring and summer in a wetland located where a dike intersects McNeil Road on the right (2.4 km.) (31.8 km.). The dike offers an excellent hike. Turn left off McNeil Road onto Neaves (Rennie) Road at the stop sign and continue north (3.8 km.) (33.2 km.). In winter, the area is an excellent site for raptors. Northern Harrier can be found, quartering the huge open fields, whilst Red-tailed Hawk and Rough-legged Hawk are viewed commonly. Short-eared Owl glide silently above the expanses of long marsh grasses, often seen during the day in the softer light of late afternoon.

A side trip can be made along Ladner Road branching off on the right just before the bridge (1.5 km.) (34.7 km.). This region of the meadows offers good possibilities for locating a rich plethora of warblers and other migrants both during spring and fall. Continue north on Neaves Road searching the fields for raptors during the winter or cranes during the summer. Scrutinize the large mixed flocks of Red-winged Blackbird and Brewer's Blackbird that feed in the agricultural fields during early October, through the winter months, for a possible Rusty Blackbird.

 Stops anywhere along the road through the Pitt-Addington Marsh Wildlife Management Area should produce American Bittern,

Sandhill Crane, a variety of waterfowl (Tundra Swan and Trumpeter Swan are sometimes found along the Pitt River or around the lakeshore in winter). Raptors are well represented with Bald Eagle, Northern Harrier, and Red-tailed Hawk. Virginia Rail, Sora, and Eastern Kingbird or Gray Catbird (both of which are rare in coastal British Columbia) could be found from the main road. Continue on (3.5 km.) (38.2 km.) where a dike intersects the road. Walk to the east to view an extensive area of bog where Sandhill Crane nest; obey signs!

After (2.6 km) (37.3 km), turn onto a rough gravel road for (1.7 km) to the left turn. This site produces Western Kingbird, Eastern Kingbird and Sandhill Crane (2 - 3 pairs). The best site for nesting Gray Catbird is the brushy areas along the west side of Rennie Road, 2 km. before reaching the boat launch. At the Wildlife Management Area boat launch (2.3 km.) (40.5 km.) is a trail leading off to the east through an area of deciduous second-growth where American Redstart have nested. Calliope Hummingbird are rare migrants coastally in spring and have been recorded in the area.

Pitt Meadows to Judson Lake

Retrace your route back to the Highway 1 East on-ramp (00.0 km.). After driving (39.8 km.) take exit 87 for Clearbrook, turning right onto Clearbrook Road. Proceed south on Clearbrook Road (making a slight left jog at King Road), parking at the end (3.9 km.) (43.7 km.). Judson Lake is off to the right. The ploughed fields in the vicinity are often used by large flocks of migrant American Pipit.

JUDSON LAKE

Judson Lake, straddling the Washington and British Columbia border, has a good selection of waterfowl especially during migrations. A scope is essential to view the Ped-billed Grebe and other waterfowl as the lake is surrounded by private property. A Little Blue Heron, the first provincial record of two, was present at the lake some years ago during the month of October through to January of the following year.

Judson Lake to Nicomen Slough and Harrison Mills

A side trip can be made for those who wish to see large populations of Bald Eagle during November through March. From Judson Lake, return to Highway 1 East (00.0 km.). Take the 92 exit at Abbotsford (5.3 km.), continuing around and under the overpass onto South Fraser Way (Highway 11). Proceed north on Highway 11 towards Matsqui, over the bridge spanning the Fraser River, and on to Mission City (13.5 km.) (18.8 km,)

At Mission City follow the signs along Horne Street for Highway 7 East (Lougheed Highway) towards Hatzic and Dewdney. At Dewdney (8.7 km.)

(27.5 km.), keep right, cross the railway tracks and the bridge over Nicomen Slough and continue east on the highway for an additional (3.5 km.) (30.0 km.).

NICOMEN SLOUGH AND HARRISON MILLS

Park beside the slough (a bulge in the Nicomen River) on the shoulder of the highway, cross the highway carefully, and continue up onto the dike. Bald Eagle gather in the hundreds during the salmon spawning in January when these white-headed scavengers are seen feeding on the decaying pink-flesh of the spawned-out salmon. Recurring floods and returning low waters cause the fish to be cast up along the upper reaches of the shoreline throughout the winter, assuring a constant supply of protein for any hungry raptor. At (8.7 km.) past Dewdney (36.2 km.), the road approaches the dike once more. Tundra Swan and Trumpeter Swan, Canada Geese, Ring-necked Duck, and other waterfowl are often found in this region of the slough in the winter months. The highway then crosses the slough again just past Hodgson Road. Cross the bridge and turn immediately onto Taylor Road. Double back along Taylor Road which provides another view point.

If you continue eastward on Highway 7 for an additional 9 km, the highway skirts Harrison Bay and the Weaver Creek fish spawning area. Each winter, hundreds of Bald Eagle concentrate on the lower reaches to feed on spawned-out salmon which are preserved in a state of modest decomposition in the cold waters. Three hundred eagles may be seen feeding, or roosting, in the large cottonwoods lining the river banks. Look for large, old-growth Douglas firs which are preferable as roosting trees. As many as 150 Bald Eagle have used a single tree, seeking protection from both wind and rain. Tundra Swan, Trumpeter Swan, Harlequin Duck, Common Merganser, gulls, Common Raven, Northwestern Crow, and American Dipper all use the river to feed on the dying salmon and the tens of thousands of fish eggs. Steller's Jay, Chestnut-backed Chickadee, Winter Wren, Golden-crowned Kinglet, and Varied Thrush are abundant in the surrounding wet forests.

Harrison Bay is just west of Harrison Mills, which is 21 kms. east of Harrison Hot Springs Resort. Eagles can be viewed from the small pullover immediately south of the Harrison River bridge and from several other sites beginning at two kilometers north on the Morris Valley Road towards the Hemlock Recreation Area, and at the Sasquatch Inn (0.5 km.) west of the bridge.

On the eastern outskirts of Harrison Mills, (from Hwy 7), take the logging road to the left (north) which leads to Chehalis Lake (approx. 18 km). The road skirts the Chehalis River en route. At the ÒTÓ junction (approx 10 km), keep right. Three Spotted Owls have been recorded along the lakeshore.

Returning through Dewdney, turn right onto Hawkins Pickle Road just past the railway tracks for a side trip to Norrish Creek. (00.0km.) After driving (2.3 km.) you will cross a set of railway tracks (keep right at the road fork), and after an additional (1.6 km.) (3.9km.) you come to the creek. Bald Eagle gather during the salmon spawning in January and American Dipper are most common at this time, feeding on the abundant salmon eggs.

Return to Highway 1 East.

Judson Lake to Cultus Lake Provincial Park

Retrace your route back to the Highway 1 East on-ramp at Clearbrook (00.0 km.). After driving (27.4 km.) (or 67.2 kilometers from the on-ramp for Highway 1 East after leaving Pitt Meadows) take the exit 119 off-ramp for Sardis and Vedder Crossing, turning right onto Vedder Road. Proceed south on Vedder Road passing through the towns of Sardis and Vedder Crossing, and then over the Vedder River. At the "Y" junction keep right onto Cultus Lake Road (5.7 km.) (33.1 km.), then right again onto Lakeshore Drive (2.5 km.) (35.6 km.) to the parking lot of Cultus Lake Provincial Park (2.5 km.) (38.1 km.).

CULTUS LAKE PROVINCIAL PARK

Walk the trail from the parking lot towards the summit of Vedder Mountain. Spotted Owl has been seen at Vedder Peak between Finn (Red-tail Creek) and Hatchery Creek, one of the few sites (although an unreliable site) for this rare owl in the province. Characteristic birds of wet coastal forests will be seen en route.

Cultus Lake Provincial Park to Hope

Retrace your route back to the Highway 1 East on-ramp. After (53.0 km.), you will arrive at Hope.

NOTES & OBSERVATIONS

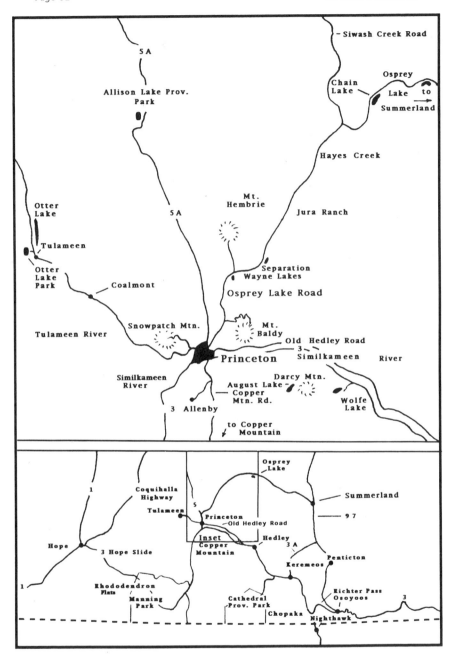

MAP 6   LOOP 5   HIGHWAY 3 ROUTE WEST

LOOP 5   HIGHWAY 3 ROUTE - WEST

HOPE

Hope is the main hub from which several loops branch.

(A) Loop 5 - Highway 3 West. Hope to Osoyoos is (248.9 km.), a 4 1/2 to 5 hour drive. From Osoyoos you can join the Okanagan Valley Loop, or continue east on Loop 7, the Highway 3 East Loop.

(B) Loop 9 - Mountains and Central Plateau Loop. Hope directly north to Cache Creek is (194 km.) (where you can also proceed onto the Trans-Canada Loop); and to Prince George (640 km.), a thirteen hour drive. From Prince George you can join the Peace River Parklands Loop at Dawson Creek (1,042 km. and a twenty-one hour drive from Hope),and thence the Alaska Highway Loop.

(C) Loop 8 - Trans-Canada Highway Loop. The start of the Trans-Canada Loop actually bypasses the first stretch of this highway, begining along Highway 3 (6.5 km.), then along the Coquihalla Highway (Highway 5) to Merritt (117.5 km.). From Merritt you can take Highway 5 and/or 5A to Kamloops (80+ km.). You can miss the Coquihalia and Highway 5 sector, driving north to Cache Creek and joining the Trans-Canada or (B) loops there. The Highway 5 sector from Hope to Kamloops is (197 km.) and (180.5 km.) from Kamloops to the Alberta/B.C. border (377 km.), a seven hour drive. From Kamloops you can join either (A) or (B) above.

We will first bird the Highway 3 Route West Loop.

Hope to Manning Provincial Park

The Route 3 Route West Loop begins at the junction of Highways 1 and 3 at Hope (00.0 km.). After driving east on Highway 3 (the Hope-Princeton Highway) for (6.5 km.) you will come to the entrance to the Coquihalla Highway (be sure to have a full tank of gas before driving the Coquihalla!). The distance through to the Manning Park Lodge is (67.2 kms.), a one and a half hour drive. Hope is an excellent place to eat and to refuel your vehicle as there are few stations between here and the park.

After driving (17.4 km.) from Hope you will reach the huge Hope Slide viewpoint. In January 1965 a minor earthquake triggered a gigantic rockfall; more than 100 million tons of rock, earth and snow slid from Johnson's Peak north of the highway, burying the road and adjacent Outram Lake to a depth of nearly 300 meters. The slide still alters the path of the highway today. The alder thickets growing from the east side of the slide produce breeding Orange-crowned Warbler and MacGillivray's Warbler.

At (36.1 km.) stop at the Rhododendron Flats rest area and nature trail. This is one of the few sites where the red rhododendron grows wild on the British Columbia mainland, the shrubs providing a colourful display in June under the canopy of the Douglas-fir forest. Blue Grouse are often heard hooting in the vicinity.

On reaching the summit of Allison Pass (58.4 km.), scan the skies for a possible Golden Eagle, or in summer for both Black Swift and Vaux's Swift. The rocky cliff-face in the old burn on the north side of the road has harboured the odd Golden Eagle.

MANNING PROVINCIAL PARK

Manning Provincial Park is a spectacular 71,400 hectare park stretching down to the Canadian/U.S. border. Highway 3 makes a "U" through the park - from the northwest corner, to the south, and then back to the northeast corner. Nestled high among the Cascade Mountains east of Allison Pass is the delightful Manning Park Resort (67.2 km.). Situated at Park Headquarters directly off of Highway 3, the lodge serves as a convenient accommodation for the birder wishing to see higher altitude species. The lodge is also located at the centre of the better birding sites within the park, and at the hub of the roads to access these sites.

East of the complex (0.9 km.) (left from Highway 3) is the park's nature house which is open in summer providing trail maps, checklists, and displays. The naturalists on duty may be able to help you find the specific species you desire. (They may know the site of an active Three-toed Woodpecker nest). Now that you are in the Cascade Range, the American Crow has become the most common black corvid, and found around the lodge.

The best boreal forest birding within the park is in the forests surrounding Lightning Lake. Drive a short distance east from the lodge to paved Lightning Lake road, turning right (00.0 km.). Proceed to the Similkameen River (1.1 km.) where American Dipper are rarely found.

After crossing the river (0.3 km.) (1.4 km.), the road passes the Rein Orchid trailhead. Hiking this interpreted nature trail could produce Spruce Grouse. After an additional (1.5 km.) (2.9 km.) the road forks; the right branch leading to the far end of Lightning Lake and beyond to the Gibson Pass ski area, the left branch to Lightning Lake day area. Keep right to the Lightning Lake Campground (2.1 km.) (5.0 km.), turning left - then right to the Spruce Bay Beach parking area (0.5 km.) (5.5 km.). A trail, including a footbridge across the lake's narrows, follows the shoreline of Lightning Lake from the parking lot. The loop could be walked in about an hour without stopping, but the interesting birding along the way should lengthen your stay.

Williamson's Sapsucker (rare, but increasingly more regular in the park) now occur at this point, their most westerly distribution. Nesting took place in 1993. Walk south along the Skyline Trail for 425 paces looking for a dead spruce snag on the left (the snag is ten paces back from the branch trail to the lake). Three-toed Woodpecker are uncommon residents of the forests surrounding the lake, the big spruces at Spruce Bay Beach are favoured. Playing a taped call of the Barred Owl near the footbridge can produce one of these elusive night predators.

Spruce Grouse, Blue Grouse, Red-naped Sapsucker, Red-breasted Sapsucker, Mountain Chickadee, Yellow-rumped Warbler, Townsend's Warbler, Dark-eyed Junco, Pine Siskin, Red Crossbill, Pine Grosbeak, and Evening Grosbeak frequent the woods around the lake. Keep a watchful eye overhead for Black Swift. Twenty Minute Lake, to the east of the road between the boat launching area and the road fork, is also an excellent area to look for Three-toed Woodpecker. Barrow's Goldeneye are regular breeders of the lake.

Proceed to Strawberry Flats (3.3) (8.3 km.), a popular cross-country skiing area. In summer, hike the Nepopekum Falls Trail at Gibson Pass (2.0 km.) (1 0.3 km.) which is long but not too strenuous. Spruce Grouse are occasional between the base of the ski run and the falls. Gray Jay, Clark's Nutcracker, Boreal Chickadee, and Golden-crowned Kinglet are common residents, whilst Townsend's Warbler are common in summer. In winter, you can drive to the ski area where winter finches will be found when the cone crop is good. Watch the roadsides in early morning for Red Crossbill, (rarely White-winged Crossbill), Pine Grosbeak, and Evening Grosbeak foraging for salt, which is spread upon the roads to melt snows.

Return to Highway 3 (00.0 km.), continuing directly across the highway junction, turning left onto the paved road that winds up the northside of the valley leading to Cascade Lookout (8.0 km.). Watch for Townsend's Solitaire and White-crowned Sparrow along the drive. A Clark's Nutcracker flying across the awesome mountain vistas will bring your attention back to birding.

The road changes to gravel from the lookout to Blackwall Meadows (7.0 km.) (1 5.0 km.). The alpine meadows in July, at an elevation of 2,000 m, provide observers with an endless carpet of colour. The wildflowers pushing through the tundra, taking advantage of the short growing season, come in every hue of the rainbow. Male Calliope Hummingbird often feed on these flowers. A dazzling electric-blue flash announces a male Mountain Bluebird, whilst Hermit Thrush and Fox Sparrow songs drift from nearby and Common Raven croak overhead. Many excellent short hiking trails loop through sub-alpine and the alpine meadows.

Heather Trail leaves the first parking lot at the Blackwall Meadows, leading ten kilometers to the Three Brothers Mountain, and beyond, for a total of twenty-one kilometers one-way for the entire trail. If you are in good shape, you can make it to Three Brothers and back in one day. The first five kilometers of trail descend through sub-alpine forest to Buckhorn Camp at 1,800 m.

Regular along the first two kilometers of the trail are Blue Grouse, Spruce Grouse, and Boreal Chickadee. A pair of Northern Hawk-Owl has nested in the large burn at Buckhorn Camp, far south of their normal range. Although unrecorded recently, a pair could resume nesting again in the future. Beyond the camp, the trail climbs through a burn area frequented by Three-toed Woodpecker; the plaintive efforts of Golden-crowned Sparrow (three whistled notes, Òoh dear meÓ) come from the birds breeding in an area just past the burn. Five kilometers into your hike past Buckhorn Camp you will be on the shoulder of Three Brothers Mountain, harbouring such alpine birds as Horned Lark, American Pipit, and Gray-crowned Rosy Finch. The edges of snow patches are favoured by these high-level avifauna, attracted by a myriad of small insects. White-tailed Ptarmigan (and very rarely Rock Ptarmigan) are occasionally found at 2,272 m on "First Brother".

Drive east for (1.5 km.) from the Manning Park Resort (68.7 from Hope) to the Beaver Pond nature trail. Species expected around the pond include: Canada Goose, Mallard, Hooded Merganser, Spotted Sandpiper, Rufous Hummingbird, Belted Kingfisher, Red-naped Sapsucker, Black-capped Chickadee, Ruby-crowned Kinglet, Swainson's Thrush, Warbling Vireo, Orange-crowned Warbler, Yellow Warbler, Common Yellowthroat, Song Sparrow, breeding Lincoln's Sparrow, and Red-winged Blackbird. The Windy Joe trailhead is situated here and White-tailed Ptarmigan, Spruce Grouse, and Boreal Chickadee are often encountered along the Windy Joe and Mount Frosty Trails, leading into alpine areas.

Look for Harlequin Duck and American Dipper along the Similkameen River (where the river parallels Highway 3 between the park and Princeton). At the East Gate to Manning Park (83.1 km.), look in the thickets around the meadow for breeding MacGillivray's Warbler.

Other common species expected in the park include:

Common Loon	Hairy Woodpecker
Common Merganser	Pileated Woodpecker
Cooper's Hawk	Olive-sided Flycatcher
Red-tailed Hawk	Western Wood-Pewee
Band-tailed Pigeon	Hammond's Flycatcher
Rock Dove	Willow Flycatcher
Northern Pygmy-Owl	Pacific-slope Flycatcher
Northern Flicker	Tree Swallow
Violet-green Swallow	Winter Wren
Northern Rough-winged Swallow	Varied Thrush
Cliff Swallow	American Robin
Barn Swallow	European Starling
Steller's Jay	Nashville Warbler
Chestnut-backed Chickadee	Chipping Sparrow
White-breasted Nuthatch	Brown-headed Cowbird
Red-breasted Nuthatch	Western Tanager
Cassin's Finch	

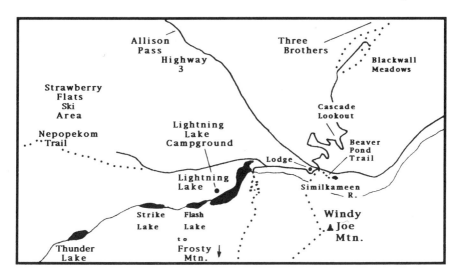

MAP 7 MANNING PARK

Manning Park to Princton

From the Manning Park Lodge to Princeton is (67.6 kms.) (or 134.8 kms. from Hope). Watch for the bluebird boxes along Highway 3 between (57.5-62.5 kms.) (124.7-129.7 kms.). Mountain Bluebird outnumber the Western Bluebird.

PRINCETON

Princeton is situated in the Similkameen Valley at the convergence of the Tulameen and Similkameen Rivers at an elevation of 550 m. This small friendly ranching town is the hub from which several paved routes branch, meandering through the surrounding tree-covered hills. Birders heading for the Okanagan seldom bird the sites around Princeton as there is an overlapping of similar species, all of which are most easily seen in the Okanagan. Regardless, access to a variety of habitats at elevations between 550 m. and 1,800 m. in open rangelands, tracts of second-growth forests of ponderoda pine, Douglas-fir, lodgepole pine, trembling aspen, Rocky Mountain juniper, black cottonwood, and mountain alder, and an expanse of sagebrush in the Allenby area south of Princeton, provide an interesting day's birding.

 From the downtown core you may take three separate loops, the Osprey Lake Road loop, the Tulameen Road loop, and the Old Hedley Road loop. A site is also accessible from Highway 3, the Copper Mountain Road loop. As some of the following birding sites are distant from ammenities it is important to get gas before starting out.

NOTE: Logging roads in the Princeton area that provide access to higher elevations may require four-wheel drive vehicles and will not be open in winter. Logging roads may have their access limited to weekends. Always obey these and heed warning signs.

 (00.0km.) From Highway 3 in Princeton, turn left onto Bridge Street (Highway 5A), then immediately right off Bridge Street following the Highway 5A signs. The Princeton Hotel (0.5 km. north on Bridge Street) has a large colony of Vaux's Swift nesting in the chimney. The trees that bear fruit along the side streets in town often have numbers of Bohemian Waxwing feeding in them during the harsh winter months. Continue north on Highway 5A towards Merritt, cross the Tulameen River bridge, turning right (east) onto the Old Hedley Road (0.9 km.). From here you can drive the Old Hedley Road , or turn left off Highway 5A onto the Tulameen Road. Drive (0.3 km.) (1.2 km.) along Old Hedley Road, turning left at the signs for Sunflower Downs, Five Mile Road, Chain Lake, and Osprey Lake onto Princeton - Summerland Road which eventually becomes Osprey Lake Road.

Osprey Lake Road follows the Hayes Creek and Troat Creek valleys through to Summerland in the Okanagan approximately 75 kilometers away. The road is paved through to Osprey Lake (41.7 km.), a well-maintained gravel road to Bull Creek, and then again paved for the remaining 15 kilometers to Summeriand. The gravel section is closed in winter past Osprey Lake.

 On the left of the Princeton - Summerland Road is the Princeton landfill (0.5 km.) (1.7 km.). Frequenting the dump are large numbers of Black-billed Magpie, American Crow, and Common Raven. Check along the wires for the next few kilometers for Western Bluebird and Mountain Bluebird in summer and Northern Shrike in winter. After driving (0.7 km.) (2.4 km.) you will reach the Sunflower Downs Race Track, behind which lies Swan Lake. Park along the gravel road running parallel to the entrance of the track and walk down the hill to the small lake. Check the broken snag at the head of the lake for a roosting Great Horned Owl. Several species of raptor may be seen in the area including Bald Eagle, Sharp-shinned Hawk, Cooper's Hawk, Red-tailed Hawk, and in winter, Rough-legged Hawk. Swan Lake can have a wide variety of waterfowl especially during migrations.

Continue along Princeton - Summerland Road to Rainbow Lake Road for the Castle RV Park and turn right (0.8 km.) (3.2 km.). After(0.7 km.) turn left for the R.V. park. A trail through the property along Allison Creek leads to a small marsh and accompaniment riparian thickets and a small lot of conifers. Tree Swallow, Violet-green Swallow, Bank Swallow, Northern Rough-winged Swallow, Cliff Swallow, Barn Swallow, Black-capped Chickadee, White-breasted Nuthatch, Red-breasted Nuthatch, Pygmy Nuthatch, House Wren, Townsend's Solitaire, Veery, Swainson's Thrush, American Robin, Warbling Vireo, Yellow Warbler, Lazuli Bunting, and Bullock's Oriole are to be expected.

Turkey Vulture, Red-tailed Hawk, and American Kestrel cruise over the neighbouring cliffs.

Return to Princeton - Summerland Road, turning right. After (0.6 km.) (3.8 km.), turn right onto an unsigned gravel road (Old Iron Mountain Road) which leads to the summit of Mt. Baldy. A passenger car is capable of travelling beyond this point in summer, however a four-wheel drive is needed in winter.

Along the drive you will pass several small ponds next to the road. Killdeer, Greater Yellowlegs, Lesser Yellowlegs, Solitary Sandpiper, Spotted Sandpiper, Long-billed Dowitcher, Common Snipe, Semipalmated Sandpiper, Least Sandpiper, Baird's Sandpiper, and Pectoral Sandpiper are seen around the pools in season. Turkey Vulture, Northern Harrier, Red-tailed Hawk, Rough-legged Hawk, Swainson's Hawk, and American Kestrel are expected in season, the larger raptors feeding on the abundant Yellow-bellied Marmots and Columbian Ground Squirrels in the area. Although uncommon, this site regularly produces Prairie Falcon in summer.

After driving about five kilometers the road levels out just below the summit. Vistas of the Similkameen Valley and surrounding countryside are breathtaking on clear days. As the property beyond the road is leased for cattle grazing, permission is necessary to leave the road and bird the hills.

After parking your vehicle, walk toward the summit checking the Rocky Mountain juniper trees in the small draws for Long-eared Owl. Once on the summit, the cliffs on the Old Hedley Road are visible where there is a small colony of White-throated Swift. Far below, the Similkameen River snakes through the burnished hills. The surrounding hills are a patchwork of deciduous and coniferous forest and open rangeland. In the small groves of riparian woodland are Ruffed Grouse, Rufous Hummingbird, Northern Flicker, Red-naped Sapsucker, Downy Woodpecker, Hairy Woodpecker, Pileated Woodpecker, Dusky Flycatcher, House Wren, Western Bluebird, Mountain Bluebird, and Warbling Vireo. In the conifers are Blue Grouse, Clark's Nutcracker, Red-breasted Nuthatch, Townsend's Solitaire, Varied Thrush, and Golden-crowned Kinglet. Horned Lark, American Pipit, Savannah Sparrow, and Vesper Sparrow occur in the pastures in season.

Return to the Princeton - Summerland Road, turning right. The first set of kilometers are the distances between points of interest, with the kilometers from the beginning of Princeton - Summerland (Osprey) Road noted second. Wayne Lake is off the road on the left at (3.0 km.) (6.8 km.). Blue-winged Teal, Cinnamon Teal, Ruddy Duck, Ring-necked Duck, and Barrow's Goldeneye nest on the lake. The reeds harbour Sora and Yellow-headed Blackbird. Eastern Kingbird, Western Wood-Pewee, and Bullock's Oriole are attracted to the habitats around the lake. When the mayflies hatch in May and early June the area is alive with insect feeders, Common Nighthawk, flycatchers, swallows, Western Bluebird, Mountain Bluebird, and warblers.

Separation Lakes lie off Osprey Lake Road on the right (2.1 km.) (8.9 km.). Look along the overhead powerlines in winter for Northern Pygmy-Owl and Northern Shrike. In summer, common waterfowl breeding on the lakes include Mallard, Gadwall, Green-winged Teal, American Wigeon, Northern Shoveler, Lesser Scaup, and Barrow's Goldeneye. American Coot and Wilson's Phalarope are abundant. Greater Yellowlegs, Lesser Yellowlegs, Long-billed Dowitcher, Bonaparte's Gull, and Black Tern, and many other waterbirds frequent the lakes on migration. In the fall, an occasional small flock of Sandhill Crane rest along the lakeshore. There are records of such rarities as White Pelican, Mute Swan, Greater White-fronted Goose, Snow Goose, and Black-necked Stilt.

Walk along the abandoned railway at the far end of the lake to a small marsh where Common Snipe and migrant shorebirds occur. Savannah Sparrow, Vesper Sparrow, and Western Meadowlark breed in the neighbouring fields. Bluebird nest boxes are placed on the fenceposts lining the road where Mountain Bluebird are especially common.

At (0.8 km.) (9.7 km.) a well-surfaced logging road, the Hembrie Mountain Road, branches off on the left. The Hembrie Mountain Road winds northward through aspens, then through a mixed forest of deciduous trees and conifers. The largest surviving ponderosa pines are found along this road. The rare Great Gray Owl has been recorded along the road and Ruffed Grouse, Blue Grouse, Cooper's Hawk, and Merlin frequent the woods. The migration of passerines is spectacular both in spring and fall with birds of casual occurrence recorded each year. The road eventually turns east and rejoins the Osprey Lake Road at Trehearne Creek, but travel beyond Mount Hembrie (4.5 km.) is not advised!

The hilly pastures on the right at (1.5 km.) (1 1.2 km.) contain a number of shallow ponds which provide protection for migrant waterfowl and shorebirds. At the Jura Ranch (1.8 km) (1 3.0 km.) look for the Nico Wynd Ranch sign, the road veers sharply to the left soon after.

At the bend is a pullover with a view of the valley and several species of bird that inhabit roadside shrubbery Ð Western Bluebird, Mountain Bluebird, Lazuli Bunting, and an occasional Spotted Towhee. Along Hayes Creek (10.3 km.) (23.3 km.) (running parallel to the road at several locations) and in the adjacent moist woods are Calliope Hummingbird, Rufous Hummingbird, Northern Flicker, Downy Woodpecker, Veery, and Northern Waterthrush. A small population of California Quail have recently become established in the Hayes Creek valley. Look for these comical little knob-topped gamebirds running across the road.

After (5.9 km.) (29.2 km.), you will cross the Siwash Creek bridge. Proceed along Osprey Lake Road (1.9 km.) (3 1.1 km.), turning left onto the rough logging road, Siwash Road, which is barely accessible by passenger car in the summer. Look and listen carefully along the first few kilometers of the road in the conifers for the light tapping of Three-toed Woodpecker and Black-backed Woodpecker. Many of the more common conifer species are also present.

After driving (41.7 km.) along the Princeton - Summerland Osprey Lake Road you will arrive at Osprey Lake and the neighbouring Chain and Link Lakes. Around the lakes are summer cabins, permanent homes, a general store, and Forest Service campsites and a road circles the lakes. On the lakes one will find Common Loon, Lesser Scaup, Barrow's Goldeneye, Bufflehead, and Common Merganser. The riparian woods are teaming with the more common passerines, while Osprey fish the lakes. Three-toed Woodpecker are found in the conifers in the area of the lake.

Retace your route back to Old Hedley Road - 5A junction.

(00.0km.) Drive west along paved Tulameen Road, towards Coalmont and Tulameen, twenty-five kilometers away. After driving (2.1 km.) the well-maintained gravel road for the Princeton Ski Resort at Snowpatch Mountain branches off on the right. At (7.2 km.) you will reach the resort where several cross-country ski trails provide summer access to sub-alpine and alpine habitats.

Along the trails in suitable habitat (including the sub-alpine) expect to find such wide-ranging species as Northern Pygmy-Owl, Common Nighthawk, Rufous Hummingbird, Hairy Woodpecker, Olive-sided Flycatcher whose unmistakable calls echo across the valley, Hammond's Flycatcher, Common Raven with their extraordinary gurgling calls, Red-breasted Nuthatch, Winter Wren, Golden-crowned Kinglet, Ruby-crowned Kinglet, Western Bluebird, Mountain Bluebird, Townsend's Solitaire, Hermit Thrush, Varied Thrush, American Robin, CassinŌs Vireo, Warbling Vireo, Yellow-rumped Warbler, Townsend's Warbler, Dark-eyed Junco, Chipping Sparrow, White-crowned Sparrow, Fox Sparrow, Western Tanager, Pine Siskin, Red Crossbill, Common Redpoll (winter), and Cassin's Finch. Higher up in the alpine Gray-crowned Rosy Finch feed around the snow patches.

Return to Tulameen Road, turning right. (the following kilometers are measured from the junction of 5A and Tulameen Road directly along the Tulameen Road). At (7.5 km.) listen on warm summer nights for the soft, hollow "boo-boot" of the Flammulated Owl emitted from some concealed perch among the ponderosa pines. Playing a tape will often bring the owls into view.

If you decide to continue to Tulameen you will pass some marvellous wetlands in the valley along the narrow and winding road. On clear days the views along the road can be stunning, the mountains magnificent, the scenery has all of the ingredients for a truly memorable tour. At Tulameen (25.0 km.), take the well-maintained gravel road running north along Otter Creek to Otter Lake Provincial Park on the left (26 km.) where Chestnut-backed Chickadee have recently established an isolated colony. Otter Lake, on the opposite side of the road, has a wintering population of Tundra Swan when the lake remains unfrozen.

Return to Highway 5A via the Tulameen Road.

Return to Highway 3 East along Highway 5A from the Tulameen Road junction, or proceed east along the Old Hedley Road. At Highway 3, turn left towards Keremeos.

(00.0km.) For Copper Mountain Road turn left onto Highway 3 East until you see the R.C.M.P. Station, turning right (south) onto paved Copper Mountain Road (0.8 km.). After (0.3 km.) (1.1 km.), turn left onto Darcy Mtn. Road for (1.0 km.) to the turn-around at the sewage lagoons where there are Wood Duck and Common Snipe during spring migration. Watch for the Bank Swallow colony en route. The sewage lagoons are posted, but birders are tolerated - one lagoon is visible without tresspassing.

Back at Copper Mountain Road, continue until you have driven (5.2 km.) from the highway, turning right onto Allenby Road which is gravel; the old Copper Mountain Mine concentrator is found along Allenby Road. At the old Allenby town site (3.0 km.) (8.2 km.), where all of the old buildings have been removed, are various introduced plants, trees, and shrubs that were planted by the past inhabitants. This habitat, the access provided by the old railway right-of-way, old tailing ponds, and neighbouring expanse of sagebrush, will guarantee a few hours of exciting birding.

Return to Copper Mountain Road and turn right (00.0 km.). At (3.5 km.) (8.7 km. from Highway 3) you will see a pond along the right side of the road that provides the reedy habitat which is a necessity for American Bittern, Virginia Rail, Sora, and Marsh Wren. The paved portion of the road ends at the Similco Mines open pit mine after approximately (17.5 km.).

Return to Highway 3, or Return to the Old Hedley Road.

(00.0km.). Paved for most of its length, Old Hedley Road parallels Highway 3 East on the opposite side of the Similkameen River, passing under rocky bluffs and eventually connecting with Highway 3 East, eight kilometers west of Hedley at Sterling Creek.

Driving this historical route is a delightful alternative to Highway 3 for those on their way to the Okanagan with extra time. As you leave Princeton, look for Common Raven nesting on the dome-shaped mountain (2.4 km.). Along the swifter sections of the river are colourful Harlequin Duck, and in calmer stretches Common Merganser. A small White-throated Swift colony frequents the cliffs along the road (2.1 km.) (4.5 km.) and Common Poorwill and Rock Wren, although infrequent, are possible in the area. At (10.9 km.) watch for a feeding station along the rightside of the road where a flock of California Quail come to feed. In winter Northern Pygmy-Owl perch on the overhead wires and fence posts along the road next to fallow fields. After (2.0 km.) (12.9 km.) you will see a Bald Eagle nest on the left. After (32.8 km.) you will join Highway 3. After an additional (32.0 km.) (64.8 km.) you will reach Ashnola River Road for Cathedral Provincial Park.

Princeton to Cathederal Provincial Park

Continue along Highway 3 East from the junction of Highway 5A (00.0 km.). The drive from Princton to Keremeos is (67.5 km.). (4.2 km.) before reaching Keremeos (63.3 kms.) The Ashnola River Road branches south (right) off Highway 3 providing access to Cathederal Provincial Park (keep right on pavement after driving about one kilometer).

(00.0km.). It is about ten kilometers from the highway to the beginning of the Ashnola Forest Development Road, where the road becomes gravel. After an additional (1 2.0 kms.) (22.0 km.) you will pass a privately-owned bridge across the Ashnola River on your left (next to Clark's Cabin) which gives access to the Cathederal Lakes Resort's property. Continue straight ahead. After an additional (1.5 km.) beyond the bridge, a road branches off on the left that leads (0.8 km.) (24.3 km.) to a parking lot, campground, and a footbridge spanning the Ashnola River. If you own a four-wheel vehicle you could cross the privately-owned bridge and drive the sixteen kilometers to the Cathederal Lakes Resort's lodge at Quiniscoe Lake. If you are camping, a short trail links the footbridge (mentioned above) with the privately- owned four-wheel road that leads to the lodge and the lakes area of the park. It will take six to seven hours to hike the sixteen kilometers from the Lakeview Trailhead Campground, climbing 1,300 meters; overnighting at one of the wilderness campsites at Lake of the Woods, or Pyramid, Scout and Quiniscoe Lakes is a must! Toilets and firewood are proaded at both Lakeview and Buckhorn Campgrounds, but there is no drinking water!

CATHEDERAL PROVINCIAL PARK

Cathedral Park is a 33,000 hectare mountain wilderness, the alpine meadows at 2,400 m, dotted with shimmering azure lakes and brightly-coloured alpine wildflowers. Granite pinnacles rise dramatically over the lakes, their serrated peaks etched against a cerulean sky. Lakeview Mountain towers majestically at 2,628 m. Passing south of Ladyslipper Lake and the Ramparts is a monolithic quartz crag eroded by the action of the wind over the millenia. Stone City, as this monzonite formation is known, appears not unlike some futuristic city. En route to the Stone City is the Devil's Woodpile, a scattering of rubble-rock formations. Following the Rock City are eroded basalt rocks that have created jagged, gigantic figures and a huge split in the granite face of the mountain known as the "Giant Cleft".

Douglas-fir predominates in the lower elevations of the park, interspersed with copses of cottonwood and aspen along rivers. Lodgepole pine and Engelmann spruce are found in still higher elevations, giving way to sub-alpine fir, alpine fir, and western larch, and finally to false heather and red alpine blueberry in alpine meadows.

Daytime temperatures in July and August often reach 25 C to 35 C with average temperatures in the 10 C to 18 C range.

The recommended way to see all of the breathtaking scenery is to reserve a room at the privately-owned Cathederal Lakes Resort, set in sub-alpine forest on the shores of Quiniscoe Lake at 2,072 m.

Quiniscoe Lake, and the accompanying lodge, is the hub from which trails radiate to most of the park's scenic attractions. A trail leads north of the lodge, meeting with a junction of the main trail (0.6 km.) leading to Red Mountain (3.0 km.), and on to the base of Quiniscoe Mountain (5.0 km.). The main trail continues on to a junction with another trail leading from Glacier Lake (6.0 km.). From this junction a trail continues on to the Devil's Woodpile, Stone City (8.5 km.), and beyond to the Giant Cleft (10.3 km.). It will take four hours for a round-trip to Quiniscoe Mountain, six to eight hours for a round-trip to Stone City.

Prairie Falcon and White-tailed Ptarmigan are two reliable specialities of the park, both are found in the alpine meadows. The Prairie Falcon nests and is found hunting over the alpine meadows and perched on precarious cliffs, usually around Red or Quiniscoe Mountains west of the lodge. Use caution as both Golden Eagle and Peregrine Falcon also nest on the mountain. White-tailed Ptarmigan, even though common, may be difficult to locate because of their abilities of camouflage. Search in the rocky rubble areas where their mottled summer plumage will make them close to invisible. Sit still and watch for movement. Try the rocky-slopes of Quiniscoe Mountain and around Stone City. Gray-crowned Rosy Finch are found on, and around, glaciers and birds will be seen picking insects from the ice on the edge of the trail near Quiniscoe Mountain.

Spruce Grouse are found on trails through the sub-alpine forests and should be seen on the trails around Quiniscoe Lake. Gray Jay and Clark's Nutcracker are constant companions around the lodge. Boreal Owl's short series of rapid, hollow ÒhooÓ notes have been heard along the trails surrounding the lodge. Three-toed Woodpecker should be found on these trails during the day. Mountain Chickadee, Boreal Chickadee, Varied Thrush, Yellow-rumped Warbler, and Dark-eyed Junco are commonly seen throughout the area of the lodge.

Cathederal Park to Chopaka

Return to, or continue along Highway 3 East through Keremeos (00.0km.) (202 kms. from Hope). After (24.8 km.) turn right onto Nighthawk Road which leads to the U.S.A./Canada border crossing (2.6km.) and on to Nighthawk in Washington state. The road is signed at the turnoff for the border crossing.

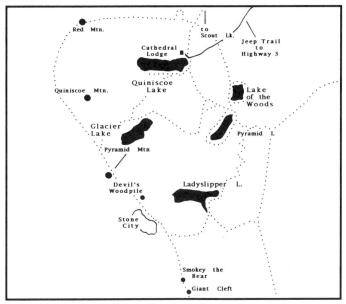

CHOPAKA

Chopaka, as this region is known (the actual town of Chopaka is on the next road further west), is the best site for Sage Thrasher in British Columbia. Sage Thrashers are unreliable here at the northernmost limits of their range, their populations fluctuating from year to year. When the thrashers are present, they are best observed at dawn and again at dusk when they are most active. Drive slowly along the road towards the border listening for the thrashers singing in flight or from the tops of the sagebrush lining the road. Their unforgetable sweet song consists of a continuous series of warbled phrases. Listen also for Grasshopper Sparrow as Chopaka is one of the better sites for this rare and local species. Vesper Sparrow, Lark Sparrow, Brewer's Sparrow, and Western Meadowlark are common along the road. Check for sparrows at the triangular patch of grasses formed at the junction of Highway 3 by the exit and enter roads.

Chopaka to Richter Pass

(00.0km.) Continue along Highway 3 East for an additional (10.8kms.), until you see the Richter Pass sign. A gravel road leads from the left side of the road (north) to the site of a proposed observatory on the summit of Mount Kobau. A Sage Sparrow spent three weeks along the road. Construction was suspended because of high costs, but the road leads almost sixteen kilometers to alpine meadows.

RICHTER PASS

Richter Pass, at an elevation of 682 m, is the most southerly pass in Canada between the Similkameen and Okanagan Valleys. "No Trespassing" signs designate the land adjacent to the highway through the pass as private property. The passes' lakes, Richter, Little Richter, Bruder, Yellow and Spotted are shallow and rimmed with the white of alkaline.

Scoping the lakes, especially Spotted Lake (2.8 km.) (1 3.6 km.) from the shoulder of the highway will produce such breeding species as Northern Pintail, Blue-winged Teal, Ruddy Duck, Redhead, Barrow's Goldeneye, Wilson's Phalarope, and Yellow-headed Blackbird. Eared Grebe and Cinnamon Teal, although uncommon, could occur. These mineral-rich sloughs are alive with migrant geese, ducks and shorebirds during spring and fall.

Over the adjacent sagebrush at dusk a nasal peent will announce the first Common Nighthawk. Many of these night aerialist-feeders skim the lakes and hills each evening for the insect banquet, relieving those daylight hawkers, the swallows: Tree Swallow, Violet-green Swallow, Bank Swallow, Northern Rough-winged Swallow, Cliff Swallow, and Barn Swallow are common. Competing for the insect morsels are Eastern Kingbird, Western Kingbird, and the unusual Lewis' Woodpecker. The Lewis' Woodpecker (unwoodpecker-like) catches insects in the air and flies rather like a corvid. Roadside bushes and shrubbery may harbour California Quail, Lazuli Bunting, or BullockÕs Oriole; whilst Vesper Sparrow songs enliven the neighbouring sagebrush.

From Spotted Lake continue along Highway 3 East an additional (4.4km.) (1 8.0 km.), turning right onto Old Richter Pass Road. (00.0km.). After driving (1.6 km.), turn left onto gravel Kruger Mtn. Road (Western Bluebirds on wires) which becomes a rough narrow road passable with a passenger car leading (2.7 km.) (4.3 km.) to Blue Lake, passing a small pond en route. Several species of hawk will be observed soaring over the region and Golden Eagle the prized raptor. From the top of a Douglas-fir a robin-like song will reveal the presence of a Western Tanager. Of the more common dry forest and adjacent sagebrush-bunchgrass community species expected are: American Kestrel, California Quail, Mourning Dove, Great Horned Owl, Common Poorwill, Rufous Hummingbird, Western Wood-Pewee, Say's Phoebe, Townsend's Solitaire, Chipping Sparrow, and Cassin's Finch. House Wren are common in the denser thickets along the lakeshore.

(00.0km.) Return to Highway 3 East, turning right. At this point the highway quickly decends towards Osoyoos where you will get your first fabulous views of the famed Okanagan Valley. After driving (6.8 km.) (11 4.1 km. from Princeton) you will arrive at the junctions of Highways 3 and 97 at Osoyoos. From Osoyoos you can join the Okanagan Valley Loop, or continue along the Highway 3 Route East Loop.

NOTES & OBSERVATIONS

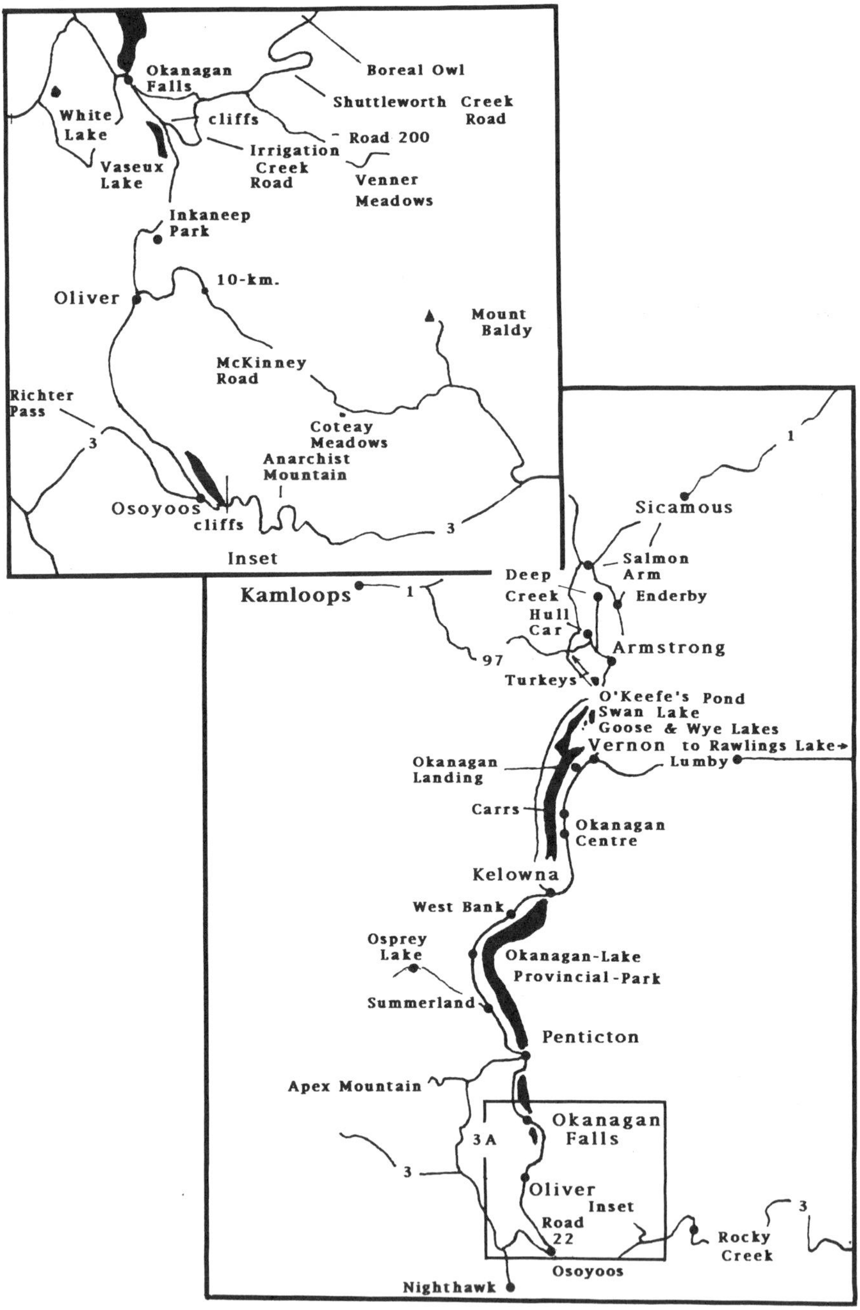

Okanagan
Falls

Boreal Owl

White
Lake

cliffs

Shuttleworth Creek
Road

Road 200

Irrigation
Creek
Road

Vaseux
Lake

Venner
Meadows

Inkaneep
Park

10-km.

Oliver

Mount
Baldy

McKinney
Road

Richter
Pass

3

Coteay
Meadows
Anarchist
Mountain

Osoyoos
cliffs

3

Inset

Kamloops

1

Deep
Creek

Salmon
Arm

Sicamous

1

Enderby

Hull
Car

Armstrong

97

Turkeys

O'Keefe's Pond
Swan Lake
Goose & Wye Lakes
Vernon to Rawlings Lake

Okanagan
Landing

Lumby

Carrs

Okanagan
Centre

Kelowna

West Bank

Osprey
Lake

Okanagan-Lake
Provincial-Park

Summerland

Penticton

Apex Mountain

Okanagan
Falls

3A

3

Oliver
Inset

Road
22

3

Rocky
Creek

Osoyoos

Nighthawk

MAP 9   THE OKANAGAN VALLEY

LOOP 6   The Okanagan Valley

Okanagan and pocket-desert, the two are synonymous when the student of ornithology reflects on this region. Visions of expansive gray-green sagebrush flats with Sage Thrasher dashing between brush like tiny roadrunners; the endless canary-like song of the Brewer's Sparrow emitted from the pungent sage tops; the electric blue of a male Mountain Bluebird perched on a gnarled, weathered-gray fence post; White-headed Woodpecker climbing the rough yellow-bark of an ancient ponderosa in an ambient pine forest; moonlike landscapes of salt-encrusted alkaline lakes, their surfaces dotted with tiny whirlpools created by the feeding of Wilson's Phalarope; a sea of golden grasslands bathed in sunlight, over which the incredible Long-billed Curlew's call is carried on balmy breezes upward to the great cerulean skies: But the Okanagan is much more than this!

High above, surrounding this isolated, sun-drenched valley, is a high mountainous plateau that extends southward from the high arctic. The varying erosional resistance of the rocks of this plateau has left an irregular surface with many high points of resistant rock creating the spectacular high mountain peaks of the Okanagan Highlands. Apex Mountain, Baldy Mountain, and Mount Brent at 2,200 + meters in altitude have, on their slopes, subalpine boreal forests and taiga-like alpine meadows. This accident of geomorphology has allowed both northern and southern avifauna to colonize the area, producing a fascinating and unique assemblage of species.

In the forests of Douglas fir, ponderosa pine, spruce, hemlock, and sub-alpine fir are a myriad of montane forest specialities from noisy Clark's Nutcracker to diminutive Calliope Hummingbird, the smallest bird in Canada; from the tame but elusive Spruce Grouse to the secretive Three-toed Woodpecker, tapping lightly in some dark shadow; from wheeling flocks of fringillidae overhead - materializing into those irruptive inhabitants of coniferous woods - White-winged Crossbill to mottled White-tailed Ptarmigan camouflaged against lichen-covered alpine rock high above treeline.

With the Georgia Depression, the Okanagan Valley is the next significant destination for the birder in British Columbia.

Osoyoos to Road No. 22

Go east on Highway 3 watching signs for Rocky Creek and Creston. From Osoyoos you may proceed east on Highway 3 for the Highway 3 East Route Loop or turn north for the Okanagan Loop.

From the junctions of Highways 97 and 3 in Osoyoos (00.0 km.) drive north on Highway 97 towards Oliver. After driving (7.8 km.) (or 12.4 km. south of Oliver), turn right onto Road No. 22 which is directly north of Osoyoos Lake.

ROAD No.22

(00.0km.) The road immediately passes between hayfields, the best site for Bobolink in the valley. As the surrounding pastures are private property, you must stay on the road; although birdfinding from the road will be highly successful. Watch for Eastern Kingbird, Western Kingbird, and Western Bluebird on the overhead wires and fence posts. Tree Swallow, Violet-green Swallow, Bank Swallow, Northern Rough-winged Swallow, Cliff Swallow, and Barn Swallow hawk low over the fields for insects. Grasshopper Sparrow, although sporatic, has nested in years when a field is left fallow. A domestic herd of American Bison are present in the pastures.

Continue over the bridge across the Okanagan River (1.0 km.). You can walk or drive either of the dike roads, be sure to close the gates after passing through! A walk along the dike to the right (south) will bring you to a small cattail marsh with both Yellow-headed Blackbird and Red-winged Blackbird; both of these blackbirds and Brown-headed Cowbird are usually seen in mixed flocks feeding in the pastures. This dike road also gives access to a patch of riparian woods at the northern end of Osoyoos Lake, one of the best sites for Long-eared Owl, Gray Catbird, and Yellow-breasted Chat in the valley. Osprey, Black-crowned Night-Heron, American Bittern, Sora, Willow Flycatcher, Black-capped Chickadee, Veery, Red-eyed Vireo, Yellow Warbler, Bullock's Oriole, and Lazuli Bunting all occur in the woods or cattail marshes in season. Late evening is the best time to see the irregular/rare night-herons as they leave their roosts to feed along the river banks. At this time a Short-eared Owl may begin its evening hunt. A careful search of the woods may reveal a Long-eared Owl sitting on his stick platform nests. If your daylight search goes unrewarded, a Long-eared Owl or a Great Horned Owl could be enticed to call after dark; (Northern Saw-whet Owl has also been recorded).

Just over the bridge (0.6 km.) (1.6 km.), park at the old farm buildings that comprise the historic ranch-site. Say's Phoebe are always present, nesting in the buildings, while Lark Sparrow are found on the flats above; Sage Thrasher is a slim possibility. The sagebrush flats contains one of the most impressive stands of prickly-pear cactus in British Columbia. Proceed uphill through the flats to the cliffs known as "The Throne" where there are White-throated Swift and Rock Wren; there is a chance of seeing Canyon Wren. A pair of Prairie Falcon have nested on "The Throne" during the spring-early summer of 1993-94. Chukar (uncommon) are present around the rocky bluff and talus slopes. Lewis' Woodpecker and Clark's Nutcracker occur in the pines.

Turn right onto the unpaved road (if you wish you may continue to drive the rough gravel road through the Inkaneep Indian Reserve to Oliver). After driving (0.2 km.) (1.8 km.) from the old ranch is a Burrowing Owl re-introduction site. Scope the hillside above the road (left) looking for the owls on posts or standing sentry duty at the entrance to their man-made burrows (the burrows consist of hollows with black plastic pipes projecting from them). A.B.A. rules prohibit anyone from counting these birds on any lists!

Road No. 22 to Oliver

 Return to Highway 97 and turn right toward Oliver (00.0 km.). After driving (12.4 km.) (20.2 km. from Osoyoos), turn right at the second set of traffic lights on Highway 97 in downtown Oliver.

Oliver to McKinney Road

(00.0km.), turn right (east), crossing over the Okanagan River bridge, keeping right onto paved McKinney Road at the "Y" junction (0.4 km.) following the "H" sign for the hospital. Past the hospital you will cross a cattleguard (0.6 km.) (1.0 km.), entering the Inkaneep Indian Reserve. Black Sage Road meets with Camp McKinney Road here (a good road to bird en route between Oliver and Osoyoos). Do Not leave the McKinney Road for the next ten kilometers as you are in an Indian Reserve!

McKinney Road

McKinney Road is "the" mandatory site to visit in the Okanagan Valley for anyone with a keen interest in seeing as many of the specialities as possible in one day. The McKinney Road passes through a wide range of habitats and accompanying avifauna.

At the intersection of Black Sage and McKinney Roads we start at (00.0 km.). McKinney Road is paved for the first sixteen kilometers and excellent gravel afterwards.

At (00.8 km.) you will see a Bank Swallow colony on the northside of the road. Gray Partridge, Gray Catbird, Lazuli Bunting, and Bullock's Oriole should be found in the neighbouring roadside habitat. After driving (2.2 km.) (3.0 km.) there is a gravel bank that produces Horned Lark and Gray-crowned Rosy Finch in winter. Drive an additional (1.0 km.) (4.0 km.) to the sagebrush flats supporting Long-billed Curlew, Vesper Sparrow, Lark Sparrow, and Brewer's Sparrow. After an additional (2.0 km.) (6.0 km), check the rocky slopes and scattered ponderosa pines above the road for Chukar, Lewis' Woodpecker, and Rock Wren; while the surrounding deciduous brush and woods will produce Gray Catbird, Nashville Warbler, Lazuli Bunting, and Bullock's Oriole.

Drive an additional (2.0 km.) (8.0 km.). Near an orange home, the road crosses over a small creek. Calliope Hummingbird and Black-chinned Hummingbird often feed at the sapsucker wells drilled into the neighbouring trees. The rare White-headed Woodpecker has occurred in the area. After (2.0 km.) (10.0 km.) the road passes over a second cattle guard. This is the site that has become legendary for Gray Flycatcher in Canada, the first nesting occurring here. The flycatchers are reliable at this location from early May through early July singing their vigorous tri-syliabic songs from the tops of the larger ponderosa pines; arrive early in the morning when the males are singing. Be cautious in your identification as Dusky Flycatcher are also found commonly at this site (although are usually found in association with deciduous shubbery along the moist creeks in the draws). Two other "empids", Willow Flycatcher and Pacific-slope Flycatcher also occur along the small creeks in the vicinity. Mourning Dove, White-breasted Nuthatch, Pygmy Nuthatch, Townsend's Solitaire, and Cassin's Finch will be found in the ponderosa pines.

A short way (1.0 km.) up the McKinney Road, a rough dirt road branches off on the left. Drive down this road until another road branches off on the right. Turn onto this road; a small clearing is soon encountered. Dusky Flycatcher are common around the clearing, with both Red-naped Sapsucker and Williamson's Sapsucker often in the area.

After (2.0 km.) (12.0 km.) there is a fork, keep to the left for McKinney Road. A reliable Flammulated Owl is found in the triangular patch of forest between the roads at this intersection in summer. On warm summer nights the soft "boo-boot" is emitted from an inconspicuous perch between kilometers 12 and 13; spotlighting these small owls is difficult. Great Horned Owl and Northern Pygmy-Owl may also be heard here. In the surrounding forests of Douglas-fir and ponderosa pine are Pileated Woodpecker, Steller's Jay, Clark's Nutcracker, Mountain Chickadee, White-breasted Nuthatch, Red-breasted Nuthatch and Pygmy Nuthatch.

Just past (4.0 km.) (16.0 km.) the road passes over Baldy Creek. Old logging roads branch off north through areas of spruce, Douglas-fir, and larch along both sides of the Baldy Creek Valley. Avifauna of this forest-type include: Barred Owl, Williamson's Sapsucker, Black-backed Woodpecker, Three-toed Woodpecker, Hammond's Flycatcher, Steller's Jay, Mountain Chickadee, Brown Creeper, Red-breasted Nuthatch, Winter Wren, Golden-crowned Kinglet, Yellow-rumped Warbler, Townsend's Warbler, Dark-eyed Junco, Pine Siskin, and Red Crossbill.

After an additional (2.2 km.) (18.2 km.) there are birch woods that harbour Red-naped Sapsucker, Downy Woodpecker, Orange-crowned Warbler, and MacGillivray's Warbler. At kilometer 20 you will pass over yet another cattleguard. The conifer forest here has a variety of woodpeckers including Williamson's Sapsucker, Hairy Woodpecker and Pileated Woodpecker.

Drive just beyond (3.8 km.) (22.0 km.) to Coteay Meadows, a sedge marsh, visible through the woods on the right (south) side of the road. Trails (cross-country ski trails in winter) lead to the west side of the pond and beyond to subalpine. After the snow has melted, the "Gold-dust Trail" provides access to a mixed forest of spruce, Douglas-fir, and larch, sedge meadows, and to beaver ponds. Green-winged Teal, Ring-necked Duck, Virginia Rail, Sora, Common Yellowthroat, Lincoln's Sparrow and Rusty Blackbird (uncommon) are found around the ponds, while Williamson's

Sapsucker, Red-naped Sapsucker, Hairy Woodpecker, Three-toed Woodpecker, Hammond's Flycatcher, Gray Jay, and Townsend's Warbler are found in the forests.

After (2.7 km.) (24.7 km.) there is a small beaver pond with accompanying Northern Waterthrush and you may possibly see the sedate Pine Grosbeak. In the logging slash between kilometers 26 and 27 are Dusky Flycatcher and the stunningly beautiful Mountain Bluebird. A patch of magnificent old-growth larch after driving (2.7 km.) (27.4 km.) supports Barred Owl, Northern Pygmy-Owl, Red-naped Sapsucker and Williamson's Sapsucker.

After (6.4 km.) (33.8 km.) there is a junction, the left road leading to the main skiing area in the southern Okanagan Valley, the Mount Baldy ski area. The right, Mt. Baldy Road, leading to Highway 3 between Bridesville and Rock Creek thirteen kilometers away. The junction is surrounded by fragmented sub-alpine forest which harbours Spruce Grouse, Gray Jay, Mountain Chickadee, Boreal Chickadee (uncommon), Winter Wren, Hermit Thrush, Varied Thrush, Wilson's Warbler, Fox Sparrow and Pine Grosbeak.

Turn left at the junction for Mount Baldy; after (7.0 km.) (40.8 km.) you will reach the main ski area. Follow the signs for the ski cabins, left of the main ski area, and park at the end of the highest road. A four-wheel drive track leads up the left ridge of the mountain to the summit at 2,304 meters. If you climb to the barren alpine ridges they could possibly reward your efford with White-tailed Ptarmigan and American Pipit.

Mount Baldy to Anarchist Mountain and Osoyoos

From the Mount Baldy junction (33.8 km.) (see above), turn right and continue to Highway 3, twelve kilometers away (en route, keep left at the smaller sideroad and then right at the 'T" junction along Mount Baldy Road). At Highway 3 and the Rock Creek bridge, (46.8 km.), turn right onto Highway 3 for Osoyoos or left for the continuation of the Highway 3 Route East. Osoyoos is (39.7 km.) away.

(00.0km.) At (7.5 km.) you will arrive at the summit of Anarchist Mountain. After driving (14.3 km.) (19.8 km.) you will reach a rest area in ponderosa pine forest; a good spot to search for the rare White-headed Woodpecker.

After driving an additional (5.3 km.) (25.1 km.) the dirt Long Joe Road on the right leads (0.5 km.) to a log house with hummingbird feeders, which are visible without trespassing! Western Wood-Pewee, Dusky Flycatcher, House Wren, and Cassin's Finch are common in the shrubbery along the length of the dirt road. Among the more common Rufous Hummingbird and Calliope Hummingbird at the home's feeders are a few Black-chinned Hummingbird. The exquisite White-headed Woodpecker has been seen along this road, or in the general area, especially in winter.

After driving an additional (3.5 km.) (28.6 km.) there is a viewpoint over the valley where Swainson's Hawk and Prairie Falcon are possible. Chukar crow from the ochre boulders below and the beautiful Lazuli Bunting sing from amongst the vegetated rocky outcrops. Lewis' Woodpecker and Rock Wren are common.

Just outside of Osoyoos, at the foot of Anarchist Mountain, a gated dirt sideroad leads off from the right (6.0 km.) (34.6 km.). Walk (1.3km.) to the base of the cliffs. The non-migratory Canyon Wren-sings its loud silvery song, a decelerating, descending series of liquid "tee's" and "tew's" from the deep crevices. Prairie Falcon are possible on the steep cliff-faces. After an additional (5.1 km.) (39.7 km.) you will arrive at the junction of Highways 3 and 97.

Return to Oliver.

Oliver to Inkaneep Provincial Park

(00.0km.) Proceed north on Highway 97 from the northern set of traffic lights in downtown Oliver. After driang (8.0 km.) (28.5 km. from Osoyoos) you will see the entrance to Inkaneep Provincial Park on your right.

INKANEEP PROVINCIAL PARK

Look for the rare Loggerhead Shrike in the dry area adjacent to the park's northern parameter along the highway right-of-way. You will be lucky indeed to find one; spring is best.

Inkaneep Park to McIntyre (irrigation) Creek Road

(00.0km.) Continue north on Highway 97 from Inkaneep Provincial Park towards Okanagan Falls. After (2.0 km.) you will see the Pine Bluff Motel and opposite it is the K.O.A. campground. There is an abundance of hummingbird feeders which have mainly Calliope Hummingbirds. a few Rufous Hummingbirds and the odd Black-chinned Hummingbird.

After driving an additional (6.2 km.) (8.2 km.) you will see the Vaseux Provincial campground on the right. McIntyre Creek Road branches off Highway 97 to the right (0.3 km.) (8.5 km.) north of the Vaseux Lake Provincial Campground (35.2 km. north of Osoyoos) (or 6.1 km. south of the community of Okanagan Falls).

McINTYRE (IRRIGATION) CREEK ROAD

(00.0km.) The gravel road passes under the Vaseux cliffs, possibly the best site in Canada to see Canyon Wren (0.1 km.).

The Canyon Wren is a permanent resident of the cliff tops and talus-slopes, their beautiful song of cascading notes tumbling down from high above like a musical waterfall. Sping is the best season to find the wren when the song is repeated frequently, echoing from the cliff face. The Rock Wren is more common, usually frequenting the lower talus-slopes, but not arriving until late May. White-throated Swift fly past the cliffs, upon which they nest, at tremendous speeds. Proceed (0.7 km.) (0.8 km.), Chukar are permanent residents, found in the brushy and rocky margins at the base of the cliffs. In winter, flocks of these colourful introduced Asian gamebirds gather at the feeders provided for the Rocky Mountain Big Horn Sheep. Calliope Hummingbird feed at the purple flowers of thistles along the road when they are in bloom. California Quail, Nashville Warbler, and Lazuli Bunting sing from brushy hillsides and the enigmatic Lewis' Woodpecker often fly-catch from the neighbouring pines where Black-billed Magpie, Say's Phoebe, Pygmy Nuthatch, and Cassin's Finch will also be found.

At (2.4 km.) (3.2 km.) you will pass under powerlines where Clark's Nutcrackers are frequently observed. On the right, after driving an additional (0.5 km.) (3.7 km.), there is a corral. A walk of about 25 m. in a south-west direction from the corral will bring you to a grove of birch trees that harbour Red-naped Sapsucker.

In summer, Black-chinned Hummingbird, Calliope Hummingbird, and Rufous Hummingbird feed at the sapsucker "wells", possibly one of the better sites in the Okanagan to observe all of the hummingbird species. In the surrounding dry forests are Western Wood-Pewee, Western Kingbird, Clark's Nutcracker, Mountain Chickadee, Pygmy Nuthatch, Western Bluebird, Townsend's Solitaire, and Cassin's Finch. Keep left at the corral, the road then continues northeast to Shuttleworth Creek Road (3.8 km.) (7.5 kms.) away. The road gets narrower and bumpier the further you go, but is passable in a passenger car. One of the favoured locales in Canada for the White-headed Woodpecker is among the ponderosa pines along this sector of Irrigation Creek Road. The woodpeckers often feed on the seeds of the great mullein weeds growing low along the roadside. At night, the red eye-glow of Common Poorwill will be picked-up in the car's headlights. Hypnotized by the lights, an observer can get out of their vehicle and approach quite closely. This is possibly the best site for Common Poorwill in the valley.

McIntyre (Irrigation) Creek Road to Vaseux Lake

Turn right onto Highway 97 North (00.0 km.). After driving (0.5 km.) pull over into the large parking area on the left next to the northeast corner of Vaseux Lake. The north shore of the lake includes a *Typha/Scirpus* marsh, wet meadows, birch, alder, and willow thickets. American White Pelican (casual), Western Grebe, Red-necked Grebe, Homed Grebe, the odd American Bittern (reeds), Tundra Swan, Trumpeter Swan (rare), Mute Swan (rare), Canada Goose, Snow Goose (casual), Mallard, Gadwall, Green-winged Teal, American Wigeon, Northern Shoveler, Canvasback, Ring-necked Duck, Greater Scaup, Common Goldeneye, Common Merganser, Virginia Rail and Sora (common in reeds), and American Coot occur at the lake in season. Many of the waterfowl remain through the winter if all or part of the lake remains unfrozen.

Vaseux Lake to the Shuttleworth Creek (201) Road

At Highway 97 and the north end of Vaseux Lake, proceed north towards Okanagan Falls (00.0 km.). After driving (4.7 km.) look for a Weyerhaeuser sign and turn right onto the unsigned gravel road. Road 201, also known as the Shuttleworth Creek Road, branches off Highway 97 (0.9 km.) south of the community of Okanagan Falls (40.4 km. from Osoyoos).

SHUTTLEWORTH CREEK ROAD (Road 201)

(00.0km.).The preceeding logging roads have kilometer markers alongside the roads. Proceed to the stop sign (0.9 km.) and continue straight ahead for (0.1 km.) (1.0 km.), keeping right. After driving an additional (1.5 km.) (2.5 km.), turn right at the stop sign. At (7.3km.) you will meet with the Irrigation Creek Road that begins (0.3 km.)north of the Vaseux Lake Campground. After (12.5 km.)(15.0 km.) Road 200 branches off to the right. Turn right onto Road 200 for an additional (0.5 km.) (15.5 km.).

A Williamson's Sapsucker nests on the left at the edge of the road about 50 feet off the ground, a reliable site; watch from the clearing. Stop at precisely (2.8 km.) (18.3 km.) and look for the highly visible nesting holes of a Black-backed Woodpecker on the right ten feet off the ground, again a reliable site. Williamson's Sapsucker also nest on the left side of the road around kilometer 14. Road 200 continues on to Venner Meadows at (6.1 km.) (24.4 km.). Three-toed Woodpecker have nested in the short stumps in the meadows off to the right.

(00.0km.) Return to the 201 and 200 Road junction, turning right onto Road 201; be sure to keep left after (4.8 km.). After driving an additional (3.9 kms.) (8.7 km.) (23.7 kms. along Road 201 from Highway 97) you will pass over a cattle guard. A dirt road branches off to the left about 75 ft. past the cattle guard.

Park your vehicle and walk down this dirt road about 10 m. and walk off to the right through the thick woods towards the small lake, checking the trees that rim the lake for four man-made nesting boxes. A Boreal Owl raised young successfully in one of these boxes in 1992 and was still being heard in 1994. The best season to check the owl boxes is late April through mid-May, but a taped call could get a response at other times, March is best. (Caution of winnowing Common Snipe later in the year which sound similar to Boreal Owls at a distance).

Return to Highway 97.

Shuttleworth Creek (201) Road to Okanagan Falls Park

(00.0km.) Continue northward to the community of Okanagan Falls (0.9 km.) (41.3 km. from Osoyoos). The name of the town is somewhat misleading as there are no longer falls; the water course has long since been dammed and channelled. Look for hummingbird feeders around the motels and homes in town. Black-chinned Hummingbird, Calliope Hummingbird, and Rufous Hummingbird are recorded in early April through late June; only Rufous occurs later. Turn left in town following Highway 97. After crossing over the Okanagan River bridge (0.6km.) (1.5 km.), turn left onto Green Lake Road where you will soon come to the entrance to Okanagan Falls Provincial Park on your right (O6 km.) (2.1 km.).

OKANAGAN FALLS PROVINCIAL PARK

This small campground is centered in the best birdfinding region of the Okanagan. The park is situated in riparian woodland on the channel-like Okanagan River that links Skaha Lake and Vaseux Lake. For budget birders without transportation it is the ideal place to stay, as well as a good site of its own. The park is within easy walking distance of many of the lower altitude habitats.

Birding within the park and the adjacent riparian woodlands along the edges of the Okanagan River in summer will produce the following species; breeding birds arrive in late March - early May:

Killdeer	Red-naped Sapsucker
Spotted Sandpiper	Downy Woodpecker
California Gull	Eastern Kingbird
Golden Eagle	Western Kingbird
Red-tailed Hawk	Western Wood-Pewee
Osprey (U)	Willow Flycatcher
American Kestrel	Steller's Jay
California Quail	American Crow
Mourning Dove	Black-capped Chickadee
Great Horned Owl	White-breasted
Nuthatch	Common Nighthawk
Marsh Wren	Vaux's Swift
Veery	White-throated Swift
American Robin	Northern Flicker
Gray Catbird	Cedar Waxwing
European Starling	Warbling Vireo

Yellow Warbler
Common Yellowthroat
American Redstart
Spotted Towhee
Lark Sparrow
Red-winged Blackbird
Brown-headed Cowbird
House Finch

Northern Waterthrush
Yellow-breasted Chat
Black-headed Grosbeak
Song Sparrow
Yellow-headed Blackbird
Brewer's Blackbird
Bullock's Oriole
Evening Grosbeak (erratic)

Okanagan Falls Provincial Park to White Lake

(00.0km.) At (0.2 km.) there is a water control dam on the Okanagan River. Here you will occasionally find Barrow's Goldeneye and American Dipper through the year. Along the river are flocks of swallows hawking for insects every evening with Tree Swallow, Violet-green Swallow, Bank Swallow, Northern Rough-winged Swallow, Cliff Swallow, and Barn Swallow represented in good numbers. Harlequin Duck occur in some stretches of the river during the winter months. Black-headed Grosbeak and Lazuli Bunting inhabit the thickets along the lake shore. If you wish to see Yellow-breasted Chat they may be found in the dense thickets along the old railway right-of-way at the southwest end of the lake. Bobolink are occasionally seen on the meadows at the south end of the lake.

Continue up Green Lake Road from Okanagan Falls Provincial Park into dry forest to Green Lake after driving (6.2) (6.4 km.). The lake often has pairs of Redhead and Barrow's Goldeneye. In the ponderosa pines there are Mountain Chickadee; the rare White-headed Woodpecker is possible. Continue to Mahoney Lake (2.0 km.) (8.4 km.) which also has breeding Redhead and Barrow's Goldeneye. After an additional (4.3 km.) (12.7 km.) paved Green Lake Road branches off to the left. Long-billed Curlew are found in fields along this road just past the fork; be sure to bear left at the fork after driving (1.4 km.). Continue along White Lake Road, always keeping to the right. Check on the road at night for the next two and a half kilometers for Common Poorwill; their eyes will appear as twin red beads in the car's headlights.

At (2.3 km.) (15.0 km.) the dry forest will open to a large sagebrush basin, one of the most expansive areas of this habitat in British Columbia. As you are turning the bend in the road and first see the open country before you, check the hillsides to your right for Gray Partridge. The partridge are found irregularly in open country in southern regions of the valley, it is best to look for them around the northern valley's extensive farmlands of alfalfa or grain. After driving an additional (3.8 km.) (18.8 km.) park your car opposite alkaline White Lake and walk off into the sage brush. The weedy area directly to your right has produced Grasshopper Sparrow, listen carefully for the indistinct high, thin chip notes, followed by an insect-like buzz. The "purer" tracts of sagebrush are filled with the common birds of this habitat; Vesper Sparrow, Brewer's Sparrow, and Western Meadowlark. Sage Sparrow is possible in the basin with two former records, so check your sparrows carefully. Sage Thrasher is always a good possibility here, occurring erratically from year to year, but has been found lately in the Chopaka region with more regularity. Prairie Falcon occurred in the past and an individual could still fly through.

Check White Lake in summer for Northern Pintail, Wilson's Phalarope, and in late summer and fall for migrant Red-necked Phalarope and other migrant shorebirds. Sandhill Crane are common transients in the basin, White Lake being the best site in the Okanagan Valley, from mid-April to mid-May and again from mid-September through mid-October. Horned Lark are common transients, uncommon in summer and winter.

At (1.2 km.) (20.0 km.), turn right at the "T" junction (this corner for White Lake Road is signed for "Oliver" if you are coming in from the opposite direction of our loop). After (0.4 km.) (20.4 km.) you will see a water tank on your right. A walk in the direction of the water tank will bring you to an expanse of golden grassland where a pair of Long-billed Curlew nest. As you approach their territory they will rise from the grasses, circling, their call ringing loudly and repetitively, a musical, ascending "cur-lee". The water tank often attracts thirsty birds such as Say's Phoebe and Mountain Bluebird, or a Lazuli Bunting from the brush on the northeast slope above the road. Chukar gather to drink and are heard calling from the tops of the rocks here in the early morning.

After an additional (0.4 km.) (20.8 km.) you will pass by the entrance road to the White Lake radio-astronomy observatory on your right. At (1.1 km.) (21.9 km.) there are shale beds that contain plant fossils, opposite these is a damp area where Common Snipe are heard "winnowing" in spring. After (1.8 km.) (23.7 km.) there is a small marsh on the right that is worth a short stop. From here back to Highway 97/3A, after an additional (4.3 km.) (28.0 km.), the road will again enter dry forest interjected with open ranchlands; watch for Mourning Dove and Townsend's Solitaire.

At the junction of White Lake Road and Highway 97 (28.0 km.), you could return to Okanagan Falls; turn right for an additional (4.6 km.) (32.6 km.), or turn left for Penticton.

White Lake Road to Apex Mountain ski area

The junction of White Lake Road and Highway 97 is (46.5 km.) north of Osoyoos. (00.0 km.) From this junction, drive north on Highway 97 for (0.7 km.) turning left onto Highway 3A for the Apex Mountain ski area. Drive 20 kms. along 3A, turning right on a secondary paved road, following the ski signs for an additional (1 2 km.) (32.5 km.); then turn left onto a gravel road at the ski signs. This corner can be reached from downtown Penticton

(see below). Follow the twisting gravel road uphill towards the summit of
Apex Mountain at 2,247 m (13 km.) (45 km.).

White Lake Road to Penticton

 If you do not wish to go to Apex Mountain, proceed north on Highway
97 from the White Lake Road junction to the Penticton bypass (9.1 km.)
or (56.3 km. north of Osoyoos). After crossing the Okanagan River
bridge, turn left following Highway 97 North. Turn left onto Fairview Road
(2.9 km.) (12.0 km.) and over the Okanagan River bridge (where Fairview
Road becomes Green Mountain Road, hence Apex Mountain Road): drive 19
kms. to the junction with the gravel road mentioned above. The roads in
Penticton are signed for Apex Alpine Ski Resort, a thirty minute drive.

APEX MOUNTAIN SKI AREA

 Apex Mountain is principally known as the most easily accessed site
in the Okanagan Valley to search for White-tailed Ptarmigan; you
will need luck to locate one. The alpine ridges are a short hike from the ski
area. Other high-level avifauna such as Spruce Grouse and Three-toed
Woodpecker should be looked for in the surrounding spruce forests.

PENTICTON

(00.0km.) From the Highway 97 bypass, proceed north for (4.8km.),
turning left and following the signs for the continuation of Highway
97. After an additional (1.1 km.) (5.9 km.), turn left just past the
Okanagan River bridge onto West Bench Drive. Proceed along West Bench
Drive for (0.8 km.) (6.7 km.), passing over a narrow wooden bridge, and
veering right onto Bartlett Road for (0.5 km.) (7.2 km.). At the "T" junction
with West Bench Drive (again!), turn right, then immediately left onto Bartlett
Drive (0.1 km.) (7.3 km.). Stay on Bartlett Drive for (1.4 km.) (8.7 km.) passing
a gravel pit (and a Bank Swallow colony), taking the unsigned gravel road
leading straight ahead. Proceed along the gravel road into the narrow
canyon to the fork in the road (2.3 km.) (11.0 km.). If you stay on pavement
into the new suburb, drive around looking for the many hummingbird feeders
where Black-chinned Hummingbird, Calliope Hummingbird, and Rufous
Hummingbird are easily found.

Several owl nest boxes, which usually house Northern Saw-whet Owl
(infrequently Flammulated Owl) have been placed on trees in the area
amongst the mixed forest of Douglas-fir and ponderosa pine. Finding the
boxes placed along the southern slope is difficult without help from their
owner. The Flammulated Owl is consistently found at the road fork each
summer - this is the best site to see the owl in the Okanagan Valley! Play your

tape to bring the owl into view. Do not be anxious of using your spotlight continuously as it is the easiest way of locating the owl as it flies silently around you. California Quail, Red-breasted Sapsucker, Western Wood-Pewee, Say's Phoebe, Red-breasted Nuthatch, House Wren, Townsend's Solitaire, Veery, Nashville Warbler, Spotted Towhee, and Western Tanager will not be overlooked in the daylight hours.

Penticton to Westbank Marsh

(00.0km.) From the junction of West Bench Drive and Highway 97, drive north on Highway 97 for (9.1 km.). In winter, turn right at the traffic lights onto Johnstone Road, Woods Avenue, and left onto Miller Street (0.8 km.) to Trout Creek Point. Both transient and wintering Redhead are abundant off the point on Okanagan Lake.

At Summerland (4.6 km.) (13.7 km.) you can access Osprey Lake Road. (00.0 km.) Turn left at the traffic lights onto Prairie Valley Road, then left again (0.8 km.) still on Prairie Valley Road. After (0.4 km.) (1.2 km.) stop at the stop sign and proceed straight ahead for Osprey Lake Road (following dump signs).

Drive an additional (10.7 km.) (24.4 km.) north along Highway 97 to the entrance to Okanagan Lake Park on your right. After an additional (23.3 km.) (47.7 km.) (13.2 km. south of Kelowna) you will arrive at Westbank.

WESTBANK MARSH

(00.0km.) From Westbank, turn left onto Old Okanagan Highway driving north. At (2.0 km.), Old Okanagan Highway jogs slightly to the right at Shannon Lake Road. Just past this intersection on the left of Shannon Lake Road is a small, reed-fringed wetland that is on private property. Red-winged Blackbird will try to drive you from their territories, sweeping low over your head, while the Yellow-headed Blackbird's song of harsh, rasping notes, ending with a long, descending buzz, will add to the avian cacophony percolating from the bullrushes. Mallard, Blue-winged Teal, Cinnamon Teal, Sora, Marsh Wren, and migrant shorebirds are to be expected.

Westbank to Green Bay, Kelowna

(00.0km.) After driving (8.3 km.) further north along Highway 97, turn right onto Boucherie Road at the Esso gas station for Green Bay (which is 4.9 km. from the east end of the Okanagan Lake Bridge and the intersection of Harvey and Abbott Streets). Take the right fork immediately after leaving the highway. Proceed along Boucherie Road for (5.5 km.) (11.7 km.), turning sharply to the left at the Green Bay Resort turnoff. Continue along the winding road past the resort, keeping on the main road which ends, after curving left between two homes, as a dirt track.

GREEN BAY

Park at the roads termination with the shore of Okanagan Lake. Common Tern, an uncommon Okanagan transient, is most often recorded here in May, and again from mid-July through September. In winter, Common Loon, Western Grebe, Red-necked Grebe, Horned Grebe, Gadwall, Canvasback, Greater Scaup, White-winged Scoter (casual summer and winter), Surf Scoter (rare), Bufflehead, Common Merganser, and American Coot sit offshore on this deep, sapphire blue lake. Snow Geese, a casual Okanagan migrant, are occasionally found in April and May.

Green Bay to Kelowna

Retrace your route back to Highway 97, turning right towards Kelowna (00.0 km.). After driving (3.9 km.) you will arrive at the junction for Kelowna at Westside. Turn left, crossing the 1,400 m. long floating bridge over the Okanagan Lake at Siwash Point (1.0 Km.) (4.9 km.). After (2.0 km.) (6.9 km.) you will arrive in Kelowna. Kelowna is (60.9 km. north of West Bench Drive in Penticton).

KELOWNA

Kelowna, the "City of Sunshine, Beaches and Smiles", is located on the shores of Lake Okanagan, approximately halfway between Penticton and Vernon. Set amidst magnificent scenery - a mosaic of extensive forest-clad mountains, low rolling hills and sparkling lakes once Kelowna has worked its magic, the spell never fades; a visit at anytime of year - and you will want to return to this fascinating place.

The Kelowna region has several sites which offer the birder an excellent array of species. Although the birding is somewhat similar to the birding opportunities that exist in the southern sector of the valley, fewer "specialities" are represented.

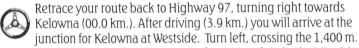

The following four sites, in and around Kelowna, are visited as three loops starting from the east end of the Okanagan Lake Bridge in Kelowna.

1. Okanagan Lake Bridge to Knox Mountain Park and Glenmore Ponds

2. Okanagan Lake Bridge to Woodhaven Nature Conservancy

3. Okanagan Lake Bridge to Mission Tow Path.

Okananagan Lake Bridge to Knox Mountain Park

 (00.0km.) From the east end of the Okanagan Lake Bridge, proceed east along Highway 97 (Harvey Avenue) for (0.3 km.), turning left at the first set of traffic lights onto Abbott Street. Abbott Street changes itsname to Bernard Avenue after a right-angled bend to the right next to the White Sails Memorial (0.1 km.) (0.4 km.). Proceed east on Bernard Avenue for (0.4 km.) (0.8 km.), turning left at the third set of traffic lights onto Ellis Street. Continue an additional (2.2 km.) (3.0 km.) to the Knox Mountain Park gates. Stop at Sutherland Park, situated along the lakeshore just before reaching Knox Mountain Park, if you wish to scan for a similar list of waterfowl found at Green Bay.

KNOX MOUNTAIN PARK

A paved road leads through the park (3.2 km.) to the top of Knox Mountain at 647 m; an excellent network of trails branch off into the woods. This area has a rich mixture of ecosystems and is home to a wide variety of dry interior avifauna. White-throated Swift and Rock Wren inhabit the rocky outcrops, while along the numerous trails one should find Rufous Hummingbird breaking all the laws of aerodynamics as they search out blossoms, the enigmatic Lewis' Woodpecker, Pileated Woodpecker, Steller's Jay, Clark's Nutcracker, American Crow, White-breasted Nuthatch, Red-breasted Nuthatch, Pygmy Nuthatch, Mountain Bluebird, Townsend's Solitaire, Veery, the beautiful Western Tanager, and Cassin's Finch. Bohemian Waxwing's winter ranges vary widely and unpredictably with large flocks visiting scattered locations. Although appearing as early as late fall, Bohemian Waxwings become most common after the first of January feeding on the available berries and small fruits.

Knox Mountain Park to Glenmore Ponds

On leaving Knox Mountain Park, retrace your route back along Ellis Street to Bernard Avenue, turning left (00.0 km.). At the intersection of Ellis Street and Bernard Avenue, continue east along Bernard Avenue, crossing the railway overpass (2.6 km.), after which Bernard curves left and becomes Glenmore Drive. Proceed past the Kelowna Golf and Country Club on your right. After driving (8.3 km.) (10.9 km.), you will arrive at the Kelowna Landfill, where a healthy population of Ring-billed Gull, American Crow, and Common Raven feed. Proceed along Glenmore Drive for an additional (1.7 km.) (10.0 km.) to the first Glenmore Pond, and (2.0 km.) (12.0 km.) to the second.

GLENMORE PONDS

In the summer, Glenmore Ponds' reed and rush beds are frequented by breeding Pied-billed Grebe, Mallard, Northern Pintail, Redhead, Ruddy Duck, Virginia Rail, Sora, the gaudy Yellow-headed Blackbird, and Red-winged Blackbird. An occasional Northern Harrier can be found here too, quartering the marsh. Wilson's Phalarope in their rich breeding dress pirouette on the water, whilst outside of the breeding season migrant Semipalmated Plover, Red-necked Phalarope (uncommon), Long-billed Dowitcher, Semipalmated Sandpiper, Least Sandpiper, and Pectoral Sandpiper occur; Greater Yellowlegs and Lesser Yellowlegs parade sedately in the background.

Okanagan Lake Bridge to Woodhaven Nature Conservancy

(00.0km.) From the Okanagan Lake Bridge, drive east along Highway 97 (Harvey Ave.) for (0.3 km.), turning right onto Pandosy Street, which eventually becomes Lakeshore Drive. Proceed along Lakeshore Drive checking several beach accesses along the way for waterfowl, gulls, and shorebirds. Local rarities such as American White Pelican, American Avocet, and Parasitic Jaeger have been recorded along this stretch of shoreline. At (7.1 km.) (7.4 km.), turn left onto DeHart Road for (0.4 km.) (7.8 km.), then right onto Gordon Drive. Stay on Gordon Drive for (0.4 km.) (8.2 km.), turning left onto Raymer Road. Continue along Raymer Road through a sharp right and left to the Woodhaven Nature Conservancy at 4711 Raymer Road (1.6 km.) (9.8 km.). A sign for the reserve is displayed on a tree next to the chain-link fence.

WOODHAVEN NATURE CONSERVANCY

The private twenty-two acre Woodhaven reserve encompasses three distinct biotic zones, open to the public at this time. Characteristic breeding avifauna of dry forests are present, many remaining through the winter: Ruffed Grouse, Vaux's Swift, White-throated Swift, Red-naped Sapsucker, Steller's Jay, Clark's Nutcracker, American Crow, Mountain Chickadee, Red-breasted Nuthatch, White-breasted Nuthatch, Pygmy Nuthatch, Varied Thrush, Townsend's Solitaire, Townsend's Warbler, Black-headed Grosbeak, Bullock's Oriole, Red Crossbill, and Evening Grosbeak. As the sunlight penetrates the canopy it may illuminate the splendid plumage of a Western Tanager. Nocturnal excursions can be fantastic with Great Horned Owl, Northern Pygmy-Owl, and Northern Saw-whet Owl. Fortunate birders could see one of these owls dozing at one of their favourite daytime roosts.

Okanagan Lake Bridge to Mission Creek Tow Path

On leaving the Glenmore Ponds, retrace your route south on Glenmore Drive past the Golf and Country Club, proceeding straight ahead onto Spall Road. Turn left after crossing the railway tracks onto Highway 97 (from downtown Kelowna, just proceed east on Highway 97) (00.0 km.). Continue east on Highway 97 from the Spall Road intersection, turning right at the Orchard Park Shopping Centre onto Benvoulin Road (1.4 km.). Drive south along Benvoulin Road, passing the Father Pendozi Mission historical point of interest on the left, turning left onto Casorso Road (4.6 km.) (6.0 km.). Proceed east along Casorso Road, parking on the east side of the Mission Creek bridge (0.5 km.) (6.5 km.). Tow-paths follow the banks of the river from the bridge, both to the north and south. The north path leads upstream (1.6 km.) to the K.L.O. bridge, the south downstream for (0.8 km.), ending at another bridge.

MISSION CREEK TOW PATH

The riparian woods along the creek support such breeding species as American Kestrel, California Quail, Lewis' Woodpecker, Hairy Woodpecker, Downy Woodpecker, Pileated Woodpecker (uncommon), Black-capped Chickadee, American Dipper, Veery, Nashville Warbler, American Redstart, Bullock's Oriole, and Western Tanager. When the hummingbird-attracting flowers are still in bloom on the banks jewel-like Black-chinned Hummingbird, Calliope Hummingbird, and Rufous Hummingbird dart about. Raptors are well represented, scanning for potential prey from virtually every fencepost. Osprey are seen regularly in the area, while Peregrine Falcon and Prairie Falcon are irregularly observed. In winter, Gyrfalcon, Snowy Owl, Northern Shrike, Winter Wren, and Bohemian Waxwing inhabit the area.

Kelowna to Vernon

For those proceeding straight through Kelowna from Westside along Highway 97, proceed across the Okanagan Lake floating bridge into Kelowna (2.5 km.) (9.3 km.). Here Highway 97 becomes Harvey Avenue and we will start at (00.0 km.) from the east end of the floating bridge. Continue following the Highway 97 signs passing Benvoulin Street on your right after (4.7 km.) for Mission Creek Tow Path (see above), then on to the junction with Highways 33 South and 97 North (0.6km.) (5.0 km.). After an additional (9.1 km.) (14.1 km.) you will pass the Kelowna Airport. After driving an additional (12.4 km.) (26.5km.), turn left at the traffic lights on paved Oceola Road, driving west toward the community of Okanagan Centre (1.2 km.) (27.7 km.), then right following the shoreline of Okanagan Lake towards the community of Carrs. Whisky Island, offshore near Carrs (7.0 km.) 34.7 km.), harbours a gull breeding colony.

For those continuing straight through from Kelowna to Vernon proceed along Highway 97. As you approach Vernon, Kalamalka Lake will be on your right. In the past, Prairie Falcon nested on the bluff above Cosens Bay on the northeast side of the lake. After driving (53.3) kms from downtown Kelowna you will arrive in Vernon.

Approaching Vernon along Hwy 97 from the south, turn right (8.1 km.) at the sign for Kekuli Bay Provincial Park. After (0.6 km.) turn right for an additional (2.2 km.) to the park. Check the weedy fields for Gray Partridge.

Continue north along Hwy 97 to 30th Ave. and turn left (0.3 km.). Proceed along 30th Ave. which son changes its name to Bella Vista Road. Bella Vista takes a sharp curve to the left, soon after which you make a right turn onto Fleming Rd. (6.5 km.) (6.8 km.). Proceed to the 7400 block of Fleming and check the fallow fields and the hills above for Gray Partridge which are easily found throughout the year. The partridge are permanent residents, frequenting a feeder in the immediate area, especially during winter.

VERNON

The city of Vernon, nestled between the convergence of four valleys in the northern end of the Okanagan, has few of the Great Basin specialities, but the surrounding commons rank high as the best area of the valley to search for Gray Partridge, Swainson's Hawk, Grasshopper Sparrow, and Clay-colored Sparrow.. It is best site for American Redstart. The jewel-like males singing during the summer from the small groves of second-growth deciduous woods. The redstarts often fan their tail and spread their wings, emblazoned with striking orange or yellow flashes, as they actively pursue insects in the foliage. Both redpolls are erratic during winter, Common Redpoll being rare to abundant, while Hoary Redpoll are rare to casual; both can occur in the birch and alder groves anywhere in the region. Gyrfalcon, Snowy Owl, and Bohemian Waxwing are possible during the winter months, usually appearing after mid-January.

A drive along any of the orchard-lined country roads through the commons will produce Northern Shrike, which are fairly common in winter, and the ubiquitous House Finch, which are abundant residents. Watch for Gray Partridge in the extensive farmlands of alfalfa or grain, especially in winter when small flocks become conspicuous, feeding upon the harrowed snow-covered fields.

At the second intersection in Vernon you may turn east along Highway 6 for Lumby, or west along 25th Avenue for Okanagan Landing. South of Okanagan Landing you will find the delightful Ellison Provincial Park, sixteen kilometers away.

Vernon to Okanagan Landing and Carrs

 From the second intersection in south Vernon (see above), turn left along 25th Avenue following the signs for Okanagan Landing, (7.5 km.) away.

OKANAGAN LANDING and CARRS

 Diligent examination of the more common gulls on the beaches anywhere near Okanagan Landing during winter could produce Glaucous Gull and Thayer's Gull, both of which are casual.

Continue south along the Okanagan lakeshore from Okanagan Landing towards Carrs. After driving an additional (8.5 km.) (16.0 km.) you will find Ellison Provincial Park on your right. After (7.5 km.) (23.5 km.) you will arrive at Carrs. Herring Gull nest at Whisky Island, lying offshore from Carrs in Okanagan Lake. The island is also one of the few known nesting colonies of Ring-billed Gull (common resident) in the province. California Gull are commonly found lurking on the periphery of the colony, except during the winter when they are rare. Bonaparte's Gull are common in the area during migrations.

Vernon to Rawlings Lake

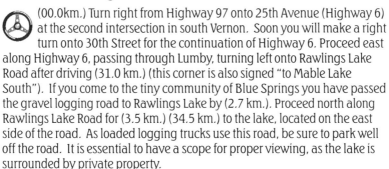 (00.0km.) Turn right from Highway 97 onto 25th Avenue (Highway 6) at the second intersection in south Vernon. Soon you will make a right turn onto 30th Street for the continuation of Highway 6. Proceed east along Highway 6, passing through Lumby, turning left onto Rawlings Lake Road after driving (31.0 km.) (this corner is also signed "to Mable Lake South"). If you come to the tiny community of Blue Springs you have passed the gravel logging road to Rawlings Lake by (2.7 km.). Proceed north along Rawlings Lake Road for (3.5 km.) (34.5 km.) to the lake, located on the east side of the road. As loaded logging trucks use this road, be sure to park well off the road. It is essential to have a scope for proper viewing, as the lake is surrounded by private property.

RAWLINGS LAKE

Rawlings Lake has an excellent cattail marsh, supporting the characteristic breeding avifauna of interior marshes: Pied-billed Grebe, Redhead, Ruddy Duck, Marsh Wren, Common Yellowthroat, the resplendent Yellow-headed Blackbird, and the beautiful Red-winged Blackbird will be among the interesting species that are encountered.

The surrounding rangelands are peppered with ponderosa pine stands which harbour American Kestrel, Lewis' Woodpecker, Clark's Nutcracker, Black-billed Magpie, American Crow, Mountain Chickadee, White-breasted Nuthatch, Red-breasted Nuthatch, Pygmy Nuthatch, and other characteristic species of dry forests. Nashville Warbler and Lazuli Bunting break the silence as they sing from the shrubs on the and sunlit slopes.

Vernon to Swan Lake

(00.0km.) From the second intersection in downtown Vernon, drive north along Highway 97 for (4.0 km.) to the south end of Swan Lake where you will find the marshes. The lake is situated immediately west of the highway, three kilometers, to ten kilometers north of Vernon. A scope is very useful to scan the far edges of the lake.

SWAN LAKE

Swan Lake has large numbers of breeding waterfowl, with the only breeding population of Western grebe in the Okanagan Valley. Red-necked Grebe also nests and remains during the winter, albeit in smaller numbers. Eared Grebe are uncommon transients, with Horned Grebe remaining commonly through the winter months. Mallard are common residents as long as the lake remains ice-free. Gadwall are fairly common transients, uncommon during the rest of year, while Green-winged Teal are also common transients, uncommon during the winter months. American Wigeon are abundant transients, uncommon during the remainder of the year. Northern Pintail are common, except during winter, while Northern Shoveler are common transients, breeding commonly on the lake, although rare during the winter. Redhead are abundant transients and winter visitors, with Ring-necked Duck mainly as transients. Greater Scaup and Common Merganser are abundant during the winter. American Coot are common residents. Northern Harrier float over the fields and marshes throughout the year. Rough-legged Hawk and Short-eared Owl are fairly common raptors that are seen hunting the long marsh grasses during the winter.

Swan Lake to Goose Lake

(00.0km.) From Swan Lake drive north to the junction of Highways 97 and 97A. (6.0 km.) (10 km. from Vernon). If you wish you can drive straight through on 97A to the Trans-Canada Highway (65 km.) or through to the Trans-Canada Highway on Highway 97 (79 kms.). Turn left onto Highway 97, driving an additional (1.4 km.) (7.4 km.) and turn left onto Old Kamloops Road; a paved road running along the west side of Swan Lake. After (5.2 km.) (12.6 km.), turn right onto paved Goose Lake Road for (0.5 km.) (13.1 km.), keeping right onto gravel to the deadend at the south end of Goose Lake (1.2 km.) (14.3 km.); Wye Lake lies to the south of the road.

GOOSE and WYE LAKES

Gray Partridge, Swainson's Hawk, Grasshopper Sparrow, and Clay-colored Sparrow are often found in the extensive hilly pastures surrounding both Goose and Wye Lakes. Grasshopper Sparrow will be found in any remaining weedy pastures; listen for the brief grasshopper-like buzz. Clay-colored Sparrow are found in the lakeside thickets, attracted to the flowerheads in the brushy fields surrounding both lakes. Large rafts of Common Merganser winter on Goose Lake while it remains ice-free. Wye Lake, south of Goose Lake, is excellent for shorebirds with similar species as those found at O'Keefe's Pond (see following page). With perseverance, Gray Partridge may be flushed from the area, exploding from your feet with a great clattering of wings.

Goose Lake to O'Keefe's Pond

Retrace your route back to Highway 97, turning left (00.0 km.). After driving (3.1 km.) you will see the O'Keefe Historic Ranch site and stop of interest. After an additional (0.5 km.) (3.6 km.) you will see O'Keefe's Pond on the right. After (0.6 km.) (4.2 km.) is Westside Road that runs the length of the west side of Okanagan Lake. After driving (3.0 km.) south along this paved road you will reach the North Arm of Okanagan Lake where Tundra Swan are uncommon transients and winter visitors.

If the shores of O'Keefe Pond are not mud-fringed try the pond on the left (1.4 km.) further west along Highway 97 towards Kamloops.

O'KEEFES POND

Captivating names conjure up images which are not disappointed by the reality, O'Keefe's Pond is such a place. O'Keefe's Pond is the best site in the Okanagan for shorebirds; a refuelling stop on their journey to-and-from their Arctic breeding grounds. Semipalmated Plover appear as uncommon fall migrants, rare during spring. Both Black-bellied Plover and American Golden-Plover are rare fall migrants. Greater Yellowlegs, Lesser Yellowlegs, Spotted Sandpiper, Least Sandpiper (uncommon spring; common fall), Baird's Sandpiper (rare spring; uncommon fall), Stilt Sandpiper (uncommon fall), Short-billed Dowitcher (casual fall), Long-billed Dowitcher (uncommon fall), and Common Snipe (fairly common summer; uncommon winter) are among the small waders feeding along the ponds shoreline: Red-necked Phalarope, Solitary Sandpiper, Semipalmated Sandpiper, Western Sandpiper, Pectoral Sandpiper are uncommon transients, both in spring and fall. Waterfowl are also well represented with Blue-winged Teal, Cinnamon Teal and Wilson's Phalarope breeding commonly along the vegetated shores.

O'Keefe's Pond to Wild Turkey Country

 (00.0km.) From the O'Keefe Historic Ranch proceed along Highway 97 towards Kamloops. Turn at the first road on the left which parallels the edge of the golf course. Although erratic from year-to-year, several Grasshopper Sparrows inhabit the brushy edges of the gravel section.

(0.00 km.)From O'Keefe's Pond, turn right onto paved St. Anne's Road running north. Gray Partridge frequent the roadside fields, especially in winter. Turn right after (1.1 km.) and begin to scan the fields and meadows along the road. The last remaining Wild Turkeys in the Okanagan occured at the farms (3.0 km.) up the St. Anne Rd.

Back onto Highway 97, after (13.3 km.), turn right onto paved Salmon River Road that leads to Enderby. This junction is (60.2 km.) before reaching the Trans-Canada Highway; (28.7 km.) from the second intersection in downtown Vernon.

Wild Turkey Country

Wild Turkey a rare introduced resident, and now virtually non-existant, occurred near Enderby, along Knob Hill Road near the community of Glenemma, and around Hullcar and Deep Creek. It would seem that there are no longer Wild Turkeys in the Okanagan. Creston is the only locality where these birds are "countable". The strikingly-plumaged Wild Turkey is a bird that much prefers to scurry away through the low clumps of brush rather than fly when approached. This wary species feeds on the ground on nuts, seeds, fruits, and insects at the forest edges.

NOTES & OBSERVATIONS

NOTES & OBSERVATIONS

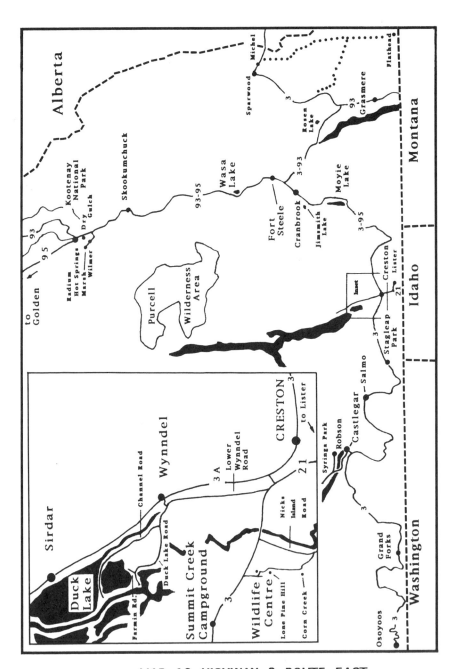

MAP 10 HIGHWAY 3 ROUTE EAST

LOOP 7 HIGHWAY 3 ROUTE - EAST

Osoyoos to Grand Forks

 (00.0km.) Proceed east on Highway 3 from Osoyoos, climbing up the steep and winding road towards the summit of Anarchist Mountain.

NOTE: Birding sites along this stretch of road to the summit are to be found under Mount Baldy to Anarchist Mountain and Osoyoos. After driving (127.5 km.) you will reach Grand Forks. Grand Forks is (377.5 km.) from Hope.

GRAND FORKS

 (00.0km.) From the downtown core of Grand Forks, return west along Highway 3 for (1.9 km.), turning right just past the railway tracks onto 4th Street West (checking for White-breasted Nuthatch in the pines around the railway station). Turn right at the stop sign (1.2 km.) (3.1 km.), continuing north for an additional (0.7 km.) (3.8 km.), then turning left diagonally onto a narrow gravel road. The gravel road leads down along a hillside to Ward Lake with a reed-fringed marsh that supports breeding Pied-billed Grebe, a variety of waterfowl including the perky Ruddy Duck, the odd Black Tern, and the secretive Sora. The brilliantly attired Yellow-headed Blackbird rush about the reeds, rival males constantly chasing each other as they defend their territories.

The gravel road eventually leads back up onto the paved road. Continue north along this road for an additional (6-8 km.) birding the riverine riparian woods which harbour - amongst the myriad avian possibilities - Black-capped Chickadee, Veery, Cedar Waxwing, Northern Waterthrush, American Redstart, and Song Sparrow. Bear right over the bridge (1 5.3 km.), and right again after crossing the Granby River, returning south to Grand Forks along the east side of the valley. Lazuli Bunting occur on the and brushy slopes amongst the dry hills to the east of the road (8.0 km.) (23.0 km.), south of the rdge. After an additional (8.5 km.) (31.5 km.) you will reach Highway 3.

Grand Forks to Syringa Creek Park

(00.0km.) Proceed along Highway 3 East. Turn left (north) at the exit for Castlegar (95 km.). Continue through Castlegar on the only paved road heading north and west towards the Hugh Keenleyside Dam (10 km.) (105 km.). The dam impounds the multi-fingered resevoir known as the Arrow Lakes. After passing over the dam, turn left to the end of pavement at Syringa Creek Park (8.5 km.) (113.5 km.).

SYRINGA CREEK PROVINCIAL PARK

The rocky cliff-faces along the road past the dam to Syringa Creek Provincial Park harbour three specialities of this habitat: White-throated Swift, Canyon Wren, and Rock Wren. The bluffs along this road offer closer studies of these birds than the famous colony at Vaseux Lake. Lewis' Woodpecker are a common sight, flying corvid-like across the cerulean skies, while Nashville Warbler sing inconspicuously from the second-growth woodlands on the dry hillsides. At the edge of the road the forest gives way to sunlit, flower-laden slopes which are frequently alive with Rufous Hummingbird; Black-chinned Hummingbird and Calliope Hummingbird are possible. The park's areas of scrub and dry forest provide an interesting diversion. Amidst magnificent scenery you will also find Black Swift, Vaux's Swift, Red-naped Sapsucker, Dusky Flycatcher, the Pacific-slope Flycatcher, American Crow, Black-billed Magpie, Gray Catbird, Townsend's Warbler, and MacGillivray's Warbler.

Syringa Creek Park to Salmo

(00.0km.) Retrace your route through Castlegar and back to Highway 3 East. At the junction with Highway 3B (25.5 km.), turn sharply left for the continuation of Highway 3. After an additional (27.5 km.) (53 km.) you will arrive at Salmo; (525.5 km.) from Hope, (275.5 km.) from Osooyos.

SALMO

(00.0km.) Proceed from Salmo along Highway 3 East toward the Creston Valley Wildlife Interpretation Centre at (74.5 km.).

Salmo to Creston

(00.0km.) Proceed on Highway 3 East. At (37.0 km.) you will reach Stagleap Provincial Park at the summit of Kootenay Pass (312.5 km. from Osoyoos). There are short hiking trails that lead to alpine meadows which are cross-country ski trails in winter.

At an elevation of 1,775 m, the sub-alpine forest will produce such typical boreal species as Gray Jay, Mountain Chickadee, Boreal Chickadee, Fox Sparrow, and Pine Grosbeak. The "hit" species here is the delightful little Boreal Owl. The best time to look for this bird is in mid-winter. Pull over at the summit sign, playing a tape about one hour after dark, or one hour before dawn. If you do not get a response, try a few more sites along the highway. With perseverance, a short series of rapid, hollow "hoo's" from the dark recesses of the night forest often break the extremely cold, winter silence.

At (73.3 km.), the Summit Creek Campground and Recreational Area is on the left. At (74.5 km.) you will arrive at the paved entrance road to the Creston Wildlife Interpretation Centre; (384.5 km.) from Osoyoos. Turn right onto Evans Road (south), then left onto West Creston Road (following the park signs) for (0.5 km.) to the centre.

At (83.6 km.) (393.6 km. from Osoyoos; an eight hour drive) you will arrive in downtown Creston.

CRESTON VALLEY

The Kootenay Flats constitute one of the most important migratory staging areas for waterfowl in the interior of British Columbia. Although an extensive system of dikes has allowed agriculture to develop on the Kootenay River floodplain, natural wetlands are still abundant despite these man-made changes. The Creston Valley Wildlife Management Area (6,480 hectares) has preserved much of this natural resource, with Duck Lake one of the better birding sites in the region.

Situated immediately west of Creston, the productive wetlands are surrounded by rolling dry hills, riparian woodlands and fields, and all accessed by all-weather roads, providing the opportunities to see many of the 238 species recorded in the region. The best season to visit is mid-April to late June. The Creston-Lister region is the only centre for Wild Turkey in the province. Introduced to neighbouring Idaho, they spread northward in recent years, where they were first recorded in the Pend-d'-Oreille River Valley. The stocked turkeys have become locally established, are within the ten year limit of the A.B.A. rules and therefore "countable".

Situated on the Pacific flyway, waterfowl are abundant, especially during the early spring from late February to early April. The Creston Valley has been called the "Valley of the Swans", for the huge migrant population of Tundra Swan which are seen during spring and fall. They, and other waterfowl, occur on the open waters at the centre, in marshes off the Creston-Summit Creek Road, in Leach and Duck Lakes, and at the south end of Kootenay Lake. The dark vegetation and circulating underwater springs speeding the melting of ice at these sites guarantees an early arrival and late departure.

SUMMIT CREEK CAMPGROUND

(00.0km.) The Summit Creek Woods Trail passes through lowland hardwood woods of birch and cottonwoods and past a wetland. American Kestrel, Ruffed Grouse, Downy Woodpecker, Pileated Woodpecker, Hammond's Flycatcher, Steller's Jay, Black-capped Chickadee, Winter Wren, Swainson's Thrush, American Robin, Cedar Waxwing, Red-eyed Vireo, and Warbling Vireo are expected. The Midgeley Mountain and Dewdney Trail climbs through a mixed dry Douglas-fir and ponderosa pine forest for over six kilometers. At its higher elevations, Calliope Hummingbird, Three-toed Woodpecker, Olive-sided Flycatcher, and Mountain Bluebird wait to be discovered.

Northern Flicker cling to exposed snags while various wood warblers complete a kaleidoscope of colour. Check for an Osprey nest near the suspension bridge across Summit Creek at the picnic area. Along the creek, Belted Kingfisher are often found fishing and Spotted Sandpiper and American Dipper are seen bobbing on rock tops.

CRESTON VALLEY WILDLIFE INTERPRETATION CENTRE

A journey through the Creston Valley is a fascinating experience, taking you through a whole spectrum of habitats. Drive (1.1km.) east along Highway 3, turning right onto paved Evans Road, then left onto West Creston Road following the park signs for (0.5 km.) (1.6km.) to the centre. A visit to the Creston Valley Wildlife Interpretation Centre is recommended, located (9.1 km.) west of Creston, telephone (250) 428-9383 or write P.O. Box 1849, Creston, B.C. VOB 1GO. They have free copies of a " Checklist of Birds, Creston Valley Wildlife Interpretation Centre", which includes Duck Lake. The centre is open all year: from May 1 to October 31 it is open every day from 9:00 a.m. to 5:00 p.m., and from November 1 to April 30 it is open the same hours, but only open on weekdays.

Boardwalks and levee trails take you through the extensive marshes where you should see such breeding species as Pied-billed Grebe, Red-necked Grebe, Great Blue Heron, Mallard, Blue-winged Teal, Cinnamon Teal, Wood Duck, Ring-necked Duck, Hooded Merganser, American Bittem, Sora, American Coot, Killdeer, Common Snipe, Black Tern, Belted Kingfisher, Eastern Kingbird, Western Wood-Pewee, Tree Swallow, Yellow Warbler, Common Yellowthroat, Black-headed Grosbeak, and Brewer's Blackbird. Osprey, Red-winged Blackbird, and Yellow-headed Blackbird nests can be viewed from the visitor centre where telescopes are trained on items of interest. Under the eves of the centre are hundreds of nesting Cliff Swallow and Barn Swallow. The downslurred, cat-like mew's of the Gray Catbird drift from the dry slopes opposite the parking lot. Ask the helpful naturalists for up-to-date directions for Wild Turkey.

Return to paved West Creston Road, turning left, and proceed south to the Lone Pine Hill dike trail (1.6 km.) (3.2 km.). A footbridge spans a slough on the east side of the road leading to a dry slope on which Long-eared Owl, Great Horned Owl, Barred Owl, Common Nighthawk, Black-chinned Hummingbird, Calliope Hummingbird, Rufous Hummingbird, Red-naped Sapsucker, Pileated Woodpecker, Steller's Jay, Cassin's Vireo, Nashville Warbler, Lazuli Bunting, Spotted Towhee, and Western Tanager occur in season. An Osprey nests along the trail while Red-tailed Hawk often soar high over this area of outstanding beauty.

Proceed south along West Creston Road for an additional (0.5 km.) (3.7 km.) to the Corn Creek Dike trailhead on your left. Walk the dike to a gate at the bottom of a short hill; birders are welcomed. A similar list of species will be found to those at Lone Pine Hill and at the Interpretation Centre. After an additional (1.3 km.) (5.0 Km.), Corn Creek Woods Trail leads to a forest of Western red cedar, Western hemlock and grand fir. A similar list of species will be found here as at Lone Pine Hill.

Proceed south along West Creston Road for an additional (1.0 km.) (6.0 km.), crossing the Corn Creek bridge. A Bank Swallow colony will be found at the gravel pit beside the creek. Yellow Warbler, Nashville Warbler and MacGillivray's Warbler breed in the neighbouring woods, while Spotted Sandpiper nod and teeter constantly along the creek.

Continue south on West Creston Road, cross the yellow wooden bridge over French's Slough and on to the junction with Nick's Island South Road branching off to the left (2.5 km.) (8.5 km.). Turn left driving north along Nick's Island South Road, crossing a red wooden bridge, and passing through several fields containing large cottonwoods. Common Pheasant, Bobolink, Savannah Sparrow, and Western Meadowlark nest in these fields, while American Kestrel, Mourning Dove, Downy Woodpecker, Northern Flicker, and a variety of swallows are seen along the roadside. American Goldfinch are attracted to the seeding thistleheads in the weedy fields.

After (4.1 km.) (I 2.6 km.), turn right onto Highway 3 at the Esso station towards Creston. American Kestrel, Mourning Dove, Bank Swallow, Cliff Swallow, Western Bluebird, and Brewer's Blackbird often perch on the overhead vores, the swallows beside the bridge over the Kootenay River. Turkey Vulture often float overhead on dihedral wings, circling high in the air with just the odd tilting movement of their wings. After (3.5 km.) (16.1 km.), turn left onto Lower Wynndel Road. Creston is (2.0 km.) east of this junction along Highway 3.

Creston to Duck Lake

(00.0km.) We will proceed east along Highway 3, taking a short connecting road which crosses the railway tracks, then turn left onto Highway 3A (0.2 km.). After (1.8 km.) (2.0 km.) there is a viewing tower on the right. Just north of Wynndel (4.4 km.) (6.4 km.) turn left at the Duck Lake sign onto paved Lower Wynndel Road, following it over the railway tracks to gravel Duck Lake Road (0.8 km.) (7.2 km.). Wild Turkey are usually found in the fields along Highway 3A between Creston and Wynndel, feeding in the livestock feedlots, especially during the harsh winter months. In winter, check any bird feeding stations, orchards, and back yards with trees and shrubs bearing fruit and seeds in any of the valley towns for Bohemian Waxwing, sparrows, finches, and Evening Grosbeak. Another area to search for Wild Turkey if you are unsuccessful are the farm roads surrounding the town of Lister (4.0 km.) south of Creston and an additional (3.5 km.) east of Highway 21.

DUCK LAKE

After crossing Duck Lake and Old Goat River Channels, Duck Lake Road road reaches a "Y" junction (0.8 km.) (8.0 km.). Turn right onto Channel Road that leads to a viewing tower (5.5 km.) (13.5 km.). Cottonwoods line Channel Road where a healthy population of Red-eyed Vireo nest; Willow Flycatcher, Veery, Swainson's Thrush, Warbling Vireo, and Yellow Warbler are expected.

Situated south of Kootenay Lake, Duck Lake is a shallow lake about five kilometers in length and three kilometers in width. The tower provides an excellent viewing platform to scan the adjacent marshes. Duck Lake is the only lake in British Columbia to claim the nesting of six species of grebe. Western Grebe have a colony of 100 pairs, with a mixed pair of Clark's Grebe x Western Grebe raising a chick in 1983. The Clark's Grebe are casual, not appearing every year, and always rare. (The best advantage point to scan the Western Grebe colony is from the town of Sirdar, an additional (8.5 km.) further north on Highway 3A. From the Sirdar Public Park along Highway 3A, walk south along the railway tracks until you see the colony through open patches in the woods). Red-necked Grebe and Pied-billed Grebe are common and Horned Grebe and Eared Grebe are rare breeders. The lake provides rich habitat for a multitude of migrant waterfowl with Canada Goose, Mallard, Gadwall, Green-winged Teal, American Wigeon, Blue-winged Teal, Cinnamon Teal, Ruddy Duck, Wood Duck, Common Goldeneye, Bufflehead, and Common Merganser remaining to breed.

The main attraction at Duck Lake is the only known colony of Forster's Tern in the province. The best place to find them is in the cattail marshes on the south side of the lake where they arrive to nest in mid-April; listen for their characteristic grating, low-pitched "tzaap" calls. Black Tern also nest commonly around the lake, while Common Tern are present as migrants in August. Use the tower on site for excellent viewing: Virginia Rail, Sora, American Coot, Wilson's Phalarope, Common Snipe, Ring-billed Gull, Marsh Wren, Common Yellowthroat, Yellow-headed Blackbird, and Red-winged Blackbird nest commonly in the available reeds. Great Blue Heron and Cinnamon Teal are also abundant.

Although Duck Lake is unproductive for shorebirds (the water levels are usually too high to provide feeding) a few interesting species occur. American Avocet are rare spring migrants, and the first breeding record of Avocet for the province occured here. The hansome Black-necked Stilt is also a rare spring migrant. When migrant shorebirds are present on the exposed mud, "peep" Semipalmated Sandpiper, Western Sandpiper, and Least Sandpiper, are most common with a few Baird's Sandpiper.

Proceed along diked Channel Road below the south end of the lake to a "T" junction at the Kootenay River dike road (3.4 km.) (16.9 km.). A stop at the "T" junction with the Kootenay River (a walk is possible along the overgrown dike road leading north and south) will produce Osprey, American Kestrel, Eastern Kingbird, Swainson's Thrush, Gray Catbird, Yellow Warbler, and a number of other riparian species characteristic of the region.

The riparian woods to the north and west of the lake ring with songs. A short walk through the woodlands should produce Great Horned Owl, Black-chinned Hummingbird, Calliope Hummingbird, Rufous Hummingbird, Black-capped Chickadee, Western Wood-Pewee, Townsend's Solitaire, Swainson's Thrush, Gray Catbird, Cedar Waxwing, Red-eyed Vireo, Warbling Vireo, Yellow-rumped Warbler, Yellow Warbler, MacGillivray's Warbler, Black-headed Grosbeak, Spotted Towhee, Song Sparrow, Lincoln's Sparrow, and Bullock's Oriole. Yellow-breasted Chat have been reported in small numbers from the north end of the lake in recent years. The surrounding fields have Northern Harrier, Short-eared Owl, Savannah Sparrow and an occasional Lark Sparrow.

The dike road leading south may be passable by car, although it may be best to retrace your route back to the "Y" intersection of Channel and Duck Lake Roads. (00.0 km.) Turn right onto Duck Lake Road, then right onto Farming Road (5.1 km.). Along the drive check the fields for Ring-billed Gull, Mourning Dove, Tree Swallow, Violet-green Swallow, Bank Swallow, Northern Rough-winged Swallow, Cliff Swallow, Barn Swallow, Savannah Sparrow, Western Meadowlark, Brewer's Blackbird, and American Goldfinch. In June and July, Bobolink frequent the weedy meadows along Farmin Road.

Raptors are the crowning feature of this wonderful reserve, the sky is seldom empty of a soaring shape. Osprey are regular, fishing on the lake's plentiful bass, while Turkey Vulture, Northern Harrier, Red-tailed Hawk, Rough-legged Hawk (winter), and American Kestrel hunt the fields and marshes. Snowy Owl and Northern Hawk-Owl are found occasionally in these same fields during the winter months. Bald Eagle and Short-eared Owl are resident, nesting locally, and Northern Pygmy-Owl are often seen during the winter.

Creston to Moyie Lake Provincial Park

Retrace your route back to Highway 3A in Wynndel (00.0 km.) driving south to Creston. At Creston (8.7 km.), continue along Highway 3 East. We begin at (00.0 km.) in the centre of Creston. After (79.0 km.), Moyie Lake Provincial Park is found on the left, twenty-three kilometers south of Cranbrook. Follow the signs and one kilometer of paved road to the park.

MOYIE LAKE PROVINCIAL PARK

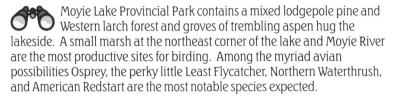 Moyie Lake Provincial Park contains a mixed lodgepole pine and Western larch forest and groves of trembling aspen hug the lakeside. A small marsh at the northeast corner of the lake and Moyie River are the most productive sites for birding. Among the myriad avian possibilities Osprey, the perky little Least Flycatcher, Northern Waterthrush, and American Redstart are the most notable species expected.

Moyie Lake Provincial Park to Cranbrook

(00.0km.) From Moyie Provincial Park proceed east on Highway 3-95 towards Cranbrook. At (13.4 km.) there is a large marsh on the east side of Highway 3-95. At (15.0 km.) you will arrive in downtown Cranbrook (94 kilometers from Creston).

CRANBROOK

The marsh south of Cranbrook along Highway 3-95 has a variety of breeding waterfowl, Black Terns, and Yellow-headed Blackbird. Turn left (west) from Highway 3-95 on the southern outskirts of Cranbrook onto paved Cross Road, signed for 12-hectare Jimsmith Lake Provincial Park, four kilometers away.

The devilishly elusive American Bittern lurk amongst the waterside vegetation, while graceful Black Tern skim the lake's surface. Widespread marsh species are well represented. The woods surrounding the lake are a magnet for birds and worth investigation. Elizabeth Lake Bird Sanctuary, an extensive marsh that attracts large numbers of waterfowl, is situated directly across from the intersection of Highway 3-95 and Cross Road. Various grebes, Canada Geese, Blue-winged Teal, Cinnamon Teal, Ruddy Duck, Redhead, Ring-necked Duck, Lesser Scaup, Common Goldeneye, Bufflehead, American Coot, Black Tern, and the more common, widespread marsh passerines are found throughout the summer months. As you drive east out of Cranbrook look for the sewage lagoons at the north end of town, they are especially good for gulls and shorebirds.

Cranbrook to points north, and points east and south

From Cranbrook you can continue north on Highway 93/95 to Fort Steele, Wasa Provincial Park, Kootenay National Park, and Wilmer Wildlife Area, hence onto the Trans-Canada Loop. We will first continue along Highway 3 East to Rosen Lake, Grassmere, and the Flathead, returning after birding these sites.

Cranbrook to Rosen Lake

 (00.0km.) From downtown Cranbrook, proceed east on Highway 3 towards Elko and Fernie. At (11.5 km.) you will pass the junction of Highways 3 and 93/95 leading to Fort Steele, Wasa, and points north. At (47.0 km.) (1.6 km. past Jaffray), turn left at the park sign onto the paved road leading (3.2 km.) (50.2 km.) north to the lake.

ROSEN LAKE

 Nestled in the Rocky Mountain Trench, Rosen Lake is an excellent site to watch for migrants, especially warblers that occur in abundance. Nowhere else in the Kootenays can the pulse and excitement of spring and autumn migrations be felt as keenly as birds funnel through on their way north to breeding grounds or south to the tropics. Around the campground at this popular recreation site are Common Loon, American Bittern, Osprey, Lewis' Woodpecker, and American Redstart. Eastern Kingbird and Western Kingbird sally forth from dead limbs after the brilliantly-coloured butterflies that occur here.

Rosen Lake to Grasmere

 Return to Highway 3 turning left towards Elko and Fernie (00.0 km.).At (1 7.0 km.), turn right onto Highway 93 South. After driving (26.0km.) (43 km.) you will arrive in Grasmere. Grasmere is (93 km.) from Cranbrook and eleven kilometers north of Roosville on the Montana/B.C. border.

GRASMERE

The arid floor of the Rocky Mountain Trench in this region of the East Kootenay's contain grasslands peppered with poderosa pine and Douglas-fir forests. A rich avifaunal community occupies the diverse habitats found in this general area. In particular, the grasslands southwest, west, and northwest of Grasmere (accessible on gravel roads), harbour Vesper Sparrow, Brewer's Sparrow, and Western Meadowlark. Along the drive watch the roadsides for Black-billed Magpie, American Crow, Chipping Sparrow, and Brewer's Blackbird. The shrubs on and sunlit slopes are summer home to Lazuli Bunting.

Grasmere to the Flathead

(00.0km.) From Grasmere, retrace your route back to Highway 3 turning east towards Elko (26 km.). At Morrissey Provincial Park (17.5 km.) (43.5 km.), proceed east on Highway 3 for an additional (1.0 km.) (44.5 km.), turning right onto the first gravel road to the east. NOTE: the following kilometers are approximated. After crossing the Elk River, turn right (south) at the "T" junction (1.0 km.) (45.5 km.). Proceed south on the well-maintained logging road, turning left after crossing Bean Creek (11.2 km.) (56.7 km.). The logging road from here follows Lodgepole Creek, climbs over a ridge, and then follows Harvey Creek downhill to a "Y" fork, an additional (32 km.) (88.7 km.). At the "Y" fork, turn right on a well-maintained logging road following the Flathead River south towards the Montana/British Columbia border (25 km.) (113.7 km.). From the "Y" junction there are several Forest Service Recreational Sites along the "Flathead Road".

The best route, albeit much longer, is to continue along Highway 3 to Sparwood and beyond to the old hotel at Michel (52.5 km. past Morrissey Provincial Park). Proceed (6.0 km.) (58.5 km.), turning right off Highway 3 (south) onto the Flathead Road - 90 kilometers to the Montana border.

FLATHEAD

The Flathead is a semi-remote high valley in the extreme southeastern portion of the province that is only accessible by logging road. There are no amenities except for bars at McGillivray, Corbin, and the two Flatheads. Except for these, the valley is uninhabited; be sure to bring your own supplies and have a full tank of gas before venturing off of Highway 3. There is actually a customs building at the British Columbia/Montana border crossing, open 9:00 a.m. to 5:00 p.m.; May to September only.

The Flathead is an astonishing area with a rich mixture of ecosystems, home to a wide variety of Rocky Mountain birds. The road passes through the valley at an average of 1,200 m above sea level with side roads above 1,600 m. The forests in the valley consist of two types: stands of second-growth lodgepole pine and older stands of western larch. There are also riparian areas of willows, aspen, and cottonwood. Several clearcuts along the valley add variety to the avifauna. Spruce Grouse are extremely common, a series of deep hoots, lower pitched than those of the Blue Grouse, will announce the males' presence. The shy and retiring Red-naped Sapsucker are also very common in the stands of aspen lining the numerous clear streams.

The following is a list of the more interesting birds to be expected:

Golden Eagle	Dusky Flycatcher
Ruffed Grouse	Hammond's Flycatcher
Common Nighthawk	Willow Flycatcher
Calliope Hummingbird	Cordilleran Flycatcher
Olive-sided Flycatcher	Steller's Jay
Gray Jay	Clark's Nutcracker
Black-capped Chickadee	Mountain Chickadee
Boreal Chickadee	Red-breasted Nuthatch

Golden-crowned Kinglet	Ruby-crowned Kinglet
Mountain Bluebird	Townsend's Solitaire
Swainson's Thrush	Hermit Thrush
Varied Thrush	American Dipper
Cedar Waxwing	Cassin's Vireo
Warbling Vireo	Orange-crowned Warbler
Flathead to Fort Steele	Yellow-rumped Warbler
Townsend's Warbler	Yellow Warbler
MacGillivray's Warbler	Wilson's Warbler
Northern Waterthrush	Common Yellowthroat
American Redstart	Lazuli Bunting
Chipping Sparrow	Fox Sparrow
Lincoln's Sparrow	Brown-headed Cowbird (U)
Western Tanager	Oine Siskin
Red Crossbill	Cassin's Finch
Evening Grosbeak	

 Retrace your route back to Highway 3, turning left (west) towards Cranbrook (00.0 km.). After driving (74 km.), turn right onto Highway 93/95 North (00.0 km.). After (6.5 km.) you will arrive in downtown Fort Steele.

FORT STEELE

The general store on Highway 93/95 in tiny downtown Fort Steele has produced an amazing array of extra-limital hummingbirds for the province at its hummingbird feeders. From June 27 through July 2, 1992 a pair of Broad-tailed Hummingbird occupied the feeder, firsts for Canada; later that month a Costa's Hummingbird appeared! You are sure to be dazzled by a profusion of those vociferous and gaudy Rufous Hummingbirds zipping in and out as they consume the sugar solution as an alternative to their natural nectar diets.

Fort Steele to Wasa Provincial Park

(00.0km.) Proceed north on Highway 93/95. At (17.0 km), Wasa Slough Provincial Bird Sanctuary is on the right. This wetland is excellent for waterfowl and the characteristic widespread species of interior marshes. At (19.0 km.), turn right onto a paved road leading (1.0 km.) along the south end of Wasa Lake to Wasa Provincial Park (20 km.).

WASA PROVINCIAL PARK

Wasa Provincial Park, lying in the Rocky Mountain Trench, is nestled among grasslands and a mixed forest of ponderosa pine and Douglas-fir.

Wasa may be the best site to observe the common breeding birds of the southeastern sector of the province as well as an important place to view migrations.

Among the one hundred species of birds recorded from the park are Franklin's Gull, Calliope Hummingbird, Least Flycatcher, Mountain Chickadee, White-breasted Nuthatch, Pygmy Nuthatch, Mountain Bluebird, Townsend's Solitaire, Bobolink, and Red Crossbill. Brilliant Western Tanagers will grab your attention, but you will come to appreciate the more somberly clad species: Brown Creeper as they peruse the rough bark of the firs, the difficult empidonax flycatchers as they dart for insects from exposed branches, and the confiding Clark's Nutcracker, which often raids the picnic grounds.

Wasa Provincial Park to Wilmer National Wildlife Area

(00.0km.) Return to Highway 93/95 North. Watch for Long-billed Curlew among the yellow grasses in the wind-blown fields between Wasa and Skookumchuck; a distance of fifteen kilometers. At (100 km.), turn left at the junction for Invermere (8.0 km. south of Radium Hot Springs). Follow the paved road to Athalmer (2.5 km.) (102.5 km.) and beyond, turning left (1.5 km.) (104.0 km.) on the paved road leading north to Wilmer (2.0 km.) (106.0 km.). At Wilmer, proceed north out of town on gravel West Side Road, keeping left at the National Wildlife sign. After (2.3 km.) (1 08.3 km.) you will arrive at the marsh. Walk the hillcrest east to the lookout.

WILMER NATIONAL WILDLIFE AREA

Wilmer National Wildlife Area, lying in the Rocky Mountain Trench on the west side of the Columbia River, is composed of bottom land marshes and ponds that are fed by both Tobby and Horsethief Creeks. Flood-tolerant sedges, willows, and cottonwoods fill the "inundation zone" of the basin, while drought-tolerant shrubs and Douglas-fir cover the and regions above.

From the lookout, nesting Red-necked Grebe, Great Blue Heron, Wood Duck, Osprey, and Bald Eagle will be noted in spring and summer. In March, migrant waterfowl begin to arrive; this being the best month to observe Tundra Swan. In the surrounding pine and fir forested uplands expect to find Blue Grouse, Northern Pygmy-Owl, Common Nighthawk, Lewis' Woodpecker, Western Kingbird, Black-billed Magpie, American Crow, White-breasted Nuthatch, and Cassin's Finch.

Wilmer Wildlife Area to Dry Gulch Provincial Park

 Retrace your route back to Highway 93/95 North (00.0 km.). At (8.5 km.) turn left at the park sign along the gravel road (1.0 km.) (9.5 km.) to the park.

DRY GULCH PROVINCIAL PARK

The arid interior Douglas-fir forest in Dry Gulch Provincial Park is the best site in the Kootenay's to observe the characteristic avifauna of this habitat. The common species include Blue Grouse, Common Nighthawk, Northern Flicker, Red-breasted Nuthatch, American Robin, Townsend's Solitaire, Cassin's Vireo, Yellow-rumped Warbler, Dark-eyed Junco, and Chipping Sparrow. Open patches of grassland harbour Vesper Sparrow.

Dry Gulch Provincial Park to Kootenay National Park

Return to Highway 93/95, turning left towards Radium Hot Springs (00.0 km.). At Radium Hot Springs (4.0 km.), Highways 93 and 95 split. If you wish to join the Trans-Canada at Golden, proceed north on Highway 95 along the Rocky Mountain Trench for (104 km.). Radium Hot Springs is (131.5 km. from the junctions of Highways 3 and 93/95). Continue east on Highway 93 from downtown Radium Hot Springs (00.0 km.).

KOOTENAY NATIONAL PARK

Kootenay National Park (1406 km.), located on the west slope of the continental divide, is a romantic place with its own special atmosphere and charm. Frequently clouds are draped across the flanks of the mountains, lending a rather mysterious air to the forests. The alpine specialities combine with the rich montane avifauna to create some of the most exciting birding in all of the province.

After (1.5 km.) ask for maps and a bird checklist at the information centre at the Kootenay National Park West Gate. On entering the park, all visitors in vehicles must stop at the booth and buy a permit either for the day or for the season.

After driving (7.0 km.) (9.0 km.), watch for the Sinclair Creek Trailhead. The trail leads to alpine meadows where the characteristic species found above timberline, White-tailed and Gray-crowned Rosy Finch, are found. After another (1.0 km.) you will reach the Sinclair Pass Summit at 1,486 m, a convenient site to search for high-level avifauna such as Three-toed Woodpecker, Black-backed Woodpecker, Hairy Woodpecker, Gray Jay, Boreal Chickadee, Hermit Thrush, Varied Thrush, and Pine Grosbeak. At (33.0 km.) (43.0 km.) you will see the George Simpson Monument and at (1.0 km.) (44.0 km.) the Simpson River Trail, easy access to Simpson and Assinaboine slides.

Avalanche slopes along the west side of the Vermillion River Valley, such as the Simpson and Assinaboine, proade brushy deciduous habitat for Warbling Vireo, MacGillivray's Warbler, Wilson's Warbler, Song Sparrow, Chipping Sparrow, White-crowned Sparrow, and Lincoln's Sparrow. Olive-sided Flycatcher, Ruby-crowned Kinglet, Hermit Thrush, Varied Thrush, Yellow-rumped Warbler, Western Tanager, Dark-eyed Junco, and Fox Sparrow frequent the cooler woods adjacent to the slides. As dusk falls, the sounds of the forest increase in fervour as several species of oW begin their nocturnal excursions and Common Nighthawk hawk for insects overhead.

NOTES & OBSERVATIONS

NOTES & OBSERVATIONS

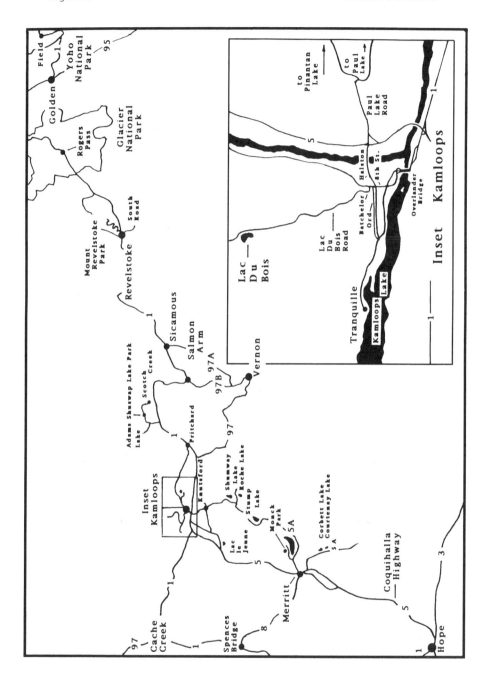

MAP 11   LOOP 8   TRANS-CANADA HIGHWAY ROUTE

LOOP 8 TRANS-CANADA ROUTE

Hope to Cache Creek

(00.0km.) For those proceeding straight through on the Trans-Canada to Cache Creek, a brief stop at Spences Bridge (147.5 km. from Hope) will produce Chukar. Explore the slopes above the south side of the Thompson River between the town of Spences Bridge and the mouth of the Nicola River. Cache Creek is reached after driving (336 km.).

Hope to Merritt

From the junctions of Highways 1 and 3 in downtown Hope, proceed east along Highway 3 for (6.5 km.), turning right at the Coquihalla (Highway 5) interchange. (00.0 km.) At (42 km.) you will reach the summit of Coquihalla Pass. After driving north on the Coquihalla Highway for an additional (12 km.) (54 km.) you will come to the toll-booth where there are washrooms.

MERRITT

In the dry hills of Nicola River's benches surrounding Merritt, Sharp-tailed Grouse perform their wild dance on traditional leks during March and April. The grouse are active at dawn, once the snow has melted from the booming grounds.

At the Kingsvale interchange, an additional (22 km.) (76 km.), the Coldwater Road leads to Brookmere and Gillis Lake, then on to the Kane Valley Road, a maintained gravel road to Merritt through rural countryside and the Coldwater Indian Reserve. A Sharp-tailed Grouse lek is found (5.8 km.) along this road, and another booming ground is found on small hill (0.8 km.) along this same road southeast from Merritt - just northeast of the Coldwater Indian Reserve. For up-to-date information on lek directions contact the Provincial Fish and Wildlife Branch office in Kamloops at tel. 250-374-9717.

Proceed north along the Coquihalla for (38 km.) (114 km.) where you will meet with the intersection for Highways 8 West leading into Merritt, and 5A South. For Highway 5A North you can turn into Merritt and then continue from downtown Merritt on 5A North, or continue along the Coquihalla for (3.5 km.) (117.5 km.), turning off at the interchange towards Nicola, Quilchena, and Kamloops.

From Merritt we can take three separate trips.

A. South on Highway 5A to Corbett and Courtenay Lakes.

B. Continue north on the Coquihalla to Lac le Jeune Provincial Park.

C. Proceed along Highway 5A North towards Kamloops, the continuation of the Trans-Canada Highway Loop.

Merritt to Corbett and Courtenay Lakes

(00.0km.) If you proceed south on Highway 5A towards Princeton from the interchange on the Coquihalla near Merritt for (14 km.) you will arrive at Corbett Lake; or (15 km.) for Courtenay Lake. Both lakes are visible on the left side of the paved highway.

CORBETT AND COURTENAY LAKES

Corbett and Courtenay Lakes, lying in the southernmost extension of the Cariboo Parklands eco-region, are nestled among low hills covered by typical steppe or bunchgrass prairie. Trembling aspen line the watercourses, while on the dry benches are a scattering of ponderosa pines. Around the margins of both Corbett and Courtenay Lakes are extensive Scirpus marshes, dominated by bullrushes. The surrounding forests are mainly of aspens, hawthorns, willows, with a dense shubbery growth of wild rose; a magnificent array of spring and summer flowers turns the entire area into a vast wild garden. The region exhibits incredible ecological diversity offering a veritable treasure chest of exiting birds.

A walk around the lakes will reveal the more common aquatic breeding species: Common Loon, Pied-billed Grebe, Red-necked Grebe, Barrow's Goldeneye, Osprey, Yellow-headed Blackbird, and Red-winged Blackbird. Tree Swallow, Violet-green Swallow, and Barn Swallow hawk for insects across the lake's surface. A hike into the hills to the west will produce the characteristic species of the region: Red-tailed Hawk, Black-billed Magpie, American Crow, Mountain Chickadee, White-breasted Nuthatch, Red-breasted Nuthatch, Mountain Bluebird, and Red Crossbill. White-winged Crossbill are occasionally found during invasions, usually in early spring. The soft pastel hues of Cedar Waxwing are revealed as they race into a fruiting bush, often to pluck berries in flight.

Merritt to Lac le Jeune Park and Kamloops

(00.0km.) From the Coldwater Interchange near Merritt, proceed along the Coquihalla Highway towards Kamloops for (50.5 km.) (164.5 km. from Hope). Turn right onto the paved road leading east to Lac le Jeune, turning right onto a gravel road to the lake (4.5 km.) (55 km.). The lake is (1.5 km.) (56.5 km.) away. The paved portion of the road swings north and junctions with the Trans-Canada Highway (5.5 km.) from Kamloops. If you wish to retrace your route back to the Coquihalla and continue north to the Trans-Canada, it is a further (25.5 km.) to the junction

with the Trans-Canada and a further (1 0.5 km.) (36 km.) into downtown
Kamloops (or 200.5 km. from Hope).

LAC LE JEUNE PROVINCIAL PARK

 The mixed forests of ponderosa pine and Douglas-fir surrounding
the lake of Lac le Jeune Provincial Park harbour nesting
Flammulated Owl. Listen for their paired hollow hoots on warm summer
nights, especially in the hills south of the lake along the various four-wheel-
drive roads. Species characteristic to the dry interior valleys are to be found
here; the magnificent scenery enhances the birding.

Merritt to Monck Park

 (00.0km.) From the intersection of Highway 8 and 5A in downtown
Merrit, proceed northeast toward Kamloops along Highway 5A. After
driving (11.4 km.) the Monck Park road branches off to the left just
before reaching the west end of Nicola Lake, after passing through the tiny
hamlet of Nicola. The Monck Park road traverses through an overwhelming
diversity of habitats with ponderosa pine and Douglas-fir forests, sagebrush,
irrigated alfalfa fields, rocky escarpments, and lakeside marshes fringed with
willow thickets. The park's gate is reached at (9.8 km.) (21.2 km.). The road
winds down to the lakeshore, offering spectacular views across Nicola Lake,
and terminates at the picnic area and boat launch.

MONCK PARK

The Nicola Valley supports most of the characteristic avifauna of
the dry interior valleys, although lacking in some of the Okanagan
specialities such as Canyon Wren and Sage Thrasher. A days birding between
late May and early July should produce about 50 to 70 species.

We start at (00.0 km.) at the beginning of the Monck Park Road. At (2.1
km.), pull over to the shoulder of the road. The road overlooks alfalfa fields, a
marsh, and the shallow west end of Nicola Lake on the south side of the road.
Several pairs of Bobolink nest, and the males can be seen in display flights
over the fields in spring as they sing their loud, bubbling "bob-o-link" song.
Bobolink are also found at other localized sites: the north end of Nicola Lake,
near the Quilchena Hotel, and at other scattered locations in the valley. Scan
the lake and marsh, using a scope, looking for Common Loon, Canada Goose,
Mallard, Blue-winged Teal, Cinnamon Teal, American Wigeon, and Redhead.

The bordering marshes are often used for nesting by Pied-billed
Grebe, American Bittern, Sora, Common Snipe, Wilson's Phalarope,
Red-winged Blackbird, and Yellow-headed Blackbird. In April and again
during the months of October through winter (as long as the lake remains ice-

free), the westernmost end of Nicola Lake is a regular stopover for migrant Tundra Swan, Canvasback, Greater Scaup, Lesser Scaup, Common Goldeneye, Bufflehead, Common Merganser, Hooded Merganser, and hundreds of American Coot. An accidental Yellow-billed Loon has been recorded during the month of December.

Scattered pondorosa pines along the north rim of the road maintains a healthy breeding population of Yellow-rumped Warbler, Clipping Sparrow, and Cassin's Finch. Beyond, Golden Eagle patrol the periphery of the the the towering escarpment, a thrilling sight to watch them gliding to and fro along the cliffs. The eagles have nested and can be seen anywhere along the cliffs as you drive towards Monck Park. Rock Wren, scarce in the valley, occur at the base of these cliffs.

After driving an additional (1.1 km.) (3.2 km.), the road closely parallels the marsh and its bordering fringe of willows, water birch, and small cottonwoods. The deciduous shrubbery will produce Eastern Kingbird, Willow Flycatcher, Yellow Warbler, Common Yellowthroat, Bullock's Oriole and Song Sparrow. The road then passes through a series of alfalfa fields, their bordering trees are home to American Kestrels, Killdeer, Mourning Dove, Barn Swallow, American Crow, Brewer's Blackbird, and Savannah Sparrow.

At (3.0 km.) (6.2 km.), turn right onto the sideroad leading to the Harmon Estates cottage sub-division nestled along the lakeshore. Past here the road swings away from the lake through an area of open ponderosa pines. Each year, a pair of Osprey add material to their already bulky nest on the huge pine snag north of the road. The Osprey can be seen fishing anywhere around the lake, while in winter two or three Bald Eagle are often present at the north end of the lake. Other snags are used by nesting Northern Flicker, Mountain Chickadee, Pygmy Nuthatch, White-breasted Nuthatch, and House Wren. The road then climbs and crosses an extensive area of sagebrush, home to Western Meadowlark, Vesper Sparrow, and Mountain Bluebird. The sagebrush flats also serve as an advantage point to look further for raptors, including Golden Eagle.

A large marsh is reached after driving an additional (1.8 km.) (0.8 km.), harbouring the characteristic widespread species of interior wetlands.

After an additional (3.4 km.) (9.6 km.), turn left onto the gravel road which follows steep forested slopes above the lake. This road eventually splits, degenerating into two four-wheel-drive roads. (The entrance to Monck Park is (02 km.) (9.6 km.) past the gravel road turnoff). Townsend's Solitaire are easily viewed as they nest in the cutbanks along the road. The predominant Douglas-fir and ponderosa pine forest is interrupted by several small aspen groves with Dusky Flycatcher, Warbling Vireo, and Orange-crowned Warbler. After driving (7.0 km.) (16.6 km.), an extensive burn supports a few pairs of Lewis' Woodpecker, rare in the valley. Common Poorwill will be heard at dusk around rock outcrops and boulders.

(00.0km.) Retrace your route back to Monck Park Road, turning right (0.2 km.) to the park gates. Common birds in the park include Mountain Chickadee, White-breased Nuthatch, Pygmy Nuthatch, Red-breasted Nuthatch, Yellow-rumped Warbler, Western Tanager, and Cassin's Finch. Great Horned Owl are frequently heard at night, and the rare Flammulated Owl has been heard on occasion, calling from the hillside above the campground. Vaux's Swift will be seen entering their nesting colony inside a large hollow pine snag near the boat launch. Few waterbirds frequent the deep waters of Nicola Lake off Monck Park in summer, really confined to the occasional Common Loon, Red-necked Grebe, and Western Grebe. Winter is a quiet season in the Nicola Lake area.

Monck Park to Stump and Shumway Lakes

Birding can also be excellent along Highway 5A on the southern and eastern sides of Nicola Lake. Retrace your route back along Monck Park Road to Nicola, turning left (00.0 km.). At (2.6 km.) Highway 5A passes through an extensive reed-fringed marsh. Early in the morning, stop and listen for the exceedingly wary American Bittern, Virginia Rail, and Sora; you will find it difficult not to see the hansome Yellow-headed Blackbird or hear the loud, rolling "wichity witchity witchity wich" of the Common Yellowthroat. The delightful little Marsh Wren are seen clinging to the reed stems.

After one kilometer (3.6 km.), a small rest area by the lakeshore provides an excellent advantage point to scan the lake for migrant loons, grebes, geese, and ducks. Further along, several large colonies of Cliff Swallow nest on the steep cliffs above the road. The sparsely-wooded hillsides above the road are home to a few Pacific-slope Flycatcher, Nashville Warbler, and Lazuli Bunting; as well as many more common, widespread dry interior species.

After (3.8 km.) (7.4 km.), the topography changes sharply as the road begins to cross the wide, flat delta of Quilchena Creek. The cultivated fields along the highway near the historic Quilchena Hotel harbour American Kestrel, Bobolink, and Sanannah Sparrow. The fringe of cottonwoods along Nicola Lake have breeding Veery, Northern Waterthrush, and one or more pairs of Osprey.

After driving an additional (2.0 km.) (9.9 km.), turn right onto Minnie Lake Road, a well-maintained two-lane gravel road that passes through relatively undisturbed native grasslands. Directly opposite the intersection of Minnie Lake Road and Highway 5A is a large shallow slough, backed by a stand of tall willows between the slough and Nicola Lake. This site is reliable for Blue-winged Teal, Cinnamon Teal, Northern Shoveler, Northern Pintail, and Wilson's Phalarope. This slough produces shorebirds, and in May and August through September is the best site in the valley for

Greater Yellowlegs, Lesser Yellowlegs, Long-billed Dowitcher, Short-billed Dowitcher, Baird's Sandpiper, and Red-necked Phalarope. Along the first (20.0 km.) of Minnie Lake Road the careful observer can consistently find Swainson's Hawk, Sharp-tailed Grouse, Long-billed Curlew, Horned Lark, Mountain Bluebird, and a wide variety of aquatic birds on the lakes and ponds beside the road.

Retrace your route back to Highway 5A, driving (24.0 km.) (33.9km. from Nicola) north to Stump Lake, an additional (7.2 km.) (41.1km.) to Trapp Lake, then (6.7 km.) (47.8 km.) to Napier Lake, or an additional (6.6 km.) (54.4 km.) north to Shumway Lake.

SHUMWAY, TRAPP, NAPIER AND STUMP LAKES

Paralleling Highway 5A are a chain of lakes and several small ponds. Shumway, Trapp, Napier, and Stump Lakes are flanked by small groves of trembling aspen, while the surrounding dry grasslands are interspersed with ponderosa pines.

The valley containing these lakes rests in a position astride a major migration flyway into the high Arctic, a position which provides observers with an endlessly changing spectacle for several weeks each spring and fall.

 The skies overhead are often filled with a constant stream of migratory waterfowl, shorebirds, raptors, and gulls as they pour northward to claim their nesting territories. Large flocks of Sandhill Crane and a few Common Tern funnel through the valley each spring and fall, while an odd ethereal flock of American White Pelican can be seen swirling against the clouds. Long-billed Curlew are frequently seen on the dry grasslands during the breeding season, while Common Loon, and many species of ducks and grebes, Black Tern, and Yellow-headed Blackbird are summer residents in the marshy habitats, especially the southern ends of Shumway and Stump Lakes. Much of the marsh habitats are easily viewed using a scope from the shoulder of Highway 5A. Numerous raptors occur along the roadside in this area, perching on fence posts and lazily scanning for unsuspecting prey.

Trapp Lake to Roche Lake

From Trapp Lake (47.8 km.), proceed north along Highway 5A for (1.0 km.) (48.8 km.), turning right onto a gravel road (this road is between Trapp and Shumway Lakes). Proceed east to Roche Lake, keeping straight at intersections (7.5 km.) (56.3 km.).

ROCHE LAKE

 Roche Lake provides the best owling in the region with Great Horned Owl, Barred Owl, and Northern Saw-whet Owl. Great Gray

Owl, North America's largest owl, is uncommon and elusive. Fortunate birders will be able to watch one in daylight as it glides silently above the meadows.

Roche Lake to Shumway Lake

Proceed north along Highway 5A, to Shumway Lake (54.4 km. from Nicola or 1 6.5 km. south of the Trans-Canada highway.

Shumway Lake to Separation Lake

Proceed north along Highway 5A for (7.1 km.) (61.5 km.) [or just southwest of Kamloops, turn south from the Trans-Canada onto Highway 5A for (9.3 km.)] to Separation Lake; evident from the roadside (on the right side of the road - driving from the south).

SEPARATION LAKE

This rich, shallow lake is nestled in a grassland setting and is an excellent site for waterfowl and shorebirds in migration, as well, as a productive breeding lake for ducks. During summer, Red-necked Grebe, Eared Grebe, Barrow's Goldeneye, Swainson's Hawk, Short-eared Owl, Say's Phoebe, Mountain Bluebird, Vesper Sparrow, Savannah Sparrow, and Yellow-headed Blackbird will be found. Delicate Wilson's Phalarope bob and pirouette about the lake, resembling toy boats. A small pond (0.8 km.) south of the lake is excellent for migrant shorebirds.

Separation Lake to Knutsford

Continue north on Highway 5A for (3.6 km.) (65.1 km.), turning right onto the Rose Hill Road. Proceed north on Highway 5A for an additional (1.6 km.) (66.7 km.) (4.2 km. south of the Trans-Canada junction) to Knutsford. The two routes described under Knutsford lead back to Kamloops through privately-owned grasslands.

KNUTSFORD

(00.0km.) From Knutsford, turn left (west) onto gravel Long Lake Road. Proceed along Long Lake Road for (1.6 km.), turning right onto gravel Goose Lake Road which parallels the north bank of Peterson Creek in part.

 Sharp-tailed Grouse breed in the area, struting about in the short grass, but are found most easily during winter in the riverine woodland. Here, in summer, the banks of the river are a rich green tapestry of foliage broken only by a magnificent red or yellow where a shrub has burst into flower, around these Calliope Hummingbird and Rufous Hummingbird dart. Much of the country surrounding Knutsford provides endless rolling ,vistas of yellow grasslands waving in the wind.

In the grasslands are tawny-coloured Short-eared Owl. Western Kingbird sally forth from weathered fenceposts after some unseen insect, while overhead Swainsons Hawk hang in the wind. American Kestrel perch on the roadside wires, Western Meadowlark sing on all sides, while Vesper Sparrow and Savannah Sparrow cling to the mauve and yellow prairie flowers. Underneath the short grasses, Horned Lark peruse the bald prairie. The road begins to climb higher into cooler forests. Secretive Blue Grouse lurk quietly next to fallen logs, while Dusky Flycatcher, Orange-crowned Warbler, Yellow-rumped Warbler, and Townsend's Warbler sing from the shady recesses.

After driving along Goose Lake Road for (6.4 km.) (8.0 km.) you will reach Goose Lake. Long-eared Owl breed in the neighbouring woods, brilliantly coloured Yellow-headed Blackbird rush about, while Marsh Wren chatter from the reeds. Western Bluebird, rare in the area may be seen south of the lake.

After (6.5 km.) (14.5 km.), you will reach a paved road, where a right turn leads north to Kamloops through country offering additional birding possibilities. A left turn leads ten kilometers south to Lac le Jeune Provincial Park.

The second loop begins (1.6 km.) south of Knutsford. Turn left (east) off of Highway 5A onto Rose Hill Road and follow it sixteen kilometers to Kamloops. In spring and summer, Long-billed Curlew and many of the grassland species mentioned previously will be found. Along this road is an excellent site from which to observe raptor and Sandhill Crane migrations in late March and April, and again in late August through October. Lapland Longspur and Snow Bunting occur in migrations and a few remain to winter. The road climbs through coniferous forests where, especially in winter, Pine Siskin, Red Crossbill, White-winged Crossbill, Common Redpoll, Cassin's Finch, and Pine Grosbeak are possible. Check the radio towers on the slopes that lead down to Kamloops for Pygmy Nuthatch.

Knutsford to Kamloops

(00.0km.) From Knutsford, proceed north to the junction with Trans-Canada Highway (5.2 km.), turning right for Kamloops. Exit the Trans-Canada Highway East at Highway 5 North (1.0 km.) (6.2 km.), proceed to the Lansdowne Street exit. Kamloops is (79.5 km.) east of Cache Creek; (362.5 km.) from the Alberta/ B.C. border.

KAMLOOPS

As you enter Kamloops, the Trans-Canada passes through a bare, parched landscape of gently rolling hills - an arid landscape kept bearable by the presence of the mighty Thompson River. The Thompson's north and south branches merge and the water then flows westward. Just west of the city, a bulge in this famed watercourse forms long, narrow Kamloops Lake. Touted as Canada's Sunshine Capital, Kamloops is known for its sunny, dry climate. It is hot and dry in summer, cold, with plenty of snow in the winter.

From Kamloops you can take three loops:

A. Knutsford; Highway 5A returning on Highway 5 via Lac le Jeune (see proceeding pages).

B. Kamloops to Lac Du Bois and Tranquille.

C. Kamloops to Paul Lake Provincial Park and Pinantan Lake.

Kamloops to Lac Du Bois and Tranquille

Exit the Trans-Canada onto Highway 5, taking the Lansdowne Street exit west into downtown Kamloops (00.0 km.). Continue along Lansdowne, then Victoria, turning right onto the Overlander Bridge spanning the Thompson River (3.7 km.). Proceed north and west along Fortune Road following the signs for Tranquille and the airport. After (2.9 km.) (6.6 km.), Fortune Road changes to Tranquille Road at the traffic lights. If you wish, you may turn right onto 8th Street for Lac Du Bois (or continue west for an additional 11.3 km. along Tranquille Road, passing the spectacular basalt columns and the hoodoos on the north side of the road - and beyond the airport - to the Fish and Wildlife Branch display board at the east end of Tranquille Pond.). Proceed north on 8th Street, passing over the Halston Road overpass, and turn left onto Batchelor Drive (1.4 km.) (8.0 km.). After (0.5 km.) (8.5 km.) paved Batchelor Drive becomes gravel Lac du Bois Road. Follow this gravel road east and north for (14.5 km.) (23.0 km.) until reaching the first major lake on the left which has Douglas-firs surrounding part of the shoreline. Watch for the recently re-introduced (and uncountable) Burrowing Owl on fenceposts in the grasslands along the drive.

LAC DU BOIS

Ponderosa pine are scattered amongst the Douglas-firs surrounding the lake. These pines are certainly the classic conifer, with their majestic stance and red, checkered bark they are symbolic of the drier slopes of the southern interior. This is prime habitat for the highly migratory Flammulated Owl. These strictly nocturnal dark-eyed owls can often be heard from the lake. To see them, hiking the roads is a necessity. Check the grasslands for Long-billed Curlew.

Lac Du Bois to Tranquille

 Retrace your route back to 8th Street, turning right (00.0 km.). After (0.1 km.) turn right off 8th Street onto Ord Road. Proceed west along Ord Road for (2.3 km.) (2.4 km.) to a large cement water tank. Search the nearby gullies for Lark Sparrow, and in the upper areas for Chukar; rocky talus slopes harbour Rock Wren. Proceed westward until you see the Empire Auto Wreckers (2.0 km.) (4.4 km.), White-throated Swift fly bullet-like across the nearby cliffs. The slopes to the west of the wreckers also have Rock Wren, Says Phoebe nest in caves at these cliffs, and Chukar are frequently found. Continue west on Ord road (short jog on Farm) to the junction with Tranquille Road, turning right (0.6 km.) (5.0 km.). After (5.4 km.) (10.4 km.), turn left (staying on pavement) and park at the parking area.

TRANQUILLE

 Do not be discouraged by the apparent agricultural or suburban nature of the area. This productive site, especially for migrants, has produced more rarities than elsewhere in the Kamloops area. Search the pond and the lane leading to the lake in front of the buildings as both provide excellent birding potential at any time of the year. Black-crowned Night-Heron, Greater White-fronted Goose, Ross' Goose, Eurasian Wigeon, American Avocet, Sharp-tailed Sandpiper, Stilt Sandpiper, Buff-breasted Sandpiper, Parasitic Jaeger, Glaucous Gull, and Caspian Tern are among the best rarities recorded here. Among the more usual species expected during migrations are thousands of Canada Geese, Tundra Swan, dabbling ducks, and shorebirds. Large groups of transient Great Blue Heron are observed during August. Check along the adjacent railway tracks for Chukar and Mourning Dove.

Proceed west along Tranquille Road, turning left onto a gravel road just before the old Tranquille Institution gates (0.9 km.) (1 1.4 km.). The gravel road runs on an angle down to the government owned shores of Kamloops Lake (1.0 km.) (1 2.4 km.). In winter, large flocks of Bohemian Waxwing, Pine Grosbeak, and Evening Grosbeak feed on the fruits and berries supplied by the crab apple trees and numerous shrubs along the shore. An occasional Bald Eagle, Northern Shrike, or Varied Thrush puts in an appearance. In summer, Lewis' Woodpecker and Bullock's Oriole are expected. Scope the lake for loons, rafts of Western Grebe, scoters, and other waterfowl during migration periods.

Kamloops and Tranquille to Paul Lake Provincial Park

Paul Lake Road can be reached by: (A) (00.0 km.) Proceed from Tranquille east along Tranquille Road, turning left onto Halston Road (5.2 km.). Follow Halston Road across the North Thompson River bridge to the junction of Highway 5 and Paul Lake Road (7.7 km.) (1 2.9 km.), or (B) (00.0 km.) Turn left off of the Trans-Canada onto Highway 5 at Kamloop's eastern town limits. Proceed north for (4.8 km.), turning right onto paved Paul Lake Road. NOTE: the land on either side of Paul Lake Road for the first (11.3 km.) is Indian reserve; birding should be conducted from the road. For permission to enter the reservation lands contact the band office, located along Highway 5 (3.7 km.) south of the Paul Creek turnoff.

For the first (6.0 km.), Paul Lake Road runs parallel to Paul Creek and provides easy access to the roadside riparian habitat.

The entire drainage for the next thirty kilometers provides good birding, some of the species expected: Great Blue Heron (colony), American Kestrel, Blue Grouse, Ruffed Grouse, Mourning Dove, Vaux's Swift, Calliope Hummingbird, Lewis' Woodpecker, Western Kingbird, Hammond's Flycatcher, Pacific-slope Flycatcher, American Crow, Black-capped Chickadee, Red-breasted Nuthatch, Golden-crowned Kinglet, Veery, Gray Catbird, Cassin's Vireo, Nashville Warbler, MacGillivray's Warbler, Western Tanager, Lazuli Bunting, Spotted Towhee, Bullock's Oriole, Cassin's Finch, and Red Crossbill.

Lewis' Woodpecker are found in the old cottonwoods near the ponds at the beginning of the road, while Northern Saw-whet Owl, Townsend's Solitaire, and Cassin's Finch frequent the Douglas-fir groves that pepper the dry southern hillsides along the valley. The riverine woodlands ring with the songs of Veery, Varied Thrush, Nashville Warbler, MacGillivray's Warbler, Lazuli Bunting, Spotted Towhee, and Bullock's Oriole. Gray-crowned Rosy Finch are occasionally found in spring on the valley slopes cloaked in sage, and Long-billed Curlew on the extensive grassy benches at Scheidam Flats. Migrating raptors, Western Meadowlark, and Vesper Sparrow are common.

Continue along Paul Lake Road for (11.3 km.) (16.1 km.), turning right onto a gravel road leading south to the Mount Harper Ski Area [be sure to keep right at the junction of the paved road leading north at (9.7 km.) (14.5 km.)]. Proceed along the gravel road into the cool higher elevations where Gray Jay, Red-breasted Nuthatch, Golden-crowned Kinglet, Hammond's Flycatcher, Cassin's Vireo, and Red Crossbill occur. Proceed along Paul Lake Road, following the signs (6.4km.) (22.5 km.) to the entrance to the campground.

PAUL LAKE PROVINCIAL PARK

The mixed forest of ponderosa pine and Douglas-fir of Paul Lake Provincial Park support nesting Great Horned Owl, Northern Pygmy Owl, and Northern Saw-whet Owl. The slopes to the north of the park entrance have nesting Flammulated Owl and hiking up steep hillsides may be required to see them, although their calls are heard from the road. Common Poorwill are often heard from here as well. At the western end of the campground, the Western Screech-Owl's hollow hooting call (that sounds rather like a bouncing ping-pong ball) will be heard on warm evenings.

White-throated Swift tear around the bluffs in which they nest each summer. A variety of species characteristic of dry woodlands are present in abundance as well as grebes and diving ducks on the lake itself.

Paul Lake Provincial Park to Pinantan Lake

Those wishing Great Gray Owl should try a nocturnal excursion, driving along the paved and gravel roads in the vicinity of Pinantan Lake during summer or winter and beyond on the gravel road running north to Warren, Pemberton, and Hyas Lakes. As this uncommon owl occasionally hunts over forest clearings during the day, especially during winter, you may wish to try a daylight excursion.

(00.0km.) Retrace your route west along Paul Lake Road, turning right onto the paved road leading to Pinantan Lake (8.0 km.). At (1.6 km.), Louis Lake has a variety of grebes and diving ducks, Northern Goshawk, and White-breasted Nuthatch. Proceed along the road to Pinantan Lake (the lake not the town) (12.4 km.) (22.0 km.). In the evening, check the tops of the fence posts lining both the main paved road and along the branch gravel road. The owls can often be lured to call by judicious use of a tape-recording of their calls. Stop periodically to play the tape or to listen for their deep, resonant "whoos". If you are unsuccessful, continue east along pavement to the town of Pinantan Lake (5.0 km.) (27.0 km.), turning left onto a gravel road that leads north for (7.0 km.) (34.0 km.), owling once more.

Pinantan Lake to Shuswap Park

(00.0km.) From the town of Pinantan Lake, proceed east along the gravel road to the T junction next to the Thompson River (10.0 km.), keeping straight at branch roads. Turn left at the T junction following the west bank of the Thompson River, then right at (2.0 km.) (12.0 km.), crossing the bridge spanning the Thompson River en route to the community of Pritchard on the Trans-Canada Highway (2.2 km.) (14.2 km.). Turn left onto the Trans-Canada and continue an additional (26.6 km.) (41.8 km.), turning left at Squilax (see below).

Kamloops to Shuswap Lake Provincial Park

(00.0km.) From the junction of the Yellowhead Highway (Highway 5) (one could start the Mountains and Central Plateau Loop from this end) and the Trans-Canada in Kamloops, proceed east along the Trans-Canada Highway towards Salmon Arm. After driving (26 km.), Highway 97 branches off to the Okanagan; one could start that loop from this end. At (64.5 km.), turn left on the paved road at Squilax over the Thompson River bridge spanning the gap between Little Shuswap Lake and Shuswap Lake. (This turnoff is ten kilometers east of Chase). After crossing the bridge do not take the left turnoff for the Adams River and Adams Lake, but keep right an additional (19.0 km.) (83.5 km.) to the park. Indian Point, on the road to Adams Lake will produce such notable species as Sora, Least Flycatcher, and Bobolink.

SHUSWAP LAKE PROVINCIAL PARK

Shuswap Lake Provincial Park is In a transition zone, a blending of wet Douglas-fir and dry ponderosa pine forests, Shuswap Lake presents an interesting diversity of avifauna. Bird checklists are available at the parks nature house which is open during the months of July and August.

Red-naped Sapsucker frequent the white birches in the region of the parking lot, their sap wells attracting Black-chinned Hummingbird and Rufous Hummingbird. In behind the nature house is a patch of forest which harbours Dusky Flycatcher, Red-eyed Vireo, and American Redstart, while the shrubs on the dry hillsides yield Nashville Warbler and Lazuli Bunting.

A list of species expected at the park in winter (many of these species are resident) includes: Common Loon, Western Grebe, Rednecked Grebe, Horned Grebe, Eared Grebe, Great Blue Heron, Tundra Swan, Trumpeter Swan, Canada Goose, Mallard, Gadwall, Green-winged Teal, American Wigeon, Northern Pintail, Redhead, Ring-necked Duck, Greater Scaup, Lesser Scaup, Barrows Goldeneye, Common Goldeneye, Bufflehead, Common Merganser, American Coot, Killdeer, Ring-billed Gull, Herring Gull, Bald Eagle, Sharp-shinned Hawk, Coopers Hawk, Northern Goshawk, Merlin, Ruffed Grouse, Common Pheasant, Northern Pygmy-Owl, Northern Saw-whet Owl, Belted Kingfisher, Northern Flicker, Downy Woodpecker, Hairy Woodpecker, Three-toed Woodpecker, Pileated Woodpecker, Stellers Jay, Gray Jay, Clarks Nutcracker, Black-billed Magpie, American Crow, Common Raven, Black-capped Chickadee, Mountain Chickadee, Chestnut-backed Chickadee, Brown Creeper, White-breasted Nuthatch, Red-breasted Nuthatch, Winter Wren, Golden-crowned Kinglet, Varied Thrush, American Robin, Northern Shrike, American Dipper, Bohemian Waxwing, European Starling, Song Sparrow, Dark-eyed Junco, Redwinged Blackbird, Brewers Blackbird, House Sparrow, Pine Siskin, American Goldfich, Red Crossbill, Pine Grosbeak, House Finch and Evening Grosbeak.

If you continue (1.6 km.) east of the park to Scotch Creek, there are Barred Owl. Playing a tape towards the mixed woods along the creek in the evening will often get a response from this dark-eyed chunky owl, a rhythmic "Who-cooks-for-you, who-cooks-for-you-all".

If it is possible to gain access to the sub-alpine meadows at Crowfoot Mountain (ask the helpful supervisor at Shuswap Lake for directions and road conditions), Spruce Grouse, Calliope Hummingbird, Three-toed Woodpecker, Gray Jay, Mountain Chickadee, and Boreal Chickadee would be typical species expected in this habitat.

Shuswap Park to Revelstoke

 (00.0km.) Return to the Trans-Canada, turning left. After driving (73.5 km.) you will meet with the junction of Highway 97A leading south towards the Okanagan Valley from the town of Sicamous. At (143.5 km.) you will pass over the Columbia River into Revelstoke at (144 km.) (21 2 km. from downtown Kamloops).

REVELSTOKE

Revelstoke has produced such rare species for the province as Lesser Black-backed Gull, Ruby-throated Hummingbird, Black-billed Cuckoo, Scissor-tailed Flycatcher, Chestnut-sided Warbler, two records of Indigo Bunting, and Brambling. A record of Rock Wren and Bay-breasted Warbler are very unusual for this sector of the province.

Recently, one or two Le Contes Sparrow have returned to summer in the large wet expanse of grasses along the Columbia River, the most southerly distribution in British Columbia.

 (00.0km.) To reach this location, turn right onto Victoria Road at the traffic lights from the Trans-Canada Highway (the only set in Revelstoke) veering right onto Railway Avenue. Drive (2.5 km.), turning left over the railway tracks onto Fourth Street. After an additional (1.1 km.) (3.6 km.), turn right immediately past the bridge over the Illecillewaet River onto a dirt road signed Saddle Club. You will soon come to a metal gate, veer left (0.1 km.) (3.7 km.). At the saddle club keep left (0.3 km.) (4.0 km.), and after an additional (0.4 km.) (4.4 km.) take the centre of three roads. After driving an additional (0.2 km.) (4.6 km.) keep right, and after (0.4 km.) (5.0 km.), turn left along the bank of the river.

In this general area and next to the highly visible old metal bridges you will find Alder Flycatcher, Yellow Warbler, and many Lazuli Bunting. Continue an additional (0.7 km.) (5.7 km.) to a small gravel pit. In the second-growth deciduous woods are American Redstart. From here the road goes down a small hill and out into the grasslands. In late summer this area will be flooded. It is best to look for the sparrows in late May and June, or listen later in the year from the airport (see below). Just past the first stretch of grasses is a small grove of trees. In this area several rarities for the province have been found including Black-billed Cuckoo, Chestnut-sided Warbler, and Bay-breasted Warbler. After driving (1.3 km.) (7.0 km.) from the gravel pit, start listening for the Le Contes Sparrow. Many Savannah Sparrow will be encountered first. Check as far as the airport (1.5 km.) (8.5 km.). In the brushy margins are Clay-colored Sparrow, Willow Flycatcher, and Common Yellowthroat.

If you come later in the year, continue one kilometer or so past the Illecillewaet River bridge (which is 3.6 km. from the Trans-Canada) to the hospital on South Road (Fourth Street changes name past the bridge). Just down the hill past the hospital is a nice patch of woods with Dusky

Flycatcher, Least Flycatcher, Veery, Gray Catbird, Red-eyed Vireo, Warbling Vireo, Tennessee Warbler, Nashville Warbler, Magnolia Warbler, Yellow Warbler, and American Redstart. Continue a bit further until you see the airport on your right (6.2 km.): listen for the Le Contes Sparrows from the back of the airport property when the first site (and best site) is flooded in late summer.

After driving (5.5 km.) past the Illecillewaet River bridge (9.1 km. from the Trans-Canada), the Upper Arrow resevoir will be on your right. Frequent stops along the resevoir in April and early May will produce several species of migrant waterfowl. If you still need some of the species typical of the extreme low elevations of the region listed above, continue to bird South Road for an additional two kilometers (11.0 km.) checking any second-growth deciduous woods.

Revelstoke to Mount Revelstoke National Park

 (00.0km.) At the bridge over the Columbia River, proceed east along Highway 1 for (1.6 km.) to the junction of the Mount Revelstoke Summit Road, turning left.

MOUNT REVELSTOKE NATIONAL PARK

Mount Revelstoke National Park (260 km.), lying in the scenic Columbia Mountains and dominated by the impressive Clachnacudainn Snowfield, offers the birder access to dense rain forest in the valleys, up to alpine tundra at the mountains summit. During June, the park should produce 50 species during your first day, including the four species of chickadee, one of the few places in British Columbia where you can accomplish this feat. More than sixty-five kilometers of established hiking trails wind through the park. The summit Road is open from late June to early October. Snow depths determine when the road is open the remainder of the year.

A drive up the road linking the community of Revelstoke to the summit of the mountain gives an excellent avifaunal cross-section of the Columbia Mountains. Summit Road runs through three distinct natural zones: dense interior rainforest (Columbia forest) at its base at 600 m containing cedar and western hemlock; sub-alpine forest above 1,300 m containing spruce, sub-alpine fir, and mountain hemlock; and alpine meadows over 1,900 m. In August, the meadows produce a magnificent array of summer flowers turning the entire region into a vast wild garden.

After driving (3.0 km.) from the begining of Summit Road, turn right at the sign for trailor parking. At the end of this short road are old scrubby fields and second-growth deciduous woods in the abandoned ski development area that harbour Rufous Hummingbird, Northern Flicker, Black-capped Chickadee, Nashville Warbler, American Redstart, and Song Sparrow.

Return to the main road. As you proceed along the Summit Road be sure to make frequent stops as the avifauna changes as elevation increases. The next six kilometers should yield the characteristic wet forest avifauna of the region including Stellers Jay, Chestnut-backed Chickadee, Winter Wren, Swainsons Thrush, Varied Thrush, Yellow-rumped Warbler, Townsend's Warbler, MacGillivrays Warbler, and Song Sparrow. After driving an additional (5.0 km.) (8.0 km.), just past the Five Mile Picnic Area, scan for the resident Blue Grouse which often display on the roadside.

After (8.0 km.) (16.0 km.) you will arrive in the sub-alpine zone, here the forest and avifauna change dramatically. Gray Jay, Common Raven, Hermit Thrush, Red Crossbill, and Pine Grosbeak are found frequently. After (3.0 km.) (19.0 km.), in the small wet flats opposite the cabin, Black Swift, Vauxs Swift, Three-toed Woodpecker, Olive-sided Flycatcher, Mountain Chickadee, and Boreal Chickadee are characteristic species of this zone that are often recorded.

After an additional (9.0 km.) (25.0 km.) stop at the Balsam Lake Picnic Area, just below the summit, where Gray Jay, Common Raven, and Fox Sparrow are typical denizens of these elevations. At the summit (1.0 km.) (26.0 km.), there is an excellent network of hiking trails through the alpine meadows, an endless panorama of rugged mountains dappled with snow and vast expanses of tundra pockmarked with pools and laced with patches of taiga.

The trail north to Eva Lake has had a nesting pair of Northern Hawk-Owl in recent years, and the trail east to Jade Lake Pass (eight kilometers in length and a strenuous climb to 2,160 m) will yield such alpine specialities as: a Golden Eagle silently soaring overhead, a family of White-tailed Ptarmigan well camouflaged against the lichen-dominated tundra rocks on the slopes, American Pipit, and a resplendent group of Gray-crowned Rosy Finch eking a meagre living from the edges of snow-patches. August is the best month to bird the meadows, as snow melts late at these elevations.

Mount Revelstoke National Park to Glacier National Park

(00.0km.) From the bridge over the Columbia River, travel east along the Trans-Canada towards Golden and the Alberta border watching for Band-tailed Pigeon. Stop at the viewpoint and pull over along the Trans-Canada at (14.7 km.). Although Black-throated Green Warbler are scarce in this region of the province, one has been found in this area on several occasions.

After (3.3 km.) (18.0 km.) you will reach the western gate of Mount Revelstoke Park. The Columbia forest lining the highway for the next thirteen kilometers through the southern fringe of the park are permanent home to Stellers Jay, Common Raven, and Chestnut-backed Chickadee. During May and June, the ultimate prize is to see the beautiful Western Tanager which can be regularly heard singing their robin-like songs from the dark recesses of the Douglas-firs.

After an additional (0.5 km.) (26.7 km.), the Skunk Cabbage Picnic area is found on the right. Look along the small creek, using the footbridge, for American Dipper. Black-headed Grosbeak and Magnolia Warbler are found in the willow-alder brush near the start of the Skunk Cabbage trail, which loops through a variety of wetland habitats. Rufous Hummingbird, Townsend's Warbler, Yellow Warbler, Common Yellowthroat, and Western Tanager are present along the walk, made more enjoyable by the sights of the large, chrome yellow skunk cabbages glowing on the marsh floor. Merlin have nested in the area.

Continue east along the Trans-Canada for (2.6 km.) (29.3 km.) to the next picnic area on the left. As a left turn is quite dangerous, proceed further east until you can make a safe U-turn. Follow the signs to the Giant Cedars Picnic Area where a small creek will usually produce an American Dipper. The Giant Cedars trail, beginning at the edge of the picnic site, will produce the characteristic species of the Columbia forests. Nothing rivals the giant ancient cedars, walking among them is an experience few people will forget. A hike along the short boardwalk through the old-growth stand of western red cedar will produce Chestnut-backed Chickadee, Golden-crowned Kinglet, Brown Creeper, Winter Wren, and Varied Thrush. After an additional (0-7 km.) (30.0 km.), the eastern gate to Revelstoke Park is attained. After an additional (22.3 km.) (52.3 km.) you will reach the western gate of Glacier National Park.

GLACIER NATIONAL PARK

Glacier National Park has a special magic - a feeling of tranquility and timelessness that affects every visitor. The park has several campsites and many hiking trails which take you into a fine variety of habitats - rain forest, sub-alpine surroundings, valley bottoms, wetlands, and coniferous forests. The complex topography offers a wide spectrum of life zones. May and June are the best birding months with a veritable treasure chest of exciting birding opportunities: migration pours northward and the breeding birds are in full song.

Proceed east along the Trans-Canada for an additional (13.8 km.) (66.1 km.), stopping at the viewpoint that features the old stone piers at Loop Brook. Here you will find the trailhead for the Loop Trail, providing access to rainforest and sub-alpine habitats where characteristic transition zone species occur: Stellers Jay, Chestnut-backed Chickadee, Red-breasted Nuthatch, Winter Wren, Golden-crowned Kinglet, Townsend's Warbler, and Wilson's Warbler.

From Loop Brook, proceed three kilometers eastward along the road leading to the Illecillewaet campground. At the campground, keep left, then turn right at the Wheeler Hut onto an old road at the junction. Cross over the Illecillewaet River, parking at the Glacier House viewpoint where the trailheads of several hiking trails are found. The sounds of the forest are the best clue as to what birds are about; Rufous Hummingbird, Northern Flicker, Hammond's Flycatcher, Violet-green Swallow, Stellers Jay, American Crow, Black-capped Chickadee, Chestnut-backed Chickadee, Boreal Chickadee, Mountain Bluebird, Townsend's Solitaire, Orange-crowned Warbler, Brewer's Blackbird, and Pine Siskin are all found in the general area.

Retrace your route back to the Trans-Canada Highway East. After (2.4 km.) (68.5 km.) you will reach the summit of Rogers Pass, the avalanche slopes support Fox Sparrow. The Abandoned Rails Trail starts at the information center walkway, providing an easy thirty minute walk along which Spruce Grouse may be seen. After an additional (2.5 km.) (71.0 km.) you will reach the Rogers Pass Tourist Service area.

 After driving east along the Trans-Canada for an additional (8.8 km.) (79.8 km.), pull over onto the paved viewpoint on the right. One can stand on this ridge-top surrounded by an almost unbroken vista of montane forest enjoying some of the most spectacular scenery in the country. The forested Purcell and Selkirk Ranges stretch away to the horizon, bisected by the Purcell Trench through which the sparkling Beaver Rver runs. Violet-green-Swallow and Northern Rough-winged Swallow zip across the backdrop of superb scenery. From the paved viewpoint, proceed down into the Beaver River Valley. The marsh on the left harbours many of the widespread characteristic birds of interior wetland habitat.

After driving an additional (7.2 km.) (87.0 km.) you will arrive at the eastern gateway to Glacier National Park. You will also move from the Pacific Time Zone to Mountain time, so set your clocks ahead one hour.

Glacier National Park to Golden

After driving east along the Trans-Canada for an additional (49.0km.) (136.0 km.) you will find Moberly Marsh, a slough with marsh habitat that harbours American Bittern, Sora and several species of ducks, most being Mallard, Green-winged Teal, Ring-necked Duck, and Common Merganser.

Golden is reached after driving east along the Trans-Canada for an additional (13.0 km.) (149.0 km.). Golden is also the junction with Highway 95 South to Radium Hot Springs where you may join the Highway 3 East Loop.

GOLDEN

The Canyon Creek Ranch which covers 1,200 acres, is the best birding site located near Golden.

(00.0 km.) Drive south of Golden along Highway 95 for (5.6 km.), taking the Nicholson bypass across the Columbia River. Proceed south on the Nicholson bypass a further (0.3 km.) (5.9 km.) to the entrance of the Canyon Creek Ranch. Proceed to the ranch house (1.6 km.) (7.5 km.) and obtain permission to bird the ranch where 183 bird species have been recorded.

Accidental species such as Connecticut Warbler and Indigo Bunting and regional rarities such as Arctic Tern and White-headed Woodpecker have been seen. Characteristic species seen along a drive through the ranch include Red-tailed Hawk, American Kestrel, Mourning Dove, Common Nighthawk, Calliope Hummingbird, Rufous Hummingbird, Northern Flicker, Eastern Kingbird, Western Wood-Pewee, Dusky Flycatcher, Cordilleran Flycatcher, Black-billed Magpie, American Crow, Black-capped Chickadee, Red-breasted Nuthatch, Mountain Bluebird, Swainsons Thrush, American Robin, Cedar Waxwing, Cassin's Vireo, Red-eyed Vireo, Warbling Vireo, Tennessee Warbler, Orange-crowned Warbler, Yellow-rumped Warbler, MacGillivray's Warbler, American Redstart, Savannah Sparrow, Song Sparrow, and Chipping Sparrow.

Golden to Yoho National Park

On the outskirts of Golden (0.5 km.) (149.5 km.) you will find the British Columbia InfoCentre for information on the Alberta/B.C. border. Proceeding eastward, the observant naturalist will see a different ecological component. In the Western Main Ranges of the Rockies along the continental divide, the mountains change from weathered peaks of limestones, interspersed with softer rocks such as shales, to hard, jagged peaks of resistant sandstone. The West Gate of Yoho National Park is an additional (26.0 km.) (175.0 km.) east of Golden.

YOHO NATIONAL PARK

The next fifty-two kilometers of the Trans-Canada winds its way through Yoho National Park and its many trails, rest stops, picnic sites, and other asssorted tourist facilities are made to order for periodic stops to sample the abundant mountain avifauna. No description can do justice to the awesome scenery, where all the works of man seem puny indeed: rocky peaks, cataracts, and placid emerald mountain lakes create spectacular vistas. The milky, rushing waters of Yoho and Kicking Horse Rivers rip through the scenic valleys embraced on both sides by towering mountains, many with snow-covered peaks above treeline.

Yoho National Park is an excellent site for birders to sample the characteristic avifauna of the Rocky Mountains. A few of the 207 bird species known to occur in the park are more easily found here than elsewhere in the southeastern sector of the province. Birders looking for the unexpected should visit the park in late May/early June, or late August. In June and early July, Yoho should produce between 80 and 100 species in 2 or 3 days.

The valley floors of the park are cloaked with second-growth stands of lodgepole pine where there is little birdlife indeed. In the extensive areas of old-growth Englemann and white spruce stands, the fairly common but inconspicuous boreal species, Spruce Grouse, Three-toed Woodpecker, and Boreal Chickadee are found. Other common species occupying the dark spruce thickets are Hammond's Flycatcher, Gray Jay, Winter Wren, Varied Thrush, Golden-crowned Kinglet, Yellow-rumped Warbler, Townsend's Warbler, Dark-eyed Junco, and Pine Siskin.

After entering the park from the west gate, drive (3.2km.) (178.2 km.) east along the Trans-Canada, stopping at the Leanchoil picnic site where there are more breeding species than elsewhere in the park.

Check out the willow-choked marsh east of the picnic site for Common Snipe, Willow Flycatcher, Alder Flycatcher, Yellow Warbler, MacGillivray's Warbler, Wilson's Warbler, Common Yellowthroat, Lincoln's Sparrow, and Red-winged Blackbird. The surrounding aspen groves and mixed woods harbour Northern Pygmy Owl, Red-naped Sapsucker, Least Flycatcher, Black-capped Chickadee, American Robin, Swainson's Thrush, Cedar Waxwing, Cassin's Vireo, Warbling Vireo, Tennessee Warbler, and American Redstart.

Drive east along the Trans-Canada for (1.6 km.) (1 79.8 km.) to the road and trail to Wapta Falls. A similar list of species as those found at Leanchoil picnic site will be found.

Follow the signs to the The Dearlodge Trailhead, located at the entrance to the Hoodoo Campground, a further (2.6 km.) (1 82.4 km.) east along the Trans-Canada. This self-guiding loop trail crosses an old beaver pond and wet meadows via a boardwalk, then reverses back on itself through the adjacent forest. Solitary Sandpiper and Common Snipe have been known to breed in the meadows. Ruffed Grouse, Belted Kingfisher, Hairy Woodpecker, Three-toed Woodpecker, Pileated Woodpecker, Red-breasted Nuthatch, Orange-crowned Warbler, Savannah Sparrow, and Lincoln's Sparrow are frequently observed in season. The trail to the Hoodoos that begins from the upper end of the Hoodoo Creek Campground is the best site for Cordilleran Flycatcher. (See Ken Kaufman's " The Lives of North American Birds" for the most accurate range map of this species.)

After driving east for an additional (12.4 km.) (194.8 km.), turn off the Trans-Canada onto the Emerald Lake Road. Proceed (8.4 km.) to translucent Emerald Lake. Looping the scenic lake is a four kilometer long trail which passes through a lodgepole pine forest, an open shrub-covered slide, an outwash plain of gravel, and finally through a dense mixed forest of red cedar and spruce. Along the walk during summer you should see

Common Merganser, Spotted Sandpiper, Barred Owl, Rufous Hummingbird, Northern Flicker, Pileated Woodpecker, Olive-sided Flycatcher, Western Wood-Pewee, Cliff Swallow, Barn Swallow, Steller's Jay, American Crow, Common Raven, Brown-headed Cowbird, White-crowned Sparrow, Pine Grosbeak, and, in invasion years, both Red Crossbill and White-winged Crossbill. Very few species of waterfowl use the lake in summer, while migration brings a plethora of new possibilities.

The Travel Information Centre for the park is found at the entrance to the town of Field (5.7 km.) (204.5 km.). The information staff have maps, checklists, and field guides available for sale and there are interesting displays.

Continue east on the Trans-Canada for (9.5 km.) (214.0 km.) (or 12.5 km from east gate) to the northbound turnoff leading to the Yoho Valley Road and Takakkaw Falls. The sub-alpine habitat at the base of the falls is attained after driving along pavement for fourteen kilometers: the double swtchback is not as fearsome as it first looks.

The spectacle of the melt-water spilling 284 m over the vertical rocky Mountainside is one of natures masterpieces. As the waters thunder over the edge, rainbows arch through the fine spray that rises high into the air. Hiking trails lead from the Takakkaw parking lot further upslope to alpine habitat. The wooded cliffs above the parking lot are filled with the slow, high pitched whistles of Varied Thrush. Those who wish to visit ptarmigan country can do so along one of the well-maintained hiking trails; best after late July, since snow melts late at this elevation. The new Iceline Trail is possibly the best hike for those who wish to see alpine species. As you break out above treeline, while you may not luck into a Golden Eagle, White-tailed Ptarmigan, American Pipit, or Gray-crowned Rosy Finch, you can be assured of some of the finest mountain scenery in the world.

After driving an additional (8.0 km) (222.0 km.) east along the Trans-Canada, stop at Wapta Lake. Wapta Lake is only five kilometers from the Alberta border and the continental divide. At the large marsh at the lakes eastern end are Common Snipe, Tree Swallow, and Common Yellowthroat. Canada Goose, Ring-necked Duck, Barrow's Goldeneye and Harlequin Duck breed. Waterfowl migrate late during spring when the lake remains frozen, but use the lake frequently during autumn migrations from August through October. Fairly common spring migrants, possibly until early June, include Surf Scoter and White-winged Scoter.

Lake O'Hara, at 2,000 m in elevation, is an emerald lake located in a spectacular alpine setting. To reach the lake, and the characteristic birds found in the surrounding alpine meadows, requires a strenuous eleven kilometer hike south of Wapta Lake. Osea Lake, the best area for White-tailed Ptarmigan and Gray-crowned Rosy Finch, can be reached along five kilometers of trail from Lake O'Hara. American Dipper occurs along the fast-flowing rivers in the area. Boreal Owl, Clark's Nutcracker, Mountain

Chickadee, Townsend's Solitaire, Hermit Thrush, and Pine Grosbeak inhabit the forests near timberline. The best strategy for birding this area is to stay overnight at the strategically placed Lake O'Hara Lodge or at a walk-in campground.

NOTES & OBSERVATIONS

NOTES & OBSERVATIONS

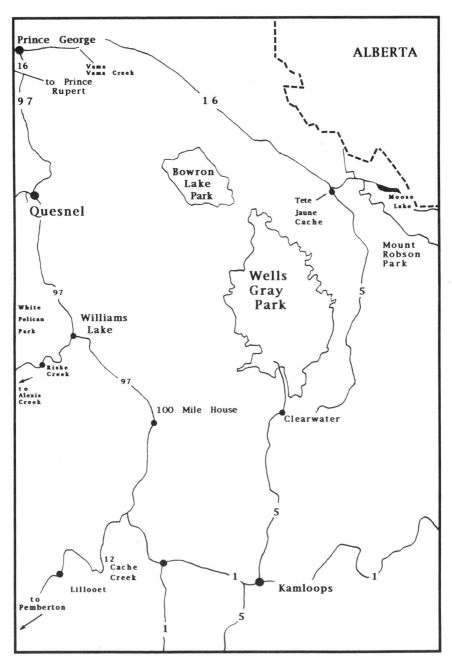

MAP 12   LOOP 9   MOUNTAINS AND CARIBOO PLATEAU

LOOP 9 MOUNTAINS AND CARIBOO PLATEAU

Hope or Kamloops to 100 Mile House

From Hope, drive north on Highway 1 (the Trans-Canada) to Cache Creek (194 km.). En route you can make a brief stop at Spences Bridge (147.5 km. from Hope) if you want to see Chukar. Explore the slopes above the south side of the Thompson River between the town of Spences Bridge and the mouth of the Nicola River.

From Kamloops drive west along the Trans-Canada to Cache Creek (80.5 km.). At Cache Creek, proceed on Highway 97 North toward Clinton (00.0 km.). After driving (115.9 km.) you will arrive at 100 Mile House.

100 MILE HOUSE

There is a wetland at the log cabin by 100 Mile House Marsh, a bird sanctuary at the north edge of town along the west side of Highway 97 (look for the 39-foot-long skiis!). This wetland, behind the Tourist Infocentre, is an excellent example of a Cariboo Parklands marsh with Mallard, Ruddy Duck, Sora, Black Tern, Marsh Wren, Yellow-headed Blackbird, and Red-winged Blackbird present through summer. Many other species of "puddle duck" are also summer residents and migrants.

100 Mile House to Williams Lake - Riske Creek

Proceed on Highway 97 North towards Williams Lake. At Williams Lake (90.1 km.) (206 km.), turn left onto Highway 20 West from the centre of town following the highway signs. Proceed along Highway 20 West to the small hamlet of Riske Creek (51 km.) (257 km.). En route along Highway 20 at (35.2 km.) (241.2 km.) there is a 60 m high Loran Coast Guard tower. Just west of the tower (approx. 0.7 km.) (35.9 km), take the dirt access road that branches north off the highway into the surrounding grasslands. This road lies between Fish Lake and Meldrum Creek Roads. Turn right, cross the cattle guard and proceed onto the federally owned property (approx. 0.8 km) to a large lake on the left. Although extremely scarce in British Columbia, Sprague's Pipit have occured at this site in recent years.

RISKE CREEK, BECHER'S PRAIRIE

Becher's Prairie, lying close to the community of Riske Creek, has an excellent mixture of dry plateau grasslands and pothole marshes. Here, in the best "prairie sloughs" in the Cariboo-Chilcotin, large concentrations of migrant and nesting waterfowl find prime habitat. These wetlands support the highest densities of breeding arrow's Goldeneye and Bufflehead in North

America. The rolling grasslands in this region are the northern limit of the Long-billed Curlew in the province.

The Cariboo Parklands of central British Columbia are characteristically a patchwork of open, scattered forests of lodgepole pine and Douglas-fir, with small groves of white spruce and quaking aspen nestled among gently rolling foothills. Predominant though are major grasslands. The alkaline lakes, with a wide range of salinity, may have extensive bullrush stands along their margins, while others are bare and salt-encrusted.

(00.0km.) At the combination store and post office in Riske Creek, take the gravel road north for (7.0 km.). Bear right (northeast) onto the dirt track for an additional (1.9 km.) (8.9 km.), then turn sharply right along the gravel road towards the southeast for (11.0 km.) (19.9 km.) back to Highway 20. Along the drive (which should consume about a half-day) make regular stops to explore the potholes, open fields, and woods.

At (17.9 km.) you will find the most productive slough, Rock Lake. During late March to early April, Red-necked Grebe, Horned Grebe, Eared Grebe, and Pied-billed Grebe begin to appear. Rock Lake has a large breeding colony of Eared Grebe at its north end. Mallard, Gadwall, Northern Pintail, American Wigeon, Blue-winged Teal, Cinnamon Teal, Green-winged Teal, Redhead, Canvasback, Ruddy Duck, Lesser Scaup, Barrow's Goldeneye, and Bufflehead are present as non-breeders or breeders through the summer and also occur as migrants.

The wide-ranging mixture of habitats provide a rich diversity of avifauna. Uncommon residents include Northern Goshawk, Sharp-tailed Grouse, Three-toed Woodpecker, and the erratic White-winged Crossbill. Winter visitors include three rare owls; Northern Hawk-owl, Great Gray Owl, and Boreal Owl. Long-eared Owl are found breeding in conifer groves. Gray-crowned Rosy Finch and Snow Bunting are irregular during the winter months.

Migration brings most of the more common Pacific flyway waterfowl, the swans, ducks, and geese. Sandhill Crane and shorebirds use the sloughs as staging areas on their way to their Arctic breeding grounds. Sandhill Crane also nest in the marshes, albeit a very small population, while Greater Yellowlegs breed commonly. Long-billed Curlew call over the surrounding wind-blown grasslands.

The two North American eagles inhabit the area: overhead, a silhouette materializes into an uncommon Golden Eagle or the fairly common Bald Eagle, which nests nearby.

Willow Flycatcher sing in summer from the willows fringing the ponds, while Least Flycatcher, Dusky Flycatcher, Mountain Chickadee, and Red Crossbill are common breeders of the deciduous or mixed woodlands. Striking Mountain Bluebird nest along the fencelines, while the brilliant Yellow-headed Blackbird are abundant in the Scirpus marshes.

Horned Lark, Savannah Sparrow, and Vesper Sparrow are common on the grasslands.

Riske Creek to White Pelican Park, Stum Lake

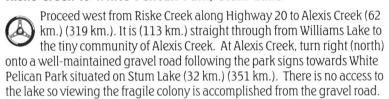 Proceed west from Riske Creek along Highway 20 to Alexis Creek (62 km.) (319 km.). It is (113 km.) straight through from Williams Lake to the tiny community of Alexis Creek. At Alexis Creek, turn right (north) onto a well-maintained gravel road following the park signs towards White Pelican Park situated on Stum Lake (32 km.) (351 km.). There is no access to the lake so viewing the fragile colony is accomplished from the gravel road.

STUM LAKE

 The huge American White Pelican nests locally at Stum Lake. While the colony is inaccessible, the birds can be seen from the road. The pelicans can be seen floating buoyantly on the lake's surface, submerging their heads as they scoop up fish in their wide, flat bills. Gregarious at all seasons, the White Pelican may even fish cooperatively in the lake's shallow waters, with several birds lining up as they herd the fish before them. Flocks are often seen soaring high in the air over the lake, wheeling in unison on motionless flat wings.

Stum Lake to West Quesnel

Retrace your route back to Williams Lake (00.0 km.). After driving (120.7 km.) you will arrive at Quesnel (326.7 km. from Cache Creek).

(00.0 km.) From the downtown core of Quesnel, turn left onto the main paved road leading west toward Bouchie Lake. After crossing the Fraser River Bridge, turn left along the west bank of the Fraser River towards the tiny community of Narcosli Creek

WEST QUESNEL

In late spring and early summer, Tennessee Warbler, Northern Waterthrush, and American Redstart are among the most interesting warblers that breed commonly in the riparian woods along the road sixteen kilometers south of the bridge. Once the vivid colours of the North American wood warbler family are appreciated, move on to search for other passerines that occur in abundance.

West Quesnel to Prince George

(00.0 km.) Proceed from Quesnel along Highway 97 North to Prince George (119.1 km.) (445.8 km. from Cache Creek - 639.8 km. from Hope).

PRINCE GEORGE

Prince George is located at the junction of the Fraser and Nechako Rivers almost slap in the center of the province.

From Prince George you may continue north to the Peace River Parklands, or drive west along the Yellowhead Highway (Highway 1 6) to Prince Rupert (734 km.), catching the ferry for the Queen Charlotte Islands. If you prefer to return south, continue to complete the Loop 9 Route starting below.

Prince George to Mount Robson Park

 From the centre of Prince George, follow the highway signs for Highway 16 East towards McBride, Jasper, and Alberta, after crossing the Yellowhead Bridge, set your odometer at (00.0 km.).

A Yellow-bellied Flycatcher site is located (47.8 km.) along the road. From the Vama Vama Creek culvert, continue east along Highway 16 until you are opposite a "New Forest Planted 1970" sign on your left (1.6 km.) (49.4 km.). A Yellow-bellied Flycatcher was present here in 1992 but may not be regular. Proceed another (0.7 km) (50.1 km.), turning right onto the small sideroad, then left after 35 m. Park your vehicle and listen about 50 m along the right hand side of this road in the habitat of young lodgepole pine and white spruce which contains a thick understory of aspen and willow. Loosely colonial, other Yellow-bellied Flycatchers could be found in this general vicinity. Although nesting took place in 1992-93, their appearance may be erratic from year-to-year.

After driving (270.4 km.) you will reach the junction of Highways 5 and 16. If you continue along Highway 16 for an additional (13.8 km.) you will arrive at the west entrance to Mount Robson Park. After an additional (1.4 km.) you will arrive at the Robson River government campgrounds. There is a turnout at the east end of Moose Lake (30.4 km. past the campgrounds, or 45.6 kilometers from the park gate)

MOUNT ROBSON PARK

The Kinney Lake Road leads to the base of Mount Robson from the park's west gate. The mixed woods along the road produce Spruce Grouse, Olive-sided Flycatcher, Dusky Flycatcher, Hammond's Flycatcher, Least Flycatcher, Alder Flycatcher, Townsend's Solitaire, Varied Thrush, Tennessee Warbler, Magnolia Warbler, Bay-breasted Warbler, Blackpoll Warbler, Northern Waterthrush, and Rusty Blackbird. Moose Lake has a marsh on its east end which supports breeding Red-necked Grebe and Horned Grebe. During migrations several species of waterfowl (including scoters) and shorebird stop over. Gray-crowned Rosy Finch occur at the higher elevations within the park.

Mount Robson Park to Well's Gray Provincial Park

 We start (00.0 km.) from the junctions of Highways 5 (Yellowhead Highway) and 16, at Tete Jaune Cache driving south on Highway 5 toward Valemont. After driving (214 km.) you will arrive at Clearwater. [Clearwater is (484.4 km.) from Prince George; (133.0 km.) from Kamloops]. Turn right (north) on paved road towards Mount Robson Park (40 km.) (254 km.). As there are no gas stations or restaurants along the road to the park, be sure to get gas and food in Clearwater.

WELL'S GRAY PROVINCIAL PARK

 (00.0km.) After driving north along the park entrance road for (16.0 km.), Spahats Creek Provincial Park will be found. The park has exquisite scenery, but is lacking in anything of ornithological interest. A short trail from the parking lot leads along the deep, creek-carved red and gray lava canyon to gaze in awe at Spahats Creek Falls, plunging ribbon-like for sixty meters. As the shadows lengthen, the golden rays of the sun illuminate the red, gray, orange and ochre colours of the canyon walls into an unlikely medley.

After (14.0 km.) (30.0 km.), look for a sign for Battle Mountain. A strenuous six or seven hour hike will take you into the sub-alpine meadows where Golden Eagle, Spruce Grouse, Mountain Chickadee, Boreal Chickadee, Hermit Thrush, and Gray-crowned Rosy Finch are found. Along Hemp Creek, an area of riparian willows just before reaching the park's gate, is an excellent site for Veery, Swainson's Thrush, Gray Catbird, MacGillivray's Warbler, Wilson's Warbler, Northern Waterthrush, and American Redstart.

At the park gate, ask the attendant for directions to any large burns within the park. Areas of recent forest fires, "burns", are often good for producing Three-toed Woodpecker, Black-backed Woodpecker, Western Kingbird, Say's Phoebe, Black-billed Magpie, Lazuli Bunting, and Bullock's Oriole.

The Ray Farm Trail is an enjoyable fifteen minute walk to a historic abandoned homestead, one of the better birding sites within the park. The willows which rim the small lake are often alive with Willow Flycatcher, Magnolia Warbler, Wilson's Warbler, and Northern Waterthrush. Another short trail leads from the farm to spring-fed mineral pools that attract finches, especially Evening Grosbeak, while in the adjacent woods there are Dusky Flycatcher, Veery, and Swainson's Thrush. Mosquitoes and no-see-ems are often very bad in the area.

At the end of the road, at Clearwater Lake and it's campground, look for Common Merganser, Osprey, American Dipper, and other characteristic avifauna of the region in the forests surrounding the lake.

Well's Gray Provincial Park to Kamloops

Retrace your route back to Clearwater, turning right onto Highway 5 South (00.0 km.). After driving (133 km.) you will arrive at Kamloops (617.4 km. from Prince George). At Kamloops you can join either the Trans-Canada Loop or the Okanagan Valley Loop, hence the Highway 3 East or West Loops.

NOTES & OBSERVATIONS

NOTES & OBSERVATIONS

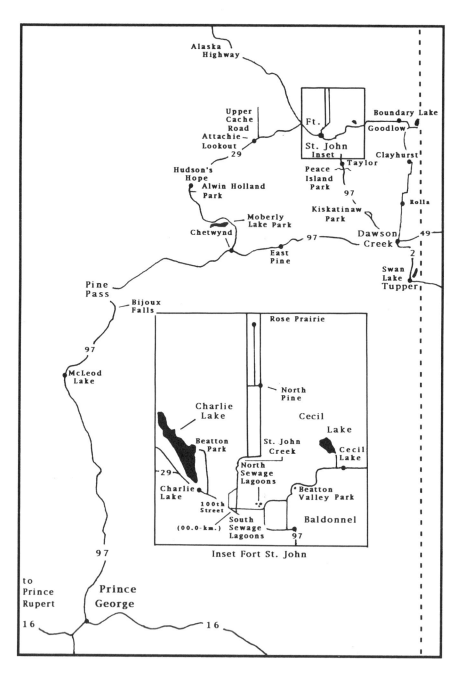

MAP 13 PEACE RIVER PARKLANDS

LOOP 10   PEACE RIVER PARKLANDS

A substantial portion of British Columbia is actually located east of the Rocky Mountain chain (and thus the continental divide), in a bio-geographical location that supports eastern avifauna characteristic of the Peace River region of Alberta. For those birders wishing to see these "eastern" birds, whose breeding distribution terminates just within the boundaries of British Columbia, a trip to the Peace River Parklands is essential. The height of migration times for passerines takes place in spring (May 20-June 1) and autumn (August 18-31), although the best time to visit is probably during late June/early July when all of the eastern specialities are present and the weather is at its finest.

Prince George to Pine Pass and Chetwynd

(00.0km.) Proceed north on Highway 97 from Prince George towards Chetwynd (302 km.) (or 402 kilometers straight through to Dawson Creek). American Dipper are observed regularly along the fast flowing river at Bijoux Falls (185.6 km.), a pleasant provincial picnic site (with washrooms) located on the west side of the highway. After driving an additional (6.2 km.) (191.8 km.) you will reach the summit of Pine Pass.

PINE PASS

Pine Pass, 935 m above sea level, is the lowest pass through the northern Rocky Mountains. It extends for 140 kilometers along Highway 97 North from the Parsnip River to Chetwynd, traversing a wide diversity of habitat. This pass is significant as it is the region where "eastern" and "western" avifauna meet - and where a few "southern" species reach the northern limits of their ranges.

Pine Pass is in a unique geographical location at the convergent zone for, and at the edge of, the range limits of such species as Red-breasted Sapsucker, Yellow-bellied Sapsucker, Dusky Flycatcher, Hammond's Flycatcher, Townsend's Warbler, Black-throated Green Warbler, and MacGillivray's Warbler. In Pine Pass, the ranges of "eastern" species such as Bay-breasted Warbler, Mourning Warbler, Canada Warbler, and Ovenbird terminate, as do "western" species such as Steller's Jay (which are rare further   east). Pacific-slope Flycatcher also occur rarely.

Access to the forest in the lower reaches of the pass is easy and direct from Highway 97 which runs through the valley, but reaching the alpine meadows involves short, but strenuous hikes. The least difficult hiking is from the viewpoint and interest sign east of Azouzetta Lake (3.6 km. from the pass summit) (195.4 km.). Hike up the mountain slopes south of the highway.

Spectacular hiking exists on the Murray Mountain Trail where your horizons will broaden almost beyond comprehension; inquire at the lodge for details, tel. (250) 565-9284. A variety of resident boreal species are found along the Murray Mountain Trail such as Spruce Grouse, Northern Hawk-Owl, and Three-toed Woodpecker; Common Redpoll and Hoary Redpoll occur during the winter months. Rock Ptarmigan and White-tailed Ptarmigan inhabit the highest peaks along with Gray-crowned Rosy Finch, which occasionally feed along the shoulder of the highway in April.

After driving an additional (36.8 km.) (232.2 km.) you will arrive at the Silver Sands Lodge. After an additional (67.3 km.) (299.5 km.) you will see the welcome to Chetwynd sign.

CHETWYND

From Chetwynd you have two choices for reaching Fort St. John and Loop 11, the Alaska Highway Route.

You can proceed east on Highway 97 to Dawson Creek and the start of the Alaska Highway (102.9 km.) then north to Fort St. John (73.7 km.) (a total of 1 76.6 km. to Fort St. John).

Or you can turn north and east along Highway 29 towards Hudson's Hope (62.6 km.) and on to the junction with the Alaska Highway (139.8 km.) (Kilometer 86.4 of the Alaska Highway), then south to Fort St. John (a total of 152.5 km. from Chetwynd to Fort St. John). A loop can be made by first continuing along highway 97, then using Highway 29 as a return loop after birding the Peace River Parklands and/or the Alaskan Highway. For those using the ferry to/from Haines, the choice of which route you take is yours, but the Highway 97 route will produce the best birding opportunities.

First listed is the Highway 29 route, followed with the continuation of the Highway 97 route to Dawson Creek. A short side trip can be made to Moberly Lake from Chetwynd, which is recommended as it is an excellent site.

Undulating along the ridges above the north bank of the Peace River, Highway 29 passes through an astonishingly varied landscape. Northern cottonwoods and white spruce dominate the rich bottomlands in remnants of northern prairie, or "breaks", on the sun-soaked southfacing slopes. Aspen parklands and black spruce muskeg are predominate on the cooler uplands.

Chetwynd to Moberly Lake Provincial Park

Continue on Highway 97 East. At (302.4 km.) (4.9 km. east of Chetwynd you will reach the Highway 97/ 29 junction (00.0 km.). Take Highway 29 North (1 9.3 km.) to the all-weather park entrance road on the left. The park is (3.2 km.) (22.5 km.) down the road, follow the park signs.

MOBERLY LAKE PROVINCIAL PARK

Moberly Lake Provincial Park is located on the southern shore of Moberly Lake. Here birders will find an interesting mixture of habitats, rich in both "eastern" and "western" avifauna. Upslope aspen parkland and white spruce forest dominate the primeval core of the forest with a few black spruce bogs and riparian stands of cottonwood or balsam poplar.

The aspen parklands maintain a healthy population of Least Flycatcher, Ovenbird, Rose-breasted Grosbeak, and White-throated Sparrow. In the boreal forest are Three-toed Woodpecker, Boreal Chickadee, Red-breasted Nuthatch, and Tennessee Warbler. The western montaine forests harbour Hammond's Flycatcher and Varied Thrush. The park is a mandatory place to visit and is one of the better sites for Black-throated Green Warbler in British Columbia. They are fairly common breeding in the conifers and mixed woods in summer. Occasionally Bay-breasted Warbler may be encountered, but their populations fluctuate from year to year. MacGillivray's Warbler is the common Oporornis, but the devilishly elusive Mourning Warbler begins to arrive in the park around June 30 in small numbers.

Moberly Lake Provincial Park to Alwin Holland Regional Park, Hudson's Hope.

Continue north on Highway 29 (00.0 km.), crossing over the Alexander Mackenzie Bridge at (38.5 km.). At (42.3 km.) (61.6 kilometers from Chetwynd) turn right down the gravel road at the sign for Alwin Holland Regional Park which is an additional (0.8 km.).

ALWIN HOLLAND REGIONAL PARK

Alwin Holland Regional Park is a small park dominated by a young aspen forest on the north shore of the Peace River and one of the few easy accesses to the banks of this river. The water-eroded channel, now dry, is a fascinating reminder of a time when the level of the Peace was not controlled by man.

Canada Geese nest offshore on the "teapot rocks", while Violet-green Swallow (uncommon this far east) are found among the Cliff Swallow that nest naturally on the cliffs. A pair of Eastern Phoebe also use the rocks to nest, building on the rock opposite the campground. While perched, the phoebes often pump and spread their tails, a habit that helps to distinguish them from the similar Western Wood-Pewee. An occasional Common Merganser and American Dipper winters along the surging river as far upstream as the north end of the highway bridge, about three and a half kilometers away. A plethora of passerines inhabit the richer forests along the river banks in summer.

Alwin Holland Park to Attachie Lookout

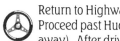 Return to Highway 29 North towards Hudson's Hope (00.0 km.). Proceed past Hudson's Hope towards the Alaska Highway (77.2 km. away). After driving (41.5 km.), you will reach the mouth of the Halfway River which has an undeveloped picnic site. The stand of white spruce and the riparian poplar-aspen forest attract Three-toed Woodpecker and Pileated Woodpecker. American Kestrel often nest in the available tree cavities of old woodpecker nests here. After driving an additional (4.0 km.) (45.5 km.) (108.1 km. from Chetwynd) you will arrive at Attachie Lookout, a rest area on the right side of the road. There is a parking area, toilet, and informative sign displayed by the B.C. Department of Highways.

ATTACHIE LOOKOUT and UPPER CACHE ROAD

Attachie Lookout is a convenient vantage point to view magnificent vistas from high above the Peace River Valley. Far below the large cottonwoods lining the northshore of the Peace River support the huge untidy bulk of a Bald Eagle nest. The landslide upstream from the confluence of the Peace River, visible from the lookout, blocked the river with an estimated ten million cubic yards of over-burden for several hours in May of 1973. Slide debris completely blocked the river channel backing up the river twenty-four feet above normal level. The fields below the lookout attract flocks of Tundra Swan and Canada Geese each spring, which are occasionally joined by a few Greater White-fronted Geese. Orange-crowned Warbler trill from the brushy hillside, while Vesper Sparrow and Clay-colored Sparrow sing in the fields below throughout the summer months.

Drive an additional (0.5 km.) (46.0 km.) east of the Attachie Lookout along Highway 29, turning left onto the Upper Cache Road (or 116th Road). This well-maintained gravel road runs north for thirty kilometers where numerous raptors occur along the roadside, scanning for prey from tree tops and fence posts.

American Kestrel hover over tiny prey items along the upper Cache Road in the ranchiands in summer. Bald Eagle, Northern Harrier, Sharp-shinned Hawk, Red-tailed Hawk, and Rough-legged Hawk (winter) favour the same open country. Resident Golden Eagle soar effortlessly over the mosaic of interconnected rivers and lakes; hidden amongst the extensive coniferous forests below are Northern Goshawk. The ranching country along the road in winter can attract fair numbers of Northern Hawk-Owl during invasion years. Drive the road looking carefully at the tops of isolated trees, particularly around the ranch buildings.

Veery, and the less common Hermit Thrush, are found locally in streamside thickets, whilst breeding Sora lurk quietly in shady recesses in the tangled marsh vegetation. Northern Waterthrush, Swamp Sparrow, Rusty Blackbird, and Common Grackle also frequent the periphery of the suitable wet habitats available at the small ponds dotting the roadside. White-winged Crossbill's harsh "chet" notes are uttered persistently from feeding flocks high in the conifers.

Attachie Lookout, Upper Cache Road to Fort St. John

(00.0km.) Proceed northeast on Highway 29 from Upper Cache Road towards the Alaska Highway (31.2 km. away).

After driving (10.2 km.) (or 164.3 kilometers from Chetwynd) there are four beaver ponds surrounded by tamaracks on the north side of the highway. The extensive marsh spreading out between them supports a remarkable selection of species.

A variety of waterfowl, Sora, Common Snipe, Lincoln's Sparrow, and Swamp Sparrow are annual breeders and migrants. Migrant shorebirds use the pond to feed, species that favour "backwater" fresh water pools such as Lesser Yellowlegs, Solitary Sandpiper, Stilt Sandpiper, and Pectoral Sandpiper are seen regularly. Several species of sparrow sing from exposed perches south of the highway shoulder in the early morning: Vesper Sparrow (uncommon), Savannah Sparrow, Song Sparrow, American Tree Sparrow, Chipping Sparrow, Clay-colored Sparrow, and White-throated Sparrow occur. Each year a tiny population of Mourning Dove use the area as an outpost. Appearing in May and gone by October, these delicate doves are rare this far north. The pond also harbours other characteristic species of this habitat such as Northern Goshawk, Least Flycatcher, Hermit Thrush, Bohemian Waxwing, Rusty Blackbird, and White-winged Crossbill.

En route to the Alaska Highway look for such raptors as Northern Harrier, Red-tailed Hawk, American Kestrel, and Merlin. At the junction with the Alaska Highway (21.0 km.) (31.2 km.) (Kilometer 86.4 of the Alaska Highway), turn right towards Fort St. John, an additional (10.8 km.) (42.0 km.), or left for Charlie Lake Provincial Park and points north.

Chetwynd to Dawson Creek

From Chetwynd, proceed east on Highway 97 for (100.9 km.), turning right (south) for an additional (1.9 km.) along Alaska Avenue (the Alaska Highway) to the Mile 0 cairn (Kilometer 0 cairn) in the Davison Creek city center.

DAWSON CREEK

Dawson Creek is Kilometer 0 of the Alaska Highway and kilometer posts alongside the Alaska Highway mark the distances - measured from Dawson Creek (the old Mile references are often used as well). We will use these kilometerages from Dawson Creek as reference, and a second kilometerage from the last main town en route. It is 1,042 kilometers from Vancouver to Dawson Creek, a further 1,470 kilometers to Whitehorse in the Yukon, 161.5 kilometers from Whitehorse to Haines Junction, and a further 245 kilometers to Haines, Alaska (a total of 2,918.5 kilometers one-way from Vancouver to Haines, Alaska)!

The Mile 0 cairn is also the starting point for Highways 49 East and 2 South, therefore we will start our trips from this point. NOTE: Those wishing to go directly to Boundary Lake can take Highway 49 East for (5.2 km.), turning left (north) onto a paved road that leads fifty kilometers through the towns of Rolla, Doe River, Shearer Dale, and hence across the Peace River towards Clayhurst. There are two different trips that can be made from Dawson Creek. The first is along Highway 2 South towards the British Columbia/Alberta border, and the second is the continuation of Highway 97 North, which now becomes the Alaska Highway beginning with Dawson Creek to Kiskatinaw Provincial Park on page 223. We begin with the route along Highway 2 South.

Dawson Creek to the Tupper area and Swan Lake

(00.0km.) Drive south from the Mile 0 cairn in Dawson Creek along 8th Street (Highway 2) towards the British Columbia/Alberta border which is reached after driving (38.1 km.). Along the highway at (30.7 km.) you will find Sudeten Provincial Park that should produce many of the eastern specialities. After (1.4 km.) (32.1 km.) you will arrive in the tiny hamlet of Tupper and turn left onto the gravel road following the signs to Swan Lake Provincial Park two kilometers away.

SWAN LAKE

Swan Lake has earned its well deserved reputation for providing some of the most exciting birding in the region, a veritable feast of ornithological riches. As the wreaths of early morning mist gradually clear, the woods become alive.

A flash of colour in this green world may signal the presence of one of several species of colourful wood warblers that return to these northern latitudes as winter loosens its grip. Eastern Phoebe, Least Flycatcher, Alder Flycatcher, Black-and-white Warbler, Ovenbird, Northern Waterthrush, Rose-breasted Grosbeak, and Baltimore Oriole are among the eastern specialities nesting at Swan Lake Provincial Park. The lake also serves as a migration stopover for many species of waterfowl with a few remaining to breed.

After birding the park return to Highway 2, turning left. Drive (4.9 km.) (37 km.), turning left onto a narrow road marked "201 " just before crossing the border. Road "201 " crosses a set of railway tracks and continues towards the southeast corner of Swan Lake.

Park off the road where it bends eastward, and walk westward along the cutline through the aspen grove toward the lake. Visible on the left will be wet, grassy meadows leading to the lakeshore. Cross the fenceline and enter these meadows; waterproof boots are a necessity.

Le Conte's Sparrow and Nelson's Sharp-tailed Sparrow breed in various areas of the large meadow that borders the lake. Le Conte's Sparrow prefer the drier grass tussocks containing a few willow shoots that are not standing in water. The rare Nelson's Sharp-tailed Sparrow, which is not annual, prefers a wetter habitat where the vegetation stands in water. Both of these sparrows are mouse-like, skulking through the matted vegetation, but can be easily observed with the aid of a scope as they sing from exposed perches in the early hours. The song of the Sharp-tail resembles the sound made as hot metal is plunged into water - "tesheeeeeeeeee", while the Le Conte's song is a short and buzzy, two syllabled hiss: "zzzz-zzt". American Bittern nervously creep along the water's edge and Black Tern, if present, dip gracefully as they pick up small insects from the surface of the water.

Dawson Creek to Kiskatinaw Provincial Park

For those wishing to drive straight through from Kilometer 0 in Dawson Creek to the 100 Street turnoff in Fort St. John, it is (73.7 km.). (00.0 km.). Kiskatinaw Provincial Park is reached from Kilometer 27.8 of the Alaska Highway, north of Dawson Creek. Turn right off the Alaska Highway (3.3 km. past Farmington) onto the paved loop of the "old" Alaska Highway, following the park signs four kilometers to the park (31.8 km.).

KISKATINAW PROVINCIAL PARK

Kiskatinaw Provincial Park is a small park on the eastern shoreline of the shallow, boulder-strewn Kiskatinaw River. Up river, by the old highway bridge, the river has cut deep into the bank revealing a broad vein of coal. Down stream from the campsite is a grove of white spruce and accompanying avifauna characteristic of the Peace River Parklands. Black-throated Green Warbler has nested in the park.

Kiskatinaw Provincial Park to Peace Island Regional Park and Johnstone Road.

From the park, turn right (north) on the "old" Alaska Highway and right after three kilometers back onto the Alaska Highway North (Highway 97 North) (00.0 km). After driving (20.0 km.) to Kilometer 54.7 km. of the Alaska Highway, turn left off of the Alaska Highway onto an all-weather gravel road just before crossing the long metal Peace River bridge - at Kilometer 55.4 of the Alaska Highway. After an additional (0.8 km.) (20.8.

km.) you will reach Peace Island Regional Park, situated on an island in the Peace River connected to the south shore by a causeway.

Turning off of the Alaska Highway at Kilometer 54.7 would put you on Johnstone Road.

PEACE ISLAND PARK ROAD and REGIONAL PARK

Peace Island Park Road lies along the south side of the Peace River and cuts through attractive mixed woodland where eastern passerines are found most easily in the area of Fort St. John. The region maintains a heathy population of colourful eastern wood warblers, a mandatory site for anyone with a keen interest in seeing a good cross-section of the eastern species.

The park harbours Canada Geese, American Kestrel, Ruffed Grouse, Barred Owl, Northern Saw-whet Owl, Northern Flicker, Yellow-bellied Sapsucker, Downy Woodpecker, Least Flycatcher, Alder Flycatcher, Blue Jay, American Crow, Swainson's Thrush, Red-eyed Vireo, Black-and-white Warbler, Mourning Warbler, Rose-breasted Grosbeak, Song Sparrow, White-throated Sparrow, Fox Sparrow, and Baltimore Oriole during the nesting season. Rarities include Cooper's Hawk, Calliope Hummingbird (has nested), White-breasted Nuthatch, Cape May Warbler, Ovenbird, MacGillivray's Warbler, and Golden-crowned Sparrow. This is the best site in the Peace River Parklands for migrant Philadelphia Vireo and the only site for the rare migrant Gray-cheeked Thrush - found with the plentiful American Robin and Swainson's Thrush flocks attracted to the red osier berries.

Peace Island Road continues past the park to the Taylor ski hill. Along the road Great Gray Owl are rare, but Gray Jay and Boreal Chickadee are quite common. Three-toed Woodpecker are usually present and so inconspicuous that one can pass only a few meters from a feeding bird without noticing it, while Downy Woodpecker, Hairy Woodpecker, and the occasional Pileated Woodpecker are found more easily. Eastern Phoebe are found nesting under the banks of the Pine River north of the ski hill. Tennessee Warbler, Orange-crowned Warbler, Magnolia Warbler, Black-throated Green Warbler, and Canada Warbler are found along the road. In winter watch for Great Horned Owl and feeding flocks of White-winged Crossbill, Common Redpoll, and Hoary Redpoll.

JOHNSTONE ROAD

Turn right onto gravel Johnstone Road off of the Alaska Highway at Kilometer 54.7. Proceed along the winding road as it meanders on benches above the Peace River, eventually skirting its southern bank. As Johnstone road is a private road, and most of the land is private property, stay on the road proper. The first five kilometers pass through aspen groves where many eastern species will be recorded so be sure to arrive early in the morning when the birds are in full-song. During the dawn-chorus you should hear Northern Flicker, Yellow-bellied Sapsucker, Downy Woodpecker, Alder Flycatcher, Blue Jay, House Wren, Swainson's Thrush, Red-eyed Vireo, Ovenbird, Rose-breasted Grosbeak, Clay-colored Sparrow, White-throated Sparrow, and Baltimore Oriole.

Park five kilometers from the highway next to the two large posts, each placed on opposite sides of the road like a gateway. A small woodlot of pines lie to the north and a sawmill to the south. Walk from here as the road gets quite rough.

 As the road dips, it passes through shady riparian woodlands where Barred Owl, Least Flycatcher, Boreal Chickadee, Tennessee Warbler, Black-and-white Warbler (uncommon), Cape May Warbler, Magnolia Warbler, Black-throated Green Warbler, Mourning Warbler, McGillivray's Warbler, Canada Warbler, and American Redstart occur. Scrutinize each Oporornis warbler species carefully as controversial hybrids of Mourning/ McGillivray's Warblers occur here at the overlapping of their ranges. This is one of the better sites for Philadelphia Vireo so check the alders beside the road. Northern Goshawk, Song Sparrow, Dark-eyed Junco, Fox Sparrow, Lincoln's Sparrow, Western Tanager, and Purple Finch are among the more common species characteristic of the boreal forests.

Johnstone Road to Cecil and Boundary Lakes or North Sewage Lagoons

 Retrace your route back to the Alaska Highway North, turning right towards Fort St. John (00.0 km.). After the community of Baldonnel, turn right onto the first paved road (8.6 km.). After an additional (4.1 km.) (12.7 km.) you will meet with 103 Road and you can turn left to the sewage lagoons or continue straight ahead for Cecil (1 4 km.) and Boundary Lakes. (NOTE: We will use downtown Fort St. John as the starting point for this trip).

Johnstone Road to Kilometer 0 in downtown Fort St. John

(00.0km.) Proceed from Johnstone Road, north along the Alaska Highway for (19.0 km.) (Kilometer 73.7 of the Alaska Highway), turning right onto 100th Street (MacKenzie Street) passing the Infocentre en route to 100th Avenue (19.9 km.) - Kilometer 0 for several trips around Fort St. John.

FORT ST. JOHN

Kilometer (00.0) for several trips around Fort St. John begins downtown at the intersection of 100th Avenue and 100th Street. Trip one leads to the North Sewage Lagoons, Cecil and Boundary Lakes; trip two leads northward to

Stoddart Creek, St. John Creek, and North Pine; trip three to the South Sewage Lagoons; and trip four is the continuation of the Alaska Highway route beginning at South Sewage Lagoons to Beatton Provincial Park. We begin with trip one.

Fort St. John to the North Sewage Lagoons

 The North Sewage Lagoons lie northeast of Fort St. John and just northwest of the Fort St. John Airport. If you pass the airport you have gone too far! From Kilometer (00.0) in the centre of Fort St. John (100th Avenue and 100th Street), drive east along paved 100th Avenue which is the main route to the airport. After reaching the outskirts of the city, 100th Avenue becomes 103 Road. Continue east on 103 Road, crossing the B.C. Railway, and after a few blocks begin to proceed through the sharp "S"-curve (approx. 4.8 km.): there is a pond on the right of the curve which is often frequented by Common Grackle. Partway through the "S"-curve, turn left onto gravel 259 Road. Proceed north along 259 Road for (1.5 km.) (6.3 km.) until you see the raised dikes of the lagoons. Park your vehicle next to the gate and walk in.

NORTH SEWAGE LAGOONS

The North Sewage Lagoons consist of a series of five large, shallow ponds that are surrounded by farmers' fields. They harbour the identical species as those at the South Lagoons but the avifauna is more varied and abundant. Check the brush and fields lining the entrance road for Merlin, Sharp-tailed Grouse, Northern Shrike, and various sparrows including Vesper Sparrow, Savannah Sparrow, Song Sparrow, Clay-colored Sparrow, Harris' Sparrow, White-crowned Sparrow, and Lincoln's Sparrow.

Shorebirds are often numerous with many species being well represented. The frequent changes of water levels in the ponds dramatically influences their abundance however. There are four distinctive seasons when the shorebirds migrations are noted: from late April until May 5 look for Hudsonian Godwit; from late May to the first week of June look for Whimbrel, Stilt Sandpiper, and the rare White-rumped Sandpiper and Buff-breasted Sandpiper. Returning juvenile shorebirds begin to arrive in early July, often in the hundreds. In September, the later shorebirds begin to arrive, often this is the best season to record the Asian accidentals: Sharp-tailed Sandpiper, Ruff, and Buff-breasted Sandpiper have been recorded a few times. Lesser Yellowlegs, Red-necked Phalarope, Long-billed Dowitcher, Semipalmated Sandpiper, Least Sandpiper, Baird's Sandpiper, and Pectoral Sandpiper are regular transients, while Killdeer and Spotted Sandpiper remain to breed. Black-bellied Plover, American Golden-Plover, Greater Yellowlegs, Short-billed DovOtcher, Ruddy Turnstone, Sanderling, and Western

Sandpiper occur with less frequency. After mid-October the lagoons will remain empty of shorebirds until next spring.

Around the short grass areas of the lagoons watch for American Pipit, Lapland Longspur (possibly a Smith's Longspur), and Snow Bunting perusing for dropped seed in the fall or early winter. The area is rarely empty of avian shapes with Tundra Swan, Sharp-shinned Hawk, Golden Eagle, Great Horned Owl, and Say's Phoebe on the list of possibilities.

Although the lagoons are subject to dramatic water-level changes and dredging, they are the best site for finding vagrants in the northeast corner of the province. Double-crested Cormorant, Great Blue Heron, Snow Goose, Brant, Wood Duck, Greater Scaup, American Avocet, Sabine's Gull, Cooper's Hawk, and Peregrine Falcon, all local rarities, have been recorded.

North Sewage Lagoons to Cecil Lake

Retrace your route back to 103 Road, turning left (00.0 km.). Drive past the turnoff to the airport (south of road), and continue east until you come to a "T" junction (approx. 5.6 km.). (NOTE: This junction can be reached from the Alaska Highway after birding the Taylor area, hence using the previous directions in reverse to the sewage lagoons). Turn left (north) at the "T" junction onto 103 Road; there is a sign for Cecil Lake. The town of Cecil Lake is fourteen kilometers away.

Soon 103 Road descends into the canyon of the Beatton River, spanned by a one-lane bridge. The narrow floodplain of the Beatton River has two good birding sites in distinctively different habitats, an effect of the varying amount of sunlight that reaches them. The arid and steep south-facing hills that lie north of the undeveloped campsite of Beatton Valley Regional Park and the cool, mixed aspen woods on the shaded south slope of the canyon.

Park your car at the park and return to the bridge, crossing to the cool spruce woods on the opposite side where you should find Least Flycatcher, Black-throated Green Warbler, Canada Warbler, Dark-eyed (Slate-colored) Junco, and Baltimore Oriole. At the park, cross the road and hike up the dry creek bed opposite the park entrance. Here, in the drier slopes, Eastern Phoebe occasionally nest under the shaded banks of the creek. Clay-colored Sparrow and White-throated Sparrow are quite common in the brushy margins.

After leaving the park, proceed east along paved 103 Road, rising out of - and onto - the north rim of the canyon where raptors will be observed in migration during April. After arriving in the tiny hamlet of Cecil Lake (19.9 km.), find the co-op store, turn around, returning back in the direction you came from (towards Fort St. John) for (0.3 km.) (20.2 km.). Turn right (north) onto a one-lane dirt road which is the most accessible public access to the southern end of Cecil Lake itself. If the road is impassable after heavy rains, just proceed on foot, as it is only one kilometer to the lake.

CECIL LAKE

Cecil Lake is a small and shallow lake once situated in an extensive area of wetlands - where drainage has reduced them to scattered remnants. The lake remains as one of the few wet habitats in the region, thus attracting great numbers of waterfowl and wetland species.

A couple of Trumpeter Swan frequent the lake each summer keeping company with the large populations of diving and dabbling ducks. Scrutinize the swans carefully as an occasional Tundra Swan has summered as well. The lake harbours Ruddy Duck, Canvasback, Redhead, Ring-necked Duck, Lesser Scaup, and a very large Eared Grebe colony. Western Grebe, Red-necked Grebe, and Horned Grebe appear as migrants. Greater White-fronted Geese are regular fall migrants from mid-August to early September. Cecil Lake claims the only record of a truly vagrant American Black Duck in B.C.; the others being introduced or wanderers from these introduced birds. Northern Harrier most likely breed at the lake, and Peregrine Falcon are seen on occasion, scanning the numerous ducks looking for a suitable prey-item. Common Grackle feed along the shoreline, their long, keel-shaped tails and pale-yellow eyes are aids in identification of the species.

Check any fallow fields in the vicinity of Cecil Lake for a possible Upland Sandpiper, one of the better locations. As you drive along the sideroads check the tops of the fencepoles and listen for the "wolf whistle" song.

Cecil Lake to Boundary Lake

Retrace your route back to the town of Cecil Lake (00.0 km.). It is (31 km.) from the town of Cecil Lake east along 103 Road to the tiny community of Goodlow. After Goodlow, drive an additional (2.5 km.) (33.5 km.) (52.5 kilometers from the sewage lagoons), where 103 Road turns sharply right (south). To reach Boundary Lake, drive an additional kilometer along the paved southbound stretch of 103 Road, turning left (east) at (approx. 34.5 km.) (before 103 Road becomes gravel) onto an unsigned gravel road. Proceed along the gravel road for (7.0 km.) (41.5 km.), passing the signed and private "Boundary Lake International Airport". This has been the most reliable site for summering Broad-winged Hawk in the province of British Columbia so watch for soaring individuals, or check the surrounding aspen forests.

After an additional (1.0 km.) (42.5 km.) past the airport you will come to a stop sign. Turn left (north) and drive slowly for a few hundred meters looking for a small road on the right that is crossed by a cattle guard. This private road is owned by an oil company and leads a short distance atop a dike to the west or British Columbia side of Boundary Lake - which straddles the B.C./ Alberta border. Although the road is private, anyone can use it but be sure not to interupt traffic by parking well-off the travelled surface. There are two other similar oil-lease dike roads that lead to the western side of the lake.

BOUNDARY LAKE

If you were to continue past these oil-lease sideroads to the north there is a large black spruce muskeg crossed by a maze of roads. Entering this area requires caution, pay close attention to directions as it is easy to get lost! Blackpoll Warbler, Palm Warbler, Fox Sparrow, and Rusty Blackbird breed in the muskeg bogs. Connecticut Warbler is possible, listen for the short series of explosive "whip-ity, whip-ity, whip-ity" notes echoing from the spruce bogs.

The lake supports a large colony of Eared Grebe; with an occasional Pied-billed Grebe occuring as a rare, local summer resident. Western Grebe, Red-necked Grebe, and Horned Grebe appear as regular migrants, as do Greater White-fronted Geese which are fall migrants from mid-August to early September. Ruddy Duck, Canvasback, Redhead, Ring-necked Duck, and Lesser Scaup breed along the marshy shoreline, and a few Yellow-headed Blackbird also use the available reed-fringed shores for nesting. Bald Eagle, Northern Harrier, and Northern Goshawk are regulars, while the odd Peregrine Falcon puts in an appearance.

Migrant shorebirds often feed along the tussocky grass margins of the lake with Black-bellied Plover, American Golden-Plover, and Stilt Sandpiper as less common regulars each fall. Hudsonian Godwit are rare, but regular, spring migrants between late April and mid-May. Ruddy Turnstone and Sharp-tailed Sandpiper are among the rarest shorebirds recorded at the lake.

Boundary Lake harbours a small colony of Black Tern. Examine any Common Tern (which are seen frequently during migrations) carefully as the occasional Forster's Tern has been seen.

The damp meadows between the gas wells and the lake are used by both Le Conte's Sparrow and Nelson's Sharp-tailed Sparrow so listen along the southern-most oil dike road.

Le Conte's Sparrow occurs annually and are the easiest to observe as they sing persistently from their perches on short willow saplings from mid-May to late July. The very rare Nelson's Sharp-tailed Sparrow, which is not annual, is best looked for in late June/early July. This Sharp-tailed Sparrow prefers the wetter habitat of longer grasses closer to the lake, as do the more common Swamp Sparrow which frequent the drowned willow tangles. A good area to look for the Nelson's Sharp-tailed Sparrow and Swamp Sparrow is the line of willows which flanks the diked road just as the road begins to advance across the lake. The locally rare Veery and Black-and-white Warbler, Savannah Sparrow, Clay-colored Sparrow, and Lincoln's

Sparrow also inhabit the willow tangles around the edges of the lake. There is a "heard only" record for the Yellow Rail, which has now been officially added to the provincial list.

Boundary Lake to Clayhurst

Retrace your route back to 103 Road (00.0 km.), turning left (south) along a short stretch of pavement and well-maintained gravel for (15 km.) The road then swinging east for an additional (5.0 km.) (20 km.) to the tiny hamlet of Clayhurst. At Clayhurst a winding gravel road (10 km.) (30 km.) leads south toward the landing where the former (and free) "Clayhurst Ferry" was run by the Department of Highways. At (30 km.) turn left (south) onto pavement and the new bridge over the Peace River (31 km.). NOTE: From this point you could drive south on pavement for fifty kilometers through farmands to Highway 49 on the outskirts of Dawson Creek, turning right for (5.2 km.) to Mile 0.

CLAYHURST

If you proceed west along the gravel road past the turnoff for the bridge (0.5 km.) you will come to Flatrock Creek. Check any of the fallow fields along the road for a possible Upland Sandpiper. The woods on the floodplain along the southern edge of the Peace River, after crossing the bridge - and before climbing the hill, have breeding Mourning Warbler and American Redstart. Although unofficial on the provincial list, a "heard only" record of Yellow Rail exists for the floodplain here. Bird from the road as it climbs up the hill where several eastern species of passerine are to be found. The distinctive short-winged silhouette of a Broad-winged Hawk could be seen soaring over the valley's woodlands.

Return to Kilometer 0 in the core of Fort St. John.

Fort St. John to Stoddart Creek

From Kilometer 0 in downtown Fort St. John, drive north along 100th Street through Fort St. John until you reach the B.C. Railway tracks, turning right (east) onto 146 Road. Proceed an additional (0.5 km.), turning left across the tracks, parking in the Northern Lights Colleges' parking lot.

STODDART CREEK

The forest to the north and east of the college consists of an extensive series of stands of old white spruce, surrounded by aspens. The old white spruce ecological communities are very rare in the region of Fort St. John.

In late spring watch and listen for these species which are subject to population fluctuations: Blue Jay, Philadelphia Vireo (rare), Black-throated Green Warbler, Bay-breasted Warbler (very rare), Cape May Warbler, Connecticut Warbler (rare), and Clay-colored Sparrow. If you miss the Blue Jay, which is very common at this site, drive slowly along 114th Avenue and 112th Avenue in Fort St. John near the 100th Street block where the birds frequent feeders.

Stoddart Creek to St. John Creek

Retrace your route back to 100th Street turning right, proceed north over the railway tracks and the Stoddart Creek bridge which is three kilometers from downtown. You are now on paved 101 Road, a rural continuation of 100th Street which runs eighty kilometers north to Prespatou. About one kilometer past the bridge keep right. Six kilometers north of the Stoddart Creek bridge, the road splits, take the right branch which descends into the valley of St. John Creek (9.5 kms. from Kilometer 0 in downtown Fort St. John).

ST. JOHN CREEK

The valley of St. John Creek can be especially good in the early fall for migrants beginning in mid-August until the end of the month. An old logging road, passable with a passenger vehicle, runs along the south side of the creek west of 101 Road. Three-toed Woodpecker and Black-throated Green Warbler may be found in summer.

St John Creek to North Pine

(00.0km.) Return to 101 Road, driving north up the hill. During the migration period watch overhead for soaring raptors. Once on top of the hill (1.4 km.), turn right onto 112th Road and continue east for (3.5 km.) (4.9 km.), then turn left (north) onto 259 Road. The next twelve kilometers northward towards North Pine is exciting country for several species. North Pine is 24.5 kilometers from downtown Fort St. John.

NORTH PINE

Common Redpoll are frequent in the fall and spring, while Hoary Redpoll can be common at times during the winter months. 259 Road and the roads that intersect from the east and west are productive for such irruptive or periodically common species as Northern Goshawk, Golden Eagle, Sharp-tailed Grouse, Snowy Owl, Northern Hawk-Owl, Northern Shrike, and Pine Grosbeak. If these irruptive species have not invaded the region, the area can be almost birdless.

The flooded fields around 248A and 252 Roads during April and early May attract flocks of Tundra Swan, Trumpeter Swan, Canada Goose, and Northern Pintail. Major movements of migrant Northern Harrier and Rough-legged Hawk, small numbers of Golden Eagle and Bald Eagle, and an occasional Peregrine Falcon are noted on clear days with light winds. Scrutinize the migrant flocks of Lapland Longspur for the rare Smith's Longspur, the odd migrant should move through the area from the Haines breeding grounds.

Return to downtown Fort St. John.

Fort St. John to the South Sewage Lagoons

(00.0km.) From Kilometer 0 in downtown Fort St. John, proceed south on 100th Street to the Alaska Highway, turning left (0.9 km.). Drive south along the Alaska Highway past the Totem Mall (on the left) (approx.4 km.) (4.9 km.), turning right on the first gravel road one kilometer past the mall (5.9 km.). This road is recognized by a large sign that displays two dirt bike racers. Proceed south along the gravel road past the sharp right bend, turning left at the bus company building. This road will lead you past a ball field and on up to the dikes of the lagoons (0.5 km.) (6.4 km.) from the highway.

SOUTH SEWAGE LAGOONS

There are four large settling ponds - attracting ducks and other waterfowl as long as the ponds remain unfrozen. Migrant Tundra Swan, and rare species such as Eurasian Wigeon and Hooded Merganser have occured. A few pairs of Eared Grebe, Mallard, Northern Pintail ' Gadwall, Green-winged Teal, Blue-winged Teal, Northern Shoveler, Canvasback, Lesser Scaup, Common Goldeneye, Barrow's Goldeneye, and Ruddy Duck are found nesting on the ponds.

 In years when the water levels are at optimum height for feeding, shorebirds can occur in numbers. Shorebird numbers, and their predictability, will usually be more reliable at the North Lagoons, however. In the third and fourth weeks of May look for the rare White-rumped Sandpiper among the more common Baird's Sandpiper and Pectoral Sandpiper. Lesser Yellowlegs, Long-billed Dowitcher, Semipalmated Sandpiper, Least Sandpiper, and Red-necked Phalarope are common transients, while Killdeer, Spotted Sandpiper, and Wilson's Phalarope breed. Black-bellied Plover, American Golden-Plover, Hudsonian Godwit, Greater Yellowlegs, Short-billed Dowitcher, Stilt Sandpiper, Ruddy Turnstone, Sanderling, and Western Sandpiper occur with less frequency.

In late May "fall-outs" of migrant passerines fill the weedy margins of the lagoons and the aspen grove to the east. This phenomenon can be staggering, as hundreds of migrants invade the trees. Roving flocks of Blackpoll Warbler and Tennessee Warbler can be present in good numbers. During these invasions there is a good chance that any extra-limital species could appear: a regional rarity in spring - Golden-crowned Sparrow, and in the fall - Harris' Sparrow, have been recorded.

South Sewage Lagoons to Beatton Provincial Park, Charlie Lake

Retrace your route back to the junction of 100th Street and the Alaska Highway (00.0 km.) (Kilometer 73.7 of the Alaska Highway). After driving (5.9 km.) north along the Alaska Highway (from the junction with 100th Street in Fort St. John), turn right off the Alaska Highway onto all-weather 271 Road, following the park signs for 8.8 kilometers to the park (enroute you will turn left at the bottom of a hill at (8.0 km.) to the gate). The turnoff is Kilometer 79.6 of the Alaska Highway.

BEATTON PROVINCIAL PARK, CHARLIE LAKE

Beatton Provincial Park, located on the eastern side of Charlie Lake, has a powerful fascination for birders, offering a rich and diverse eastern avifauna against a backcloth of superb scenery.

The park contains a small grove of old white spruce (an endangered species in the Peace River region) that attracts a few eastern warblers in the breeding season. Migrant passerines are present both in May and again in August through early September. The best season to visit the park is anytime from May to October.

The long cove below the hill and entrance gate is one of the better regions of the lake for waterfowl. Park at the gate and walk to the lakeshore.

Frequenting the lake from late August until November are Red-necked Grebe, Horned Grebe, Eared Grebe, Lesser Scaup, White-winged Scoter, Surf Scoter, and Bufflehead. In October there are Common Loon, Pacific Loon, Red-throated Loon, and Oldsquaw (the latter three are local rarities). Barrow's Goldeneye and Common Goldeneye remain on the lake as long as there is open water. Bonaparte's Gull are abundant around the lakeshore in the late summer months, remaining through to the early fall. Western Grebe, Sabine's Gull, Common Tern, Parasitic Jaeger, Ruddy Turnstone, and Willet are among the rarest species to be recorded on, or around the lake.

After scanning the lake, drive past the boat launching site and campground to the final parking area. A trail leads from the playing field into the alders, then skirts the old stand of white spruce. The trail provides an excellent opportunity to observe some of the eastern warblers, especially in late August when the breeding species are augmented with migrants. Migrants include Black-backed Woodpecker (Sept.- Oct.), Black-and-white Warbler and Townsend's Warbler (mid and late August), Magnolia Warbler, Blackpoll Warbler (most common in May), and rarities such as Philadelphia Vireo, Canada Warbler, and Golden-crowned Sparrow.

 Breeding species include Ruffed Grouse, Great Horned Owl, an occasional Northern Goshawk, Gray Jay, Yellow-bellied Sapsucker, Downy Woodpecker, and Hairy Woodpecker. Look for one or two pairs of Cape May Warbler, one pair of Black-throated Green Warbler annually, and Bay-breasted Warbler (erratic in appearance; absent some years) in the spruces. Baltimore Oriole are found around the grassy picnic area. Other park trails lead into scrubby aspen groves that harbour Ovenbird and Rose-breasted Grosbeak. White-throated Sparrow are abundant, virtually in every habitat throughout the park. Boreal species are also present with Boreal Chickadee, Red-breasted Nuthatch, and Golden-crowned Kinglet. Olive-sided Flycatcher are usually present, along with more common species such as Northern (Yellow shafted) Flicker, Western Wood-Pewee, Eastern Phoebe, Least Flycatcher, and Swainson's Thrush.

Beatton Provincial Park to Charlie Lake Provincial Park

Retrace your route back to Kilometer 79.6 of the Alaska Highway, turning right (00.0 km.). After driving (1.8 km.) you will come to the community of Charlie Lake at Kilometer 81.4 of the Alaska Highway where there is a gas station. After an additional (2.3 km.) (4.1 km.) (10. km. north from the junction of the Alaska Highway and 100th Street in Fort St. John), turn right off the highway at the "Red Barn" pub, following the park signs for Charlie Lake Provincial Park. Proceed along Lakeshore Drive to the south end of Charlie Lake.

CHARLIE LAKE PROVINCIAL PARK

Charlie Lake Provincial Park is noted for its spectacular Arctic migrations and rich assemblage of northern and eastern breeding species.

Charlie Lake has its widest point at the boat ramp, an excellent vantage point to scope the lake for water birds. Common Loon, the locally rare Western Grebe, Horned Grebe, Eared Grebe, Tundra Swan, Trumpeter Swan, Canada Geese, Canvasback, Redhead, Oldsquaw, Common Merganser, and Red-breasted Merganser are attracted to the open azure waters of the lake during the early part of their migration in May. In autumn, especially the months of September and October, Ring-necked Duck, White-winged Scoter, Surf Scoter, and Hooded Merganser join those species that are present in spring.

A trumpeting, rattling "gar-oo-oo" (audible for some distance over the bogs) will announce the presence of the local nesting population of Sandhill Crane. The gray adults are noticably stained with a ferrous solution contained in the mud, transfered to feathers of their back, lower neck, and breast as they preen with muddy bills.

June and July are especially good months for gulls; Bonaparte's Gull arrive during this time in the hundreds. Ten species of gulls have been recorded including a few Sabine's Gull annually since 1982, and the first inland record of Little Gull for the province. Dainty Franklin's Gull, with their rose-tinged breeding dress, will be present in flocks of hundreds, with Ring-billed Gull, Herring Gull, and California Gull occuring regularly in smaller numbers. Rarer gulls, Glaucous Gull and Glaucous-winged Gull should be watched for. Rare inland, Parasitic Jaeger have put in an appearance on the lake a number of times. Common Tern, and an occasional Arctic Tern, are observed during migrations.

In late May, and again from early July, shorebirds begin to appear: Black-bellied Plover, American Golden-Plover, Hudsonian Godwit, Whimbrel, Spotted Sandpiper, Red-necked Phalarope, Long-billed Dowitcher, Ruddy Turnstone, Dunlin, Sanderling, Semipalmated Sandpiper, Least Sandpiper, and Pectoral Sandpiper have all been recorded. The rare White-rumped Sandpiper and Buff-breasted Sandpiper are recorded here on occasion during the fall. During the breeding season, Lesser Yellowlegs, Solitary Sandpiper, and Common Snipe fill the air with their aerial displays.

The deciduous woodlands of the park harbour Ruffed Grouse, Black-capped Chickadee, and White-throated Sparrow, while the spruce forest and accompanying bogs hold Bohemian Waxwing, Tennessee Warbler, Rusty Blackbird, Common Grackle, and Fox Sparrow. A variety of warblers and sparrows pass through in migration (try the woods at the southeast corner of the lake).

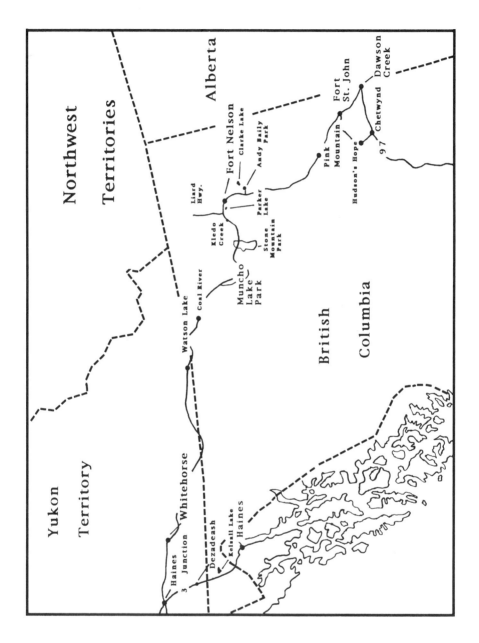

MAP 14   LOOP 11   ALASKA HIGHWAY ROUTE

LOOP 11   ALASKA HIGHWAY ROUTE

Driving distances are great in this region. It is 1,042 kilometers from Vancouver to Dawson Creek and a further 1,470 kilometers along the Alaska Highway to Whitehorse in the Yukon. To reach Haines from Whitehorse is a further 406.5 kilometers: a one-way trip from Vancouver to Haines, Alaska is 2,918.5 kilometers!

 Anyone planning on driving the Alaska Highway should purchase a copy of "The MilePost" (see Suggested Reference Materials). The Department of Transport maintains the Alaska Highway, which is now paved almost throughout its length. The exceptions are well-maintained gravel sections past the Liard Highway near Kiedo Creek (22 km.), between the Liard River and Lower Post (130 km.), and beyond Whitehorse to Haines Junction (48 km.). The Department of Transport has a few maintainance buildings along the highway, which location you should keep in mind as you pass in the case of an emergency. Few facilities are found along the Alaska Highway so be sure to always keep your gas topped-up at each station. As a precaution, carry an extra spare tire, an extra five-gallon can of gasoline, emergency rations, lots of warm clothing, a sleeping bag, and a good deet insect repellent. Boreal Owl can be found along the entire length of the Alaska Highway.

NOTE:Beginning at Fort St. John, we will use the Alaska Highway kilometer posts as reference. (Kilometer 0 of the Alaska Highway begins at Dawson Creek, however). In addition, the first kilometers used will indicate the distance from the last birding site along the Alaska Highway. Example: Pink Mountain to Trutch (90 km.) (323.0 km.); the first kilometerage is the distance between Pink Mountain and Trutch, the second the Alaska Highway kilometerage post.

For those continuing straight through to Fort Nelson from Fort St. John, proceed north on Highway 97 (the Alaska Highway) for 381 kilometers. Fort Nelson is at Kilometer 454.7 of the Alaska Highway.

Charlie Lake Provincial Park, Fort St. John to Pink Mountain

(00.0km.) From Charlie Lake Provincial Park proceed north on the Alaska Highway for (144.5. km.) (152.2 km. north of Fort St. John) to the small community of Pink Mountain at Kilometer 225.9 of the Alaska Highway. The mountain itself lies to the west of the Beatton bridge at Kilometer 232.9. Turn left off the highway following the gravel road for (13 km.), turning right onto a secondary rough gravel road which climbs toward the mountain summit. It is approximately (11 km.) (24 km.) to the summit, much of which is only accessible by fourwheel drive. Ask for directions while getting a local update of the road conditions from any of the several local gas stations. Not far north of the tiny community of Pink Mountain you enter the next time zone - in summer set your clocks back one hour!

PINK MOUNTAIN

Pink Mountain, at an elevation of 1787 m., is an isolated eastern outlier of the Rocky Mountains. This mountain deserves much investigation as its natural history is poorly known. A fire tower on the mountain's summit is usually accessible with a four-wheel vehicle. On the way up the mountain look for Ruffed Grouse at the base and Blue Grouse about halfway. The mountain alpine supports a small population of Rock Ptarmigan, while there are isolated records of both Willow Ptarmigan and White-tailed Ptarmigan. Horned Lark, American Pipit, Bohemian Waxwing, Wilson's Warbler, and Golden-crowned Sparrow also occur.

Pink mountain to Andy Baily Recreational Area

(00.0km.) From Pink Mountain continue north on the Alaska Highway towards Fort Nelson. The Alaska highway descends from the foothills to the lowlands near Trutch, 200 kilometers of the highway passing through an extensive region of low undulating lands of muskeg and black spruce. After driving (200.6 km.), to Kilometer 426.5 of the Alaska Highway, turn right just after crossing Jackfish Creek at the sign for Andy Baily Recreational Area. It is a further (14 km.) of gravel road to the park.

ANDY BAILY RECREATIONAL AREA

Andy Baily Recreational Area is open from May to October. Fort Nelson is a further 30 kilometers away on the Alaska Highway or 44 kilometers from the park. The recreational area has many eastern warblers including Mourning Warbler.

Andy Baily Recreational Area to Clarke Lake

Return to the Alaska Highway, turning right for (20.2 km.). Turn right immediately south of the Husky Gas Station at Kilometer 446.2 of the Alaska Highway, (8.1 km.) south of Fort Nelson. Proceed east along the dirt Mile 295 Road, down a hill, and cross over the Fort Nelson River via a railroad bridge.

CLARKE LAKE

The lake itself cannot be reached, this is the name given to the general area, a region of black spruce and muskeg, crossed by a maze of oil and gas lease roads that continue on for over 130 kilometers.

After crossing the Fort Nelson River, explore either left or right forks of the Mile 295 Road - making sure that you do not interupt the access of other vehicles on the petroleum leased roads. Be careful that you remember your return route as it is easy to get lost! There are no services so be sure to fill your gas tank if you expect to travel far. In wet weather a four-wheel drive vehicle is recommended.

Characteristic species you will find along these roads are: American Kestrel, Hermit Thrush, Swainson's Thrush, Solitary Sandpiper, Greater Yellowlegs, Sandhill Crane, Olive-sided Flycatcher, Bohemian Waxwing, Black-and-white Warbler, Tennessee Warbler, Orange-crowned Warbler, Magnolia Warbler, Connecticut Warbler, Mourning Warbler, Ovenbird, Rusty Blackbird, Common Grackle, Rose-breasted Grosbeak, Savannah Sparrow, Fox Sparrow, and White-throated Sparrow.

FORT NELSON

At Kilometer 454.3 of the Alaska Highway you will enter Fort Nelson, lying in the lee of the Rocky Mountains in a heavily forested region, the "Fort Nelson Lowlands", which are relatively rich in eastern passerines. Fort Nelson's magnificent mixed forests are much older and hence richer than the second-growth aspen groves further south in the Peace River country. The area of lowlands are largely forested with white and black spruce. Trembling aspen forms pure stands on the warm south-facing slopes, especially on the poplar hills from Fort Nelson west to about Kilometer 520 of the Alaska Highway. Balsam poplar is the pioneer tree on river gravels, where it attains a huge size. Black spruce muskegs are abundant, but seldom seen from the road.

This region is the northern limits in the province for the ranges of Broad-winged Hawk, Osprey, Black Tern (breeding), Barred Owl (breeding), Yellow-bellied Flycatcher, Blue-headed Vireo, Philadelphia Vireo, Canada Warbler (breeding), and Rose-breasted Grosbeak breeding), and the southern limit in the province for the ranges of Surf Scoter (breeding), and Rough-legged Hawk (summer). The region is also the western limits for Broad-winged Hawk, Cape May Warbler, Black-throated Green Warbler, Chestnut-sided Warbler (accidental), Bay-breasted Warbler, Connecticut Warbler, Mourning Warbler, Canada Warbler, and Rose-breasted Grosbeak. Approximately 157 species of birds have been recorded below 610 m, including 30 breeding species - with an additional 76 probably breeding.

The Fort Nelson Landfill, including the mixed woods behind the dump, are excellent sites to start your birding in the Fort Nelson area. Herring Gull frequent the dump, there is a Bank Swallow colony, and Canada Warbler breed in the woods. In town, Common Nighthawk feed over the buildings each evening. Western Wood-Pewee, Tree Swallow, and Cliff Swallow nest on the Fort Nelson High School. Close to town are Brewer's

Blackbird, Western Tanager, Purple Finch, Savannah Sparrow, Clay-colored Sparrow, and White-crowned Sparrow, while along the creeks there are Common Raven, American Robin, Varied Thrush, and Mourning Warbler. At the Westend Campground and RV Park at Mile 300.5 at the north end of town, both Bay-breasted Warbler and Connecticut Warbler have been recorded in early July.

FORT NELSON AIRPORT

 One of the easiest sites around Fort Nelson to locate eastern passerines is the Fort Nelson Airport.

Follow the signs from the town core along Airport Road to the airport, ten kilometers north and east of town on paved road. Leave your vehicle in the parking lot and look for the white domed building. A public road running in a north to south direction passes alongside of this building. Walk south along this road, down the hill, and through a mixed forest to the river floodplain. Sharp-shinned Hawk, Three-toed Woodpecker (their works are evident on many trees), Philadelphia Vireo, Canada Warbler, Ovenbird, Mourning Warbler, and Cape May Warbler occur in the woods. The rare Blackburnian Warbler has been recorded. Early July is the best time to "get" the best selection of warblers this far north. In late winter, Boreal Owl can be heard singing around the airports' forests.

Fort Nelson to Watson Lake

The driving distance from Fort Nelson to Watson Lake is 566.7 kilometers, Watson Lake is Kilometer 1,021 of the Alaska Highway.

Fort Nelson to Parker Lake

 (00.0km.) From the center of Fort Nelson, proceed west along the Alaska Highway, turning left onto an unsigned single-lane dirt road (13.3 km.) - Kilometer (467.6 km.) of the Alaska Highway. Proceed south an additional (1.3 km.) (14.6 km.) off the highway to the end of the road.

PARKER LAKE

 Parker Lake is a shallow boreal lake surrounded by muskeg, the muskeg contains a few Yellow-bellied Flycatcher. This well-known colony is easily reached about halfway down the narrow road. The damp sphagnum "bed" is surrounded by stunted birch, alder, willow, and black spruce. From the canopy of white spruce and birch, forming an "island" of taller trees in the midst of the receding muskeg, the liquid and leisurely "chelek" will be heard. Unlike its feisty flycatcher cousins, the Yellow-bellied

Flycatcher personifies the word timid. A scope is necessary to get excellent views as it sits on the tops of the snags. The call is less emphatic than the "chebec" of the Least Flycatcher - and never issued in a series. Another call, a sweet surwee, which is similar to the call of the Semipalmated Plover, could also be heard.

During the spring migration, in May and June, the trees lining the entrance road may teem with warblers including Black-and-white Warbler, Palm Warbler, Blackpoll Warbler, and Magnolia Warbler. From late May through July there are Red-throated Loon, Red-necked Grebe, Horned Grebe, Barrow's Goldeneye, White-winged Scoter, Surf Scoter, Wilson's Phalarope, Sora, Bonaparte's Gull, Black Tern, Common Tern, Northern Shrike, Western Wood-Pewee, Common Yellowthroat, Le Conte's Sparrow, Swamp Sparrow, and Common Grackle. An excellent site for migrants, particularly waterbirds.

Parker Lake to Beaver Lake and Kiedo Creek

(00.0km.) From Parker Lake, proceed north on the Alaska Highway for (15.9 km.), turning right onto the Liard Highway (Highway 77 North) from Kilometer 483.5 of the Alaska Highway. Continue on the well-maintained gravel highway, turning off the highway along the short road to Beaver Lake, which is well-signed (10.0 km.) (25.9 km.). The mixed forest around the lake has several "eastern" warblers. After birding the lake return to the Alaska Highway, turning right and drive twenty-six kilometers along the highway to Kilometer 509.5 and Kledo Creek.

Kiedo Creek

At Kilometer 509.5, (55.2 km. from Fort Nelson), you will find the Kiedo Creek campsite next to the Kledo Creek bridge. A short drive or walk on the road leading south of the highway opposite the campground will bring you to a few gravel pits, passing excellent spruce stands en route along its one kilometer length. The abundant mosquitoes along the road warrant the liberal use of repellent!

In the black spruce muskeg and boreal mixed forest you should find Greater Yellowlegs, Sharp-shinned Hawk, Spruce Grouse, a possible Common Nighthawk in the evening, Varied Thrush, Hermit Thrush, the perky little Least Flycatcher, Dusky Flycatcher, Connecticut Warbler, Canada Warbler, Ovenbird, Palm Warbler, White-winged Crossbill, White-throated Sparrow, Clay-colored Sparrow, Chipping Sparrow, and the resplendent Rose-breasted Grosbeak could be encountered. This is one of the better sites for Cape May Warbler and Bay-breasted Warbler.

At Kilometer 512 of the Alaska Highway (57.7 km. west of Fort Nelson), check the mature aspen forest near Miduski Creek for American Kestrel,

Common Snipe, Pileated Woodpecker, Yellow-bellied Sapsucker, Philadelphia Vireo, Black-and-white Warbler, Orange-crowned Warbler, Magnolia Warbler, Blackpoll Warbler, Ovenbird, Mourning Warbler, Wilson's Warbler, Canada Warbler, American Redstart, Rose-breasted Grosbeak, and Swamp Sparrow.

At the Kilometer 53.8.5 turnout, search the bottomland white spruce forest so typical of the Fort Nelson lowlands. A host of birds return to this harsh but beautiful landscape to take advantage of the short summer.

 Among the migrants, summer residents, and residents you should find Sharp-shinned Hawk, Bald Eagle, Ruffed Grouse, Barred Owl, Belted Kingfisher, Pileated Woodpecker, Three-toed Woodpecker, Western Wood-Pewee, Gray Jay, Boreal Chickadee, American Robin, Varied Thrush, Swainson's Thrush, Golden-crowned Kinglet, Ruby-crowned Kinglet, Bohemian Waxwing, Blue-headed Vireo, Black-and-white Warbler, Orange-crowned Warbler, Yellow Warbler, Magnolia Warbler, Chestnut-sided Warbler (an accidental record), Bay-breasted Warbler, Blackpoll Warbler, Ovenbird, Northern Waterthrush, Mourning Warbler, Wilson's Warbler, American Redstart, Western Tanager, and Rose-breasted Grosbeak.

Kiedo Creek to Stone Mountain Provincial Park

Continue north on the Alaska Highway from Kledo Creek for an additional (87.5 km.) to Mile 392 (Kilometer 597.0) at Summit Lake Lodge.

STONE MOUNTAIN PROVINCIAL PARK

This relatively new park contains some of the most outstanding scenery and wildlife in northern B.C. Stone Mountain Provincial Park is 25,691 hectares of hoodoos, snow-covered rocky peaks, a mosaic of inter-connected rivers and lakes, all creating an awesome panorama across a vast wilderness - a geological wonderland! The highway runs through the northernmost section of the park: within its boundaries are endless hiking and walk-in wilderness campsites. Several trails lead to Summit Lake and to the summit of Summit Peak. Summit Lake Lodge has rooms, a cafe, groceries, and gasoline. Just beyond the pass at Kilometer 605.7 is the Rocky Mountain Lodge with all visitor services.

The alpine can be easily reached by driving south along the seven kilometer long Micro-wave tower road that begins west of the Summit Lake gas station at Kilometer 597.4. After driving (2.5 km.) along the rough gravel road toward the tower (that can be driven without a four-wheel vehicle) you will find the trailhead for Flower Springs Lake Trail.

Along the trail are: Rock Ptarmigan, Gray Jay, Boreal Chickadee, Townsend's Solitaire, Bohemian Waxwing, Magnolia Warbler, Yellow-rumped (Myrtle) Warbler, American Tree Sparrow, Golden-crowned Sparrow, and Pine Grosbeak. Boreal Owl is a distinct possibility. At the Micro-wave tower, an old track leads south through alpine meadows where Rock Ptarmigan and Gray-crowned Rosy Finch are found. If you hike deeper into the hills to higher elevations, look at talus slopes for White-tailed Ptarmigan and in willow thickets for Willow Ptarmigan. Both American Golden-Plover and Lapland Longspur have been observed in breeding plumages during the summer, attesting to the probable nesting in the region.

At Kilometer 597.6 the highway crosses Summit Pass at 1,295 m, the highest point along the Alaska Highway, where there is a campground; dramatic sudden weather changes at this site warrent warm clothing and sleeping gear! The highest mountain towering over the area is Mount St. George at 2,261 m. This is an excellent vantage point along highway to explore the hills for ptarmigan.

Stone Mountain Provincial Park to Watson Lake, Yukon

Continue north along the Alaska Highway to the Kilometer 614 marker, exploring the hillside black spruce forest as you decend from Summit Lake for Ruffed Grouse, Gray Jay, Red-breasted Nuthatch, Brown Creeper, Winter Wren, Varied Thrush, Golden-crowned Kinglet, and Ruby-crowned Kinglet.

A drive straight through to the community of Watson Lake in the Yukon at Kilometer 1,021 of the Alaska Highway from the Summit Lake Lodge is (424 km.). There are several interesting parks en route but none hold any additional species until you reach the Haines Road.

Watson Lake to Whitehorse, Yukon

It is an additional (449 km.) from Watson Lake to Whitehorse at Kilometer 1,470 of the Alaska Highway.

WHITEHORSE

Whitehorse, on the banks of the Yukon River, is by far the largest town in the Yukon Territory. For the birder, Whitehorse is simply an airport and car rental, a convenient means to attain the birding sites along the Haines Road, thus eliminating the long-haul drive from points south.

Whitehorse, Yukon to the Haines Road, British Columbia

* NOTE: There are no maps in the "British Columbia Recreational Atlas" for the Yukon beyond Whitehorse.

 (00.0km.) Proceed west on the Alaska Highway North from the Whitehorse Airport cutoff to Haines Junction, Yukon (161.5 km.)

(Kilometer 1,635.3 of the Alaska Highway). Turn right (south) onto paved Highway 3 toward Haines, Alaska which is (245 km.) away (Highway 3 becomes Highway 7, as you cross the border into Alaska). This relatively short road passes through a unique geographical location, the meeting of the Yukon Territory, the far northwestern corner of the province of British Columbia, and the panhandle of Alaska. As you drive south along Highway 3 you will pass along the eastern perimeter of Kluane National Park.

HAINES ROAD

* NOTE: Groceries, an extra spare tire, and an emergency five-gallon can of gasoline should be purchased before leaving Whitehorse, at Haines Junction, (or at Haines, Alaska if you are coming off the ferry). The last gas station is at Haines Junction until you get to the 33 Mile Roadhouse in Alaska, 190.5 kilometers! The closest hospital and medical service is at Haines Junction. The highway has fairly heavy traffic because of the ferry service, so one does not need to feel isolated. A highway maintenance camp is situated on the west side of the highway southwest of Kelsall Lake - midway through Chilkat Pass. Contact the crew for help or use their telephone in the case of a medical emergency.

The weather can change quickly. A sudden snowstorm in the morning can be transformed into warm sunshine, prompting a mass removal of clothing only hours later. The variable and unseasonable weather here will require winter clothing - a heavy coat, rain wear, and protective waterproof footwear. This is Grizzly Bear country, use caution!

The Haines Road, running between the 59th and 61st degree of North Latitude, passes through three major avifaunal habitats. As you progress southward from the Yukon at mid-elevations, where vast, primeval dark spruce forests have never felt the axe, you will rise in elevation - passing through sub-alpine and alpine - then back down to Haines, lying in wet coastal forest.

As many birders will fly into Whitehorse, we will start our trip at Haines Junction where you should re-start your trip odometer to (00.0).

At (54.4 km.) you reach the old Lake Dezadeash Lodge and camping area.

The first section of the highway passes through spuce forest as you cross from the Yukon Territory into British Columbia at the provincial border sign (48.7 km.) (103.1 km.).

In the taiga, an area of stunted and windswept conifers, and in the surrounding boreal forests and bogs are Northern Goshawk, Spruce Grouse, Boreal Owl, Northern Flicker, Three-toed Woodpecker, Gray Jay, Black-billed Magpie, Common Raven, Boreal Chickadee, Gray-cheeked Thrush, American Robin, Northern Shrike, Bohemian Waxwing, Yellow-rumped (Myrtle) Warbler, Blackpoll Warbler, Common Yellowthroat, Dark-eyed Junco, Fox Sparrow, Lincoln's Sparrow, Rusty Blackbird, Pine Siskin, White-winged Crossbill, and Pine Grosbeak.

After (10.0 km.) (113.1 km.) you will reach the Stanley Creek bridge. From here, over Glacier Flats to Chilkat Pass, the highway crosses silt-laden streams, flowing from the Crestline Glacier. Close to the bridge the highway breaks out into willow shrub-tundra. Willow Ptarmigan are common, their range almost coinciding with the shrub-tundra zone, and American Tree Sparrow and Fox Sparrow breed in summer. Northern Hawk-Owl are frequent visitors in the fall.

After an additional (19.9 km.) (133.0 km.) you cross the Mule Creek culvert, and after (10.0 km.) (143.0 km.), you will reach an area known as "mosquito flats" surrounding Kelsall Lake, one of the better birding sites along the Haines Road. At these high elevations, birders should arrive to coincide with the breeding season, around mid-July. Peak migrations periods are in May, and again in September.

KELSALL LAKE

The most famous site in British Columbia for Arctic breeders is Kelsall Lake, lying in sub-alpine habitat. A host of birds return to the harsh but beautiful tundra landscapes of their birth to take advantage of the short Arctic-like summer.

Common breeding species in the willow thickets, along rivers that have their birthplace high amongst the snowfields, include Wilson's Warbler, American Tree Sparrow, Brewer's (Timberline) Sparrow, White-crowned Sparrow, Golden-crowned Sparrow, and Common Redpoll. Willow Ptarmigan are easily found in the widespread willow habitat in the flats along the upper tributaries of the Tatshenshini River, their strange calls create a most evocative evening chorus as the sun slowly sinks behind the mountains.

There are few crude roads and trails leading off of the highway, one leads to Kelsall Lake. The landscape is covered in many areas with impenetrable brush and willow. Common Loon and Red-throated Loon nest on the lake. Green-winged Teal, American Wigeon, Northern Pintail, Northern Shoveler, Blue-winged Teal, Harlequin Duck, Common Merganser, and Red-breasted Merganser may be seen at various times. At Kelsall Lake is a small localized colony of Bank Swallow, other widespread swallow species can also be observed.

This region is the southern limit of nesting by Wandering Tattler (rare) and Red-necked Phalarope; although unofficial, American Golden-Plover most likely nests. Short-billed Dowitcher and Least Sandpiper also nest on the flats. Breeding Lesser Yellowlegs perch on low hummocks or stunted bushes, noisily proclaiming the presence of intruders, while nesting Semipalmated Plover whistle their distinctive "chu-weet". As you wander across the marshy tundra shorebirds will be everywhere - "tewing" and "trilling" overhead, or flushing suddenly from a newly laid clutch of beautifully patterned eggs: Kilideer, Greater Yellowlegs, Solitary Sandpiper, Spotted Sandpiper, Common Snipe, and Baird's Sandpiper should be among the shorebirds observed in the area.

This region is also the southern breeding limit of the Arctic Tern. Terns plunge-dive into the lake for small fish (or into the hair on your head as you pass by their nests on the gravel bars around Kelsall Lake)! The Tatshenshini River gravel bars, west of the highway at Kelsall Lake, are also used as nest sites for both the Arctic Tern and Wandering Tattler (there is only one nesting record for the tattler, however). These terns have departed by mid-August for their epic journey southward to Antarctica.

Thousands of American Pipit and a few Horned Lark migrate through each spring and fall, while Gray-cheeked Thrush breed fairly commonly throughout the area. Other species frequenting the flats are Short-eared Owl, Say's Phoebe, and Northern Shrike; all are uncommon but seen fairly regularly.

Kelsall Lake is a mandatory site to visit for anyone wishing to see Smith's Longspur in the province. This colourful, uncommon, and highly secretive longspur is seldom seen on migration in British Columbia, passing directly over the Rocky Mountains and hence to the Great Plains. When a rare wayward individual is seen south of this location it is usually of an immature bird during autumn migration in September or October. Smith's Longspur breed in the area, but have departed by late August.

Walk the flats listening for a song suggesting a wheezy Chestnut-sided Warbler: "switoo-whideedeedew, whee-tew". The male Smith's Longspur will be singing from the top of a low, isolated spruce clump. It can best be seen using a scope, unmistakable with the golden breast afire in the low-light of morning.

CHILKAT PASS

Drive south for (4.7 km.) (147.7 km.). The summit of Chilkat Pass at 1,065 m is the highest elevation of the highway; here the wind blows constantly. The views are magnificent! Snow-covered mountains and glaciers dominate the labyrinth of smaller lakes, shallow bogs, and vast expanses of taiga lying below on the subalpine flats. Tundra lies directly alongside the road, a simple step from your vehicle to a hinterland of snow-spattered, flower-strewn, and lichen-dominated alpine meadows.

The Chilkat Pass is one of the most accesssible sites in Canada where all three species of ptarmigan occur: White-tailed Ptarmigan on the wind-swept ridges, Rock Ptarmigan (scarce) on the rocky talus slopes, and the common Willow Ptarmigan below in the lower Wliow patches. Hepburn's race of the Gray-crowned Rosy Finch are seen regularly, present in small numbers. Golden Eagle and Common Raven drift on the winds high overhead. The pass is the southern limit of nesting by the Snow Bunting, which are surprisingly quite uncommon; when found, they favour the lichen-dominated tundra on the slopes.

Two Wandering Tattler nests have been found on tam flats in the St. Elias Mountains near a glacier at the head of Nadahini Creek and along west Nadahini Creek at Chilkat Pass. Walk east from the pass towards the river looking for wide areas of small boulders interspersed with short vegetation.

There are three major routes through the coastal mountains from the Pacific to the interior of the Yukon and eastern Alaska. The Chilkat Pass is the largest and most northerly of these used by birds. Often large numbers of migrants are forced to fly low through the pass when encountering adverse weather. Greater White-fronted Geese are seen migrating through the pass in numbers each fall. Passage migrant Gyrfalcon search for their principal prey - ptarmigan - as they move through constantly in October, the numbers of birds seen would indicate that this species is not endangered. Gyrfalcon also breed and can be seen in June; immatures begin to appear in early August.

From Chilkat Pass, the highway quickly descends toward the Alaska's panhandle border, thirty-one kilometers beyond. After (7.6 km.) (155.3 km.) you will see Three Guardsmen Pass to the northeast, hidden by low hummocks along the road. To the north is the Kusawak Range, to the south is Three Guardsmen Mountain towering at 1,920 m. After an additional (8.7 km.) (164.0 km.) the highway crosses Seltat Creek, watch for Golden Eagle soaring over the uplands.

After (l4.3 km.) (178.3 km.) you arrive at Pleasant Camp where you must stop for Canada Customs and Immigration. The office is open year-round from 8:00 a.m. to midnight, Pacific time. There are no public facilities.

After (0. 5 km.) (178.5 km.) you arrive at the U.S.A./Canada border at Dalton Cache station. After (0.5 km.) (179.0 km.) is the U.S.A. Customs and lmmigrations where you must stop if you are entering Alaska. Open year-round 7:00 a.m. to 11:00 p.m. Alaska time; one hour behind Pacific time as observed in B.C. There are restrooms.

After an additional (11.5 km.) (190.5 km.) you will see the 33 Mile Roadhouse (see introduction to Haines Road for details). At the Chilkat River flats (22.9 km.) (213.4 km.) huge numbers of Bald Eagle come to feed on the spawned-out salmon annually, begining in mid-October through January. Four thousand individuals may gather here, the largest single concentration in the wodd!

After an additional (30.6 km.) (244 km.) you will arrive at the town of Haines, Alaska. In the surrounding wet, coastal forests closer to Haines are Sharp-shinned Hawk, Red-tailed Hawk, Red-breasted Sapsucker,

Hairy Woodpecker, Violet-green Swallow, Steller's Jay, Northwestern Crow, Chestnut-backed Chickadee, Winter Wren, Golden-crowned Kinglet, Ruby-crowned Kinglet, Swainson's Thrush, Hermit Thrush, Varied Thrush, Cedar Waxwing, Orange-crowned Warbler, Yellow-rumped Warbler, Townsend's Warbler, Song Sparrow, Dark-eyed Junco, Fox Sparrow, Pine Siskin, and Red Crossbill. Several coastal specialities such as loons, grebes, sea ducks, gulls, alcids, and "rock" shorebirds are found in the area of the ferry terminal.

NOTES & OBSERVATIONS

NOTES & OBSERVATIONS

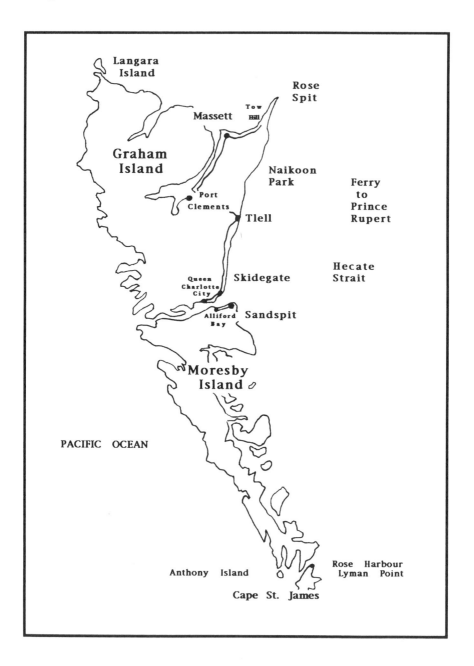

MAP 15   QUEEN CHARLOTTE ISLANDS

LOOP 12   QUEEN CHARLOTTE ISLANDS

The best opportunity to see pelagics is from a ferry aboard the Queen of Prince Rupert which navigates the waters of Hecate Strait between Prince Rupert on the mainland and Skidegate on the Queen Charlotte Islands. The sailing is quite comfortable aboard this well-equipped vessel, presenting a luxurious cruise. On the crossing of 170 kilometers you will be in truly pelagic waters for 100 kilometers of the trip. The trip duration is normally six hours (one-way), however, during winter Hecate Strait is regularly subjected to violent storms with huge swells when the trip could take twenty hours to cross. Both the Prince Rupert B.C. and Alaska Marine ferry terminals are about two kilometers southwest of downtown Prince Rupert.

Also, Vancouver Island Helicopters will take you anywhere you would like to go (weather permitting), possibly the fastest way of "getting" the Horned Puffin (although expensive with fleeting looks).

FERRY CROSSING

Among the common littoral species are Common Loon, Pacific Loon, Red-throated Loon, grebes, cormorants, sea ducks, and alcids. One of the more interesting of the littoral species one could expect to see would be Yellow-billed Loon (regular through winter, late spring, and early summer). Ninty-one breeding colonies of seabirds are directly responsible for the nearly half-a-million pairs of alcids inhabiting the coastline and adjacent pelagic waters.

Marbled Murrelet and Pigeon Guillemot occur closer to shore, with Common Murre and Rhinoceros Auklet encountered anywhere during the crossing. Ancient Murrelet are mainly summer residents, breeding in large colonies along the coast of the Queen Charlotte Islands. They are semi-pelagic feeding in large groups along tide-lines. If the timing of the ferry crossing meets with a group you are assured of seeing hundreds, especially during April, May, and June.

Tufted Puffin breed on Flatrock Island, Anthony Islets, Cape St. James, and Lyman Point; Horned Puffin are seen with Tufted Puffin at Marble Island, Cape St. James, and Kerouard Island, and is known to breed at a small unnamed islet northwest of Anthony Islet. Although the Tufted Puffin is quite common (the Horned is scarce), both of these bizzare puffins are only seen from the ferry on occasion in the fall. There are 158,000 pairs of Cassin's Auklet nesting on the Charlottes, as these alcids feed off the west coast of the islands they are infrequently observed from the ferry. Black-legged Kittiwake, as well as being in pelagic waters, are common in waters closer to the Queen Charlotte Archipelago.

The more frequently seen pelagic species that occur throughout the year are Sooty Shearwater (mainly mid-April-December), Fork-tailed Storm-Petrel (mainly mid-March-November), and Northern Fulmar (mainly October-February). In the summer months Sooty Shearwater are present in thousands and dozens of Fork-tailed Petrel will be encountered. Northern Fulmar are seen irregularly, mainly in the fall, and sometimes in numbers. Short-tailed Shearwater may occur throughout the year, the most reliable site in Canada for this species. They occur in concentrations irregularly in spring and again in August through late October; and with small numbers throughout the winter months. The difficulty of separation between Short-tailed Shearwater and Sooty Shearwater leaves the status of this species in doubt (the difficulty of identification should never be underestimated!).

Other pelagic species that are seen occasionally are: Pink-footed Shearwater and Leach's Storm-Petrel (50% chance), Buller's Shearwater (20% chance), and Flesh-footed Shearwater (1%). Pink-footed Shearwater occurs in mid-April through mid-October, while Flesh-footed Shearwater occur in early May through mid-October. Buller's Shearwater is rare during the months of late June through August and again in early November. It is most likely to be seen from the ferry during the time period of mid-September to mid-October when it is most common off the B.C. coast. Leach's Storm-Petrel usually occurs far-offshore; rare in the months of February, March and April, it could be seen off the ferry from late April through November, but is most likely in the months of June through mid-October.

Red Phalarope, Red-necked Phalarope, South Polar Skua (rare), Pomarine Jaeger, Parasitic Jaeger, Long-tailed Jaeger (rare), Sabine's Gull (regular), and Arctic Tern (rare) are other pelagic species that you have a good chance of seeing in season (see Checklist and Bargraphs for status and months).

There have been comparatively few crossings of the Queen of Prince Rupert with birders aboard that others could certainly make exciting discoveries. Black-footed Albatross, Laysan Albatross, Mottled Petrel, Common Eider, Red-legged Kittiwake, Aleutian Tern (three records for the Charlottes: May 25-June 6), Thick-billed Murre, Kittlitz's Murrelet, Parakeet Auklet, and Horned Puffin are among the realistic possibilities with the proximity of Alaskan waters. Xantus' Murrelet has been recorded once in nearby waters, 57 miles off Moresby Island in the Queen Charlotte Sound, and Parakeet Auklet well-off the southern tip of the islands. Although summer provides the birder more comfort, easy viewing, and a short-list of reliable pelagics, winter could be most exciting, with the best chance of seeing an Alaskan rarity.

Horned Puffin

For Canada listers, the paramount interest lies with observing one specific species: the Horned Puffin which has rare breeding status on the Queen Charlotte Islands. Boats may be chartered to visit the seabird colonies, in particular to see the exotic and very local Horned Puffin and the more common Tufted Puffin. The Horned Puffin are scarce, but are dependable at the Tufted Puffin colonies. The murrelets and auklets are easy to see around their colonies early in May through July, while the petrels are seen during the same time period off their colonial burrows each night.

NOTE: If you plan on renting your ownboat to see the puffins, be aware that the seas are unpredictable and unforgiving and that several of the ninty-one seabird colonies are also ecological reserves; special permission and a permit are required to visit them. Write: Director, Ecological Reserves Unit, Ministry of Lands, Parks and Housing, B.C. Provincial Government, Victoria, B.C. V8V lX4.

THE ISLANDS

Wild. Mysterious. Primordial. The rain-drenched Queen Charlotte Archipelago harbours cathedral-like forests containing ancient giants, their huge limbs festooned with exquisite epiphytic mosses and ferns; her rugged wind-swept islands, stark mountain ranges, and savage coastlines, shrouded in rain and mist for most of the year - all are enhanced by the peculiar quality of the light, which lends an ethereal beauty to the landscape.

The Queen Charlotte Archipelago, lying about 70 kilometers off the northwest coast of the mainland and 50 kilometers south of the panhandle of Alaska, consists of some 154 scattered islands stretching like an upside down triangle for 270 kilometers. Essentially still a region of wilderness, the two main islands, Graham to the north, Morseby to the south, are separated by narrow Skidegate Channel. The ocean is filled with smaller scattered islands varying in size from the larger Louise and Lyell Islands, to chains of tide-washed rocks. The Charlottes are warmed by an ocean current originating off Japan and hit with 225 cm. of rain annually. Running like a spine along the western side of the islands, the Queen Charlotte and San Christoval ranges effectively cast a rain shadow, protecting the east side from much of the Pacific onslaught. The east coast, where most of the villages are located, still receives a wet 127 cm. annually.

The best time to visit the islands is July through September, when there are fewer storms - but always be prepared for the erratic weather - sunny and calm one moment, howling winds and terrential rains the next. June and July are the best months to visit for the Horned Puffin, while autumn anti-cyclonic low pressure systems bring the best chance for Asian vagrants.

The ninty-one seabird colonies around the islands support nearly half a million pairs of breeding Leach's Storm-Petrel, Fork-tailed Storm-petrel, Pelagic Cormorant, Glaucous-winged Gull, Common Murre, Pigeon Guillemot, Ancient Murrelet, Cassin's Auklet, Rhinoceros Auklet, a few Horned Puffin, and Tufted Puffin. Marbled Murrelet most likely breed in fair numbers.

A legendary raptor breeds on the Queen Charlottes Islands in greater numbers than anywhere else in the world, where the steep shores are the last stronghold of the magnificent Peregrine Falcon. A recent survey of southern Moresby Island suggested that this relatively small area, with sixty-three nest sites (some in trees!), contained one-third of British Columbia's total population. Langara Island, a small isolated island and the northwesternmost island in the archipelago, claims a few aeries.

Peregrine nest on Cox Island on the southeast side of Langara, and at the south end of Langara, north of the Indian village of Dadens. The dark Peale's sub-species relies upon the numerous seabird colonies as their principal prey, the alcids constantly moving just offshore present an opportunistic food-source.

Bald Eagle are abundant residents on the islands, and always impressive and spectacular to any visiting birder. The sight of dozens of eagles fishing for herring at spawning season is awe-inspiring. There are over one hundred and forty nests on the east coast of Moresby Island alone, and they possibly number in the thousands in total.

Darker sub-species of the Northern Saw-whet Owl (Aegolius acadicus brooksi) and Hairy Woodpecker (Picoides villosus picoides) evolved on, and remain restricted to these isolated islands. A sub-species of Sharp-shinned Hawk (Accipiter striatus perobscurus), is known only to nest on the Charlottes, while darker coastal races of Steller's Jay and Pine Grosbeak also occur.

SANDSPIT

The Charlottes are to Canada, as the Aleutian island of Attu is to the United States, a fantasyland for listers. Vagrants with names to entice the mind of any birder: Short-tailed Albatross, Mottled Petrel, Magnificent Frigatebird, Red-faced Cormorant, Steller's Eider, Mongolian Plover, Red-legged Kittiwake, Aleutian Tern, Xantus' Murrelet, Sky Lark, Red-throated Pipit, Yellow Wagtail, Rustic Bunting, and Great-tailed Grackle. A hypothetical record of Black-tailed Gull exists. Lesser rarities include Great Egret, Emperor Goose, Snowy Plover, Bar-tailed Godwit, Curlew Sandpiper, and Brambling.

Small navigators make big mistakes - birders have learned that they can intercept some of these strays by positioning themselves at strategic points for the everpresent possibility of seeing these vagrants - Sandspit is one of these places. These islands have been poorly birded. A visitor to Sandspit in the fall has an excellent chance of seeing a new Asian extralimital for their Canadian list. Prediction of weather conditions, and consequent vagrant occurrence, is very difficult to predict.

For example during the autumn of 1991 several dramatic anti-cyclonic low pressure systems, originating in the Gulf of Alaska, produced perfect conditions to push migrants that would have normally proceeded eastward toward Asia - southward toward the Charlottes. That year did not only create the perfect weather for vagrant dispersal, but two experienced birders just happened to be visiting to intercept them. That year a Steller's Eider, Red-legged Kittiwake (beach-washed specimen), Sky Lark (a true Asian vagrant, not one of the introduced birds from the Saanich Peninsula), Yellow Wagtail, and several Red-throated Pipit were discovered.

The Sandspit Airport rests on a large grassy spit. The open, short grasslands and fields of the airport proper, once farmlands, attract migrant shorebirds such as Whimbrel; such extreme rarities as Upland Sandpiper and Buff-breasted Sandpiper are possible.

The wide tidal flats surrounding the spit harbour migrating shorebirds: Semipalmated Plover, Killdeer, Black-bellied Plover, American and Pacific Golden Plover, Greater Yellowlegs, Lesser Yellowlegs, Spotted Sandpiper, Short-billed Dowitcher, Red Knot (rare), Dunlin, Western Sandpiper, Least Sandpiper, and Pectoral Sandpiper. Thousands of Black Turnstones can be seen in the fall some years, in others they are rare or absent. A few Ruddy Turnstone are found in these flocks, mainly in the fall. There are single records of Snowy Plover, Bar-tailed Godwit, and Ruff for the spit.

A flock of Brant regularly makes the spit winter home, while Emperor Geese occur with some frequency; recorded almost annually during the past few winters. Franklin's Gull, Western Gull, and Caspian Tern are among the rarer gulls and terns that have been recorded on the islands and are possible here. Ring-billed Gull and California Gull are infrequent visitors at the spit during June and July.

As you walk the beach driftline amongst the beached logs and cast up seaweed, expect the unexpected. Brambling have been recorded a few times foraging along the shoreline, with up to five individuals in one flock.

Sandspit to Skidegate Inlet and hence terry to Skidegate

(00.0km.) From Sandspit Airport drive south on paved road to the small community of Alliford Bay (12.5 km.). Catch the ferry, crossing Skidegate Inlet to the town of Skidegate.

SKIDEGATE INLET

Located between Graham and Moresby Islands, Skidegate Inlet can be very picturesque with colourful homes perched on its south facing slopes above sheltered bays and small islets. Scan the sheltered waters from both sides (or from the ferry as you cross) for seabirds throughout the year.

Pelagic Cormorant, Black Oystercatcher, Glaucous-winged Gull, Pigeon Guillemot, and Northwestern Crow are abundant residents. Common Loon, Western Grebe, Red-necked Grebe, Brant, Greater Scaup, White-winged Scoter, Surf Scoter, Common Goldeneye, Bufflehead, and Common Murre are seen abundantly in winter. Black Turnstone, Rock Sandpiper, and Dunlin are found along the rocky shoreline in winter. As many as 160 individual Rock Sandpiper can be found around the inlet, certainly one of the few places concentrations of this size are known to occur. Surfbird are common migrants but rather uncommon during the winter months. Wandering Tattler teeter among the rocks during migration, especially in the more wave-washed regions of the shoreline. Bonaparte's Gull, Mew Gull, Herring Gull, Thayer's Gull, Glaucous Gull, and Glaucous-winged Gull are expected in season. European Starlings are common residents around town.

Skidegate to Tlell

(00.0km.) Proceed north on Highway 16 to Tlell (42 km.).

TLELL

Naikoon Park Headquarters are situated in Tlell. Situated at the south end of Naikoon Provincial Park, the mouth of the Tlell River is an excellent site for migrant shorebirds. The endless rolling sand dunes along the beautiful beach and accompanying spruce forest behind the dunes are worth exploration. During spring migration it is not unusual to see flocks of thousands of loons, grebes, geese, scaup, and scoters as they rush northward to claim their nesting territories.

Tlell to Port Clements

Proceed north on Highway 16 to the small community of Port Clements (21 km.) (63 km.). Turn left onto the main logging road leading south out of the town for (2.5 km.) (65.5 km.) to the mouth of the Yakoun River.

PORT CLEMENTS

The Yakoun, the largest river of the islands, forms a large estuary at the southern end of Masset Inlet, a major site for wintering waterfowl.

Thousands of waterfowl, mainly Trumpeter Swan, Canada Geese, Mallard, Green-winged Teal, American Wigeon, and Northern Pintail seek refuge each year. Along the Yakoun are a few stands of mature forest where giants still stand. Common Merganser breed along the calm sections of the river. The main logging road leading south from Port Clements branches into a maze of secondary logging roads. These well-maintained gravel roads give access to second-growth forests in the interior of Graham Island, where characteristic humid maritime forest avifauna will be found. Northern Saw-whet Owl frequent the moist regions around small lakes. Pacific-slope Flycatcher, Swainson's Thrush, and Wilson's Warbler are located in brushy deciduous patches. Blue Grouse, Brown Creeper, Red-breasted Nuthatch, Townsend's Warbler, and Dark-eyed Junco prefer the driest conifers on the southeast slopes, with Hairy Woodpecker, Steller's Jay, Chestnut-sided Chickadee, Winter Wren, Golden-crowned Kinglet, Hermit Thrush, Varied Thrush, Fox Sparrow, Red Crossbill, and the odd Pine Grosbeak in wetter regions. On the faster streams, regal pairs of Harlequin Duck ride the rapids and American Dipper teeter endlessly. Gravel bars are peppered with dozens of Bald Eagle.

Port Clements to Delkatia Wildlife Sanctuary, Masset

(00.0km.) Proceed north on Highway 16 to Masset (45 km.) (108 km. from Skidegate). After crossing Delkatla Inlet into Masset, continue along Hodges Avenue, then turn right onto Trumpeter Drive. The road follows the inlet, and several short walking trails meander along the shore. To see more of the sanctuary, drive along Tow Hill Road toward Naikoon Provincial Park, turning left at the sanctuary sign on Masset Cemetery Road (To reach Tow Hill Road, return along Highway 16 South from Masset for about one kilometer, turning left (east) for an additional kilometer to Masset Cemetery Road).

Bird Walk Trail is signposted off the road, then further along Masset Cemetery Road, stop at Simpson Viewing Tower. A trail leads through a wide open meadow and marshes dotted with wild-flowers to the tower.

Continue along Masset Cemetary Hill Road to the parking area and a trail to the beach. Common Loon, Red-throated Loon, Red-necked Grebe, Pelagic Cormorant, Black Scoter, White-winged Scoter, Surf Scoter, Harlequin Duck, Oldsquaw, Red-breasted Merganser, Sanderling, Mew Gull, Herring Gull, and Glaucous-winged Gull are found in season

DELKATLA WILDLIFE SANCTUARY

 Delkatia Wildlife Sanctuary, lying within the town limits of Masset, continues as an important staging area for migrants.

Flocks of hundreds or even thousands of Greater White-fronted Geese and Sandhill Crane use the sanctuary as a stopping-off point as they cross the Pacific on their long-haul migration to-or-from Alaska. The Greater White-fronted Geese arrive in mid-April on their spring migrations.

Delkatia Slough has a wide variety of habitat including grassy fields, wet coastal forest, sandy beaches, and salt flats; thus attracting a myriad of avian possibilities. In spring, Bufflehead and Common Goldeneye begin their courting behavior, while other waterfowl that have overwintered begin nesting or preparing for their long-flights: Trumpeter Swan, Canada Geese, Mallard, Green-winged Teal, American Wigeon, Northern Pintail, Northern Shoveler, Canvasback, Greater Scaup, and Common Merganser. Blue-winged Teal and Cinnamon Teal occur during migrations.

Migrant shorebirds include Semipalmated Plover, Killdeer (breeds), Black-bellied Plover, American and Pacific Golden-Plover, Whimbrel, Greater Yellowlegs, Lesser Yellowlegs, Spotted Sandpiper (breeds), Short-billed Dowitcher, Long-billed Dowitcher, Common Snipe, Dunlin, Western Sandpiper, and Least Sandpiper. Scrutinize the shorebirds carefully for the rare Sharp-tailed Sandpiper as it has been recorded among the more common Pectoral Sandpiper. Marbled Godwit, Solitary Sandpiper, Stilt Sandpiper, Red Knot, Semipalmated Sandpiper, and Baird's Sandpiper are all possible rare migrants; there is a single record of Ruff. Rocky stretches around Masset will produce the extremely common resident Black Oystercatcher.

Bald Eagle, Northern Harrier, Sharp-shinned Hawk, Red-tailed Hawk, and Peregrine Falcon hunt over the slough and adjacent woods. Short-eared Owl use the grassy sections as refuge during migration in October, while Snowy Owl are occasionally present, perched on logs along the driftline in winter.

Great Blue Heron, Mew Gull, Glaucous-winged Gull, and Northwestern Crow are abundant residents around the slough. Belted Kingfisher, Northern Flicker, Red-breasted Sapsucker, Hairy Woodpecker, Steller's Jay, Common Raven, Chestnut-backed Chickadee, Winter Wren, Golden-crowned Kinglet, Varied Thrush, European Starling, Song Sparrow, Dark-eyed Junco, Pine Siskin, and Red Crossbill are resident, while Rufous Hummingbird, Pacific-slope Flycatcher, Tree Swallow, Barn Swallow, Hermit Thrush, American Robin, American Pipit, Orange-crowned Warbler, Townsend's Warbler, Savannah Sparrow, White-crowned Sparrow, Golden-crowned Sparrow, Fox Sparrow, and Lincoln's Sparrow occur each summer. Lapland Longspur is a rare migrant in the grassy areas adjacent to the slough.

Delkatia Wildlife Sanctuary to Naikoon Provincial Park

From Masset, one of the most beautiful areas to visit is Agate Beach and Tow Hill in Naikoon Provincial Park. We begin this trip from the junction of Tow Hill Road, one kilometer south of Masset on Highway 16 (00.0 km.). The trip along Tow Hill Road takes you through kilometer after kilometer of moss-draped trees. En route you will first pass Masset Cemetery Road on the left after one kilometer. Proceed along Tow Hill Road pass the municipal campground, the site of the future Masset Municipal Airport, and Naikoon Park Motel. Just after the motel you will enter Naikoon Provincial Park (9.0 km.), after an additional (5.5 km.) (14.5 km.) you will arrive at the beach campground. Soon after the campsites is the begining of a long beach strewn with shiny, smooth, sea-worn pebbles and driftwood, separated from the road by the Chown River. After crossing the Sangan River (1.5km.) (16.0 km.), gravel surface begins. The road ends at Tow Hill (9.0km.) (25.0 km.). It is a further fifteen kilometer walk to the end of Rose Spit.

NAIKOON PROVINCIAL PARK and ROSE SPIT

The spectacular Naikoon Provincial Park lies along the eastern shore of Hecate Strait and encompasses 707 km., preserving a large block of lowland wilderness on the northeasternmost coast of Graham Island. Within the park are ninty-seven kilometers of endless sandy beaches with driftwood zones and rolling, grassy dunes and areas of low muskeg surrounded by stunted lodgepole pine, red and yellow cedar, western hemlock, and sitka spruce.

At Tow Hill, a trail leads to the top of almost-vertical cliffs rising from the beach, massive seastacks and surrounding headlands are pounded by the relentless surf. Peregrine Falcon hunt seabirds, their principal prey on these islands, from the high vantage point of the lookout. The ground and many of the trees at Tow Hill are completely cushioned in spongy yellow moss. Hiellen Riverside Trail leads through the sombre forests made more mystical by the ethereal piercing notes of Varied Thrush. Characteristic birds of wet maritime forests are found such as Red-breasted Sapsucker, Hairy Woodpecker, Steller's Jay, Chestnut-backed Chickadee, Winter Wren, Golden-crowned Kinglet, Hermit Thrush, Varied Thrush, Fox Sparrow, Red Crossbill, and Pine Siskin.

Rose Spit is a five kilometer point of land at the northeastemmost tip of the park, jutting between Dixon Entrance and Hecate Strait. This spit projects well into the surrounding sea, thus collecting passing migrants, especially shorebirds. Rose Spit is an excellent site to observe these migrations and possibly to see seabirds from the outermost tip on windy days. Gyrfalcon has been recorded, resting on the drift logs.

To reach Rose Spit requires a full day's hike from the end of the road at Tow Hill, a round-trip of thirty kilometers! The shoreline from Masset, east to

Rose Spit, and south to Tlell, is sand beach that stretches as far as the eye can see; thus the walk is on hard-packed sand. If you find the length of the walk daunting, just imagine the vagrants that could occur at the end of the spit. Along the walk, check the muskeg regions in the centre of the spit. You may find breeding Common Loon, Red-throated Loon, Sandhill Crane, Semipalmated Plover, Short-billed Dowitcher, Common Snipe, and Least Sandpiper.

Here we end our wonderful birding journey through British Columbia.

NOTES & OBSERVATIONS

NOTES & OBSERVATIONS

CHECKLIST AND BAR-GRAPHS

The following is a complete checklist of the birds occurring in British Columbia as of January 1998; a total of 470, plus 9 hypotheticals and 2 extinct species. A quick inspection of the following bar-graphs (along with the colour-coded range maps in the National Geographic's "Field Guide to Birds of North America" showing the seasonal distribution of birds) will give you all of the information of seasonal occurrence and relative abundance of the avifauna for British Columbia. As it is not possible to indicate all of the small seasonal arrival and departure dates that can, and do, occur throughout a province as vast as British Columbia (arrival and departure dates are for the southern province), the checklist and bar-graphs note only the four regions that birders will need to visit to see all of B.C.'s birds.

HOW TO USE THE BAR-GRAPHS

The first step is to consult your National Geographic "Field Guide to Birds of North America", whose maps will show which species range in the sector of the province you are birding and if they occur in summer, winter, or as a resident. If you are interested as to the exact arrival and departure dates consult the last page number in the index for the page number of that species in the checklist. Listed under Species in the checklist * indicates that the species nests in the province.

The next four columns represent the province as divided into four equal sectors with the status centered at 1) Vancouver-Victoria, 2) Okanagan Valley, 3) Peace River Parklands-Fort Nelson, and 4) Boreal Forest-Haines Road. Extra-limital records, however, are noted from the general sectors. Each of these four columns is divided into spring, summer, fall, and winter. A - represents that the species is rare at that season, a i uncommon, a l common. A - represents an extra-limital or accidental species.

The next twelve columns represent the calendar year. The varying widths of bar-graphs show the exact seasonal occurrence (arrival and departure dates for migrants) and relative abundance of the species as a whole throughout the proance and/or the status of that species in its usual range in the proance — check in the first four columns for the species seasonal status and relative abundance in the region you are birding.

BRITISH COLUMBIA CHECKLIST

Species	1	2	3	4	J	F	M	A	M	J	J	A	S	O	N	D
Common Loon*																
Yellow-billed Loon		••••	•	••												
Pacific Loon*																
Red-throated Loon*																
Western Grebe*																
Clark's Grebe																
Red-necked Grebe*																
Horned Grebe*																
Eared Grebe*																
Pied-billed Grebe*																
Short-tailed Albatross (acc)	•								•							
Black-footed Albatross																
Laysan Albatross																
Northern Fulmar																
Flesh-footed Shearwater																
Sooty Shearwater																
Short-tailed Shearwater																
Pink-footed Shearwater																
Streaked Shearwater (hypo)	•											•				
Buller's Shearwater																
Black-vented Shearwater (acc)	•••					•					••	•	••		•	•
Mottled Petrel (R)	• •					•			••							
Leach's Storm-Petrel*																
Fork-tailed Storm-Petrel*																
Magnificent Frigatebird (acc)	•							••				•				
Red-tailed Tropicbird (acc)	•									•						
American White Pelican*				••	•											
Brown Pelican																
Double-crested Cormorant*				••	•••											
Brandt's Cormorant*																
Pelagic Cormorant*																
Red-faced Cormorant (acc)	•							•								

Species	1	2	3	4	J	F	M	A	M	J	J	A	S	O	N	D
Least Bittern (acc)	•	•									•	•				
American Bittern*	‖‖‖	‖‖	‖													
Black-crowned Night-Heron*	....	...			..	..	..	..	..	..	..	..	..	..	..	..
Green-backed Heron*	‖.	••			..	..	..	—						..	..	..
Little Blue Heron (acc)	••				•									••	••	••
Cattle Egret	. ‖.	...	•		..		..	..	•	..			•	.	——	..
Snowy Egret (R)	•••						•	••				•	•		•	
Great Egret	....	••			•		..	..	..	..	..	..	..	..		..
Great Blue Heron*	‖‖‖‖		..	•	▬	▬	▬	▬	▬	▬	▬	▬	▬	▬	▬	▬
Wood Stork (acc)	•												•			
White-faced Ibis	•••	••			••	••	••	••	••	••	•		•		••	••	•• ••
Sandhill Crane*	‖.‖	‖‖	‖‖	...	..	..	—▬—	▬			.	▬	—		
Whooping Crane (sight records)			• •				•				•		
Tundra Swan	.‖‖	‖‖‖	.	‖	▬	—▬—	.	..	..	..	—▬—	▬	
Trumpeter Swan*	.‖	. ..	‖‖	‖	▬	▬	▬							▬	▬	▬
Mute Swan* (I)	‖‖	....			▬	▬	▬	▬	▬	▬	▬	▬	▬	▬	▬	▬
Greater White-fronted Goose	.‖.‖.‖.	.‖			▬	.	..	..	..	▬	
Snow Goose	.‖.‖.	.‖.	...	. .	▬	..	..	..	.	▬	
Ross' Goose	. .....	•			..	..	..	..	•			..	..	..	..	..
Emperor Goose	. ..				..	..	..	..						..	..	
Canada Goose*	‖‖‖‖‖	.	‖‖‖	▬	▬	▬	▬	▬	▬	▬	▬	▬	▬	▬	▬
Brant	...	....	•		..	..	▬	▬	..	..	..	..	..	..	..	..
Mallard*	‖‖‖‖‖	‖‖.	▬	▬	▬	▬	▬	▬	▬	▬	▬	▬	▬	▬
American Black Duck* (I)	‖‖	•														
Gadwall*	.‖‖‖‖	...	▬	▬	▬	▬	▬	▬	▬	▬	▬	▬	▬	▬
Green-winged Teal*	‖‖‖‖.	‖	▬	▬	▬	▬	▬	▬	▬	▬	▬	▬	▬	▬
Baikal Teal (acc)	•														•	
American Wigeon*	‖‖‖‖‖	‖	▬	▬	▬	▬	▬	▬	▬	▬	▬	▬	▬	▬
Eurasian Wigeon	.‖‖	....	.		—	.	..			..		.	.—
Northern Pintail*	.‖‖‖‖‖	‖	▬	▬	▬	▬	▬	▬	▬	▬	▬	▬	▬	▬
Northern Shoveler*	.‖‖‖‖	‖.	▬	▬	▬	▬	▬	▬	▬	▬	▬	▬	▬	▬
Blue-winged Teal*	‖‖‖‖	‖	.		..	..	..	▬	▬	▬	▬	..	..	..
Garganey (acc)	••	•					••	•• •	•		•	•		
Cinnamon Teal*	‖‖.‖‖	.	..	..	..	..	▬	▬	▬		..	..	..	..

Species	1	2	3	4	J	F	M	A	M	J	J	A	S	O	N	D
Ruddy Duck*																
Fulvous Whistling-Duck (acc)																
Wood Duck*																
Canvasback*																
Redhead*																
Ring-necked Duck*																
Tufted Duck																
Greater Scaup																
Lesser Scaup*																
Common Eider (acc)																
King Eider																
Steller's Eider (acc)																
Black Scoter																
White-winged Scoter*																
Surf Scoter																
Harlequin Duck*																
Oldsquaw*																
Barrow's Goldeneye*																
Common Goldeneye*																
Bufflehead*																
Common Merganser*																
Red-breasted Merganser*																
Hooded Merganser*																
Smew (acc)																
Virginia Rail*																
Sora*																
Yellow Rail (hypo)																
Common Moorhen (acc)																
American Coot*																
Black Oystercatcher*																
American Avocet*																
Black-necked Stilt																
Snowy Plover																
Semipalmated Plover*																

Species	1	2	3	4	J	F	M	A	M	J	J	A	S	O	N	D
Killdeer*																
Black-bellied Plover																
American Golden-Plover*																
Pacific Golden-Plover																
Marbled Godwit																
Bar-tailed Godwit																
Hudsonian Godwit*																
Bristle-thighed Curlew (acc)																
Whimbrel																
Long-billed Curlew*																
Far Eastern Curlew (acc)																
Willet																
Greater Yellowlegs*																
Lesser Yellowlegs*																
Spotted Redshank (acc)																
Solitary Sandpiper*																
Spotted Sandpiper*																
Terek Sandpiper (acc)																
Wandering Tattler*																
Wilson's Phalarope*																
Red-necked Phalarope*																
Red Phalarope																
Short-billed Dowitcher*																
Long-billed Dowitcher																
Stilt Sandpiper																
Common Snipe*																
Ruddy Turnstone																
Black Turnstone																
Surfbird																
Rock Sandpiper																
Red Knot																
Dunlin																
Sanderling																
Curlew Sandpiper (R)																

Species	1	2	3	4	J	F	M	A	M	J	J	A	S	O	N	D
Semipalmated Sandpiper																
Western Sandpiper																
Least Sandpiper*																
White-rumped Sandpiper (R)																
Baird's Sandpiper																
Little Stint (acc)																
Temminck's Stint (acc)																
Rufous-necked Stint (R)																
Spoonbill Sandpiper (acc)																
Sharp-tailed Sandpiper																
Pectoral Sandpiper																
Ruff (R)																
Upland Sandpiper																
Buff-breasted Sandpiper																
South Polar Skua																
Pomarine Jaeger																
Parasitic Jaeger																
Long-tailed Jaeger																
Heermann's Gull																
Franklin's Gull																
Bonaparte's Gull*																
Common Black-headed Gull (R)																
Little Gull																
Ross' Gull (acc)																
Ring-billed Gull*																
Mew Gull*																
Herring Gull*																
California Gull*																
Glaucous Gull																
(Iceland Gull) Thayer's in part (R)																
Thayer's Gull																
Slaty-backed Gull (acc)																
Lesser Black-backed Gull (acc)																
Great Black-backed Gull (acc)																

Species	1	2	3	4		J	F	M	A	M	J	J	A	S	O	N	D
Western Gull	▮																
Glaucous-winged Gull*		▮															
Black-legged Kittiwake	▮			•													
Red-legged Kittiwake (acc)	•													•			
Sabine's Gull	▮																
Ivory Gull (acc)		•		•										•	•	••	
Common Tern	▮																
Arctic Tern*				▮													
Aleutian Tern (acc)	•										••	•					
Forster's Tern*		▮															
Black Tern*		▮															
Elegant Tern (R)	••											•	••	••			
Caspian Tern*			••														
Common Murre*	▮																
Thick-billed Murre* (R)										••	••	••					
Pigeon Guillemot*	▮																
Marbled Murrelet*	▮																
Kittlitz's Murrelet (acc)	••					••	••	••	•							•	••
Xantus' Murrelet (acc)	•••											•		•			
Ancient Murrelet*	▮																
Cassin's Auklet*	▮																
Parakeet Auklet (R)	••					••	••						•	••	••	••	••
Crested Auklet (hypo)	•					?	?										?
Rhinoceros Auklet*	▮					••	••								••	••	
Horned Puffin* (R)	▮					•	••	••	••	••	••	••		••	••		
Tufted Puffin*	▮					••	••	••							••	••	••
Turkey Vulture*	▮					••	••								••	••	
Golden Eagle*	▮																
Bald Eagle*	▮																
Black-shouldered Kite (acc)	•••							•		••				•			
Northern Harrier*	▮																
Sharp-shinned Hawk*	▮																
Cooper's Hawk*	▮																
Northern Goshawk*	▮																

Species	1	2	3	4	J	F	M	A	M	J	J	A	S	O	N	D
Broad-winged Hawk																
Red-tailed Hawk*																
Swainson's Hawk*																
Rough-legged Hawk																
Ferruginous Hawk* (R)																
Osprey*																
Eurasian Kestrel (acc)																
American Kestrel*																
Merlin*																
Prairie Falcon*																
Peregrine Falcon*																
Gyrfalcon*																
Ruffed Grouse*																
Spruce Grouse*																
Blue Grouse*																
White-tailed Ptarmigan*																
Rock Ptarmigan*																
Willow Ptarmigan*																
Sharp-tailed Grouse*																
Sage Grouse (ext)		e			e	e	e	e	e	e	e	e	e	e	e	e
Northern Bobwhite (I) (ext)	e	e			e	e	e	e	e	e	e	e	e	e	e	e
California Quail* (I)																
Mountain Quail* (I) (ext?)																
Chukar* (I)																
Gray Partridge* (I)	e															
Ring-necked Pheasant* (I)																
Wild Turkey* (I)																
Band-tailed Pigeon*																
Rock Dove* (I)																
Mourning Dove*																
White-winged Dove (acc)																
Yellow-billed Cuckoo (ext)																
Black-billed Cuckoo (R)																
Barn Owl*																

Species	1	2	3	4	J	F	M	A	M	J	J	A	S	O	N	D
Short-eared Owl*																
Long-eared Owl*																
Great Horned Owl*																
Barred Owl*																
Great Gray Owl*																
Spotted Owl*																
Snowy Owl																
Western Screech-Owl*																
Flammulated Owl*																
Northern Pygmy-Owl*																
Northern Saw-whet Owl*																
Northern Hawk-Owl*																
Boreal Owl*																
Burrowing Owl*																
Common Poorwill*																
Common Nighthawk*																
Black Swift*																
Vaux's Swift*																
White-throated Swift*																
Ruby-throated Hummingbird (acc)*																
Black-chinned Hummingbird*																
Costa's Hummingbird (acc)																
Anna's Hummingbird*																
Calliope Hummingbird*																
Broad-tailed Hummingbird (acc)																
Rufous Hummingbird*																
Belted Kingfisher*																
Northern Flicker*																
Red-headed Woodpecker (acc)																
White-headed Woodpecker*																
Lewis' Woodpecker*																
Williamson's Sapsucker*																
Red-breasted Sapsucker*																
Red-naped Sapsucker*																

Species	1	2	3	4	J	F	M	A	M	J	J	A	S	O	N	D
Yellow-bellied Sapsucker*		•														
Downy Woodpecker*																
Hairy Woodpecker*																
Three-toed Woodpecker*																
Black-backed Woodpecker*																
Pileated Woodpecker*																
Eastern Kingbird*																
Gray Kingbird (acc)	•															
Thick-billed Kingbird (acc)	•															
Western Kingbird*																
Tropical Kingbird (R)	•															
Scissor-tailed Flycatcher (acc)			•													
Ash-throated Flycatcher (R)																
Olive-sided Flycatcher*																
Western Wood-Pewee*																
Eastern Phoebe*	•															
Black Phoebe (acc)	• •															
Say's Phoebe*																
Gray Flycatcher*																
Dusky Flycatcher*	•															
Hammond's Flycatcher*																
Least Flycatcher*																
Acadian Flycatcher (acc)		•														
Willow Flycatcher*																
Alder Flycatcher*																
Yellow-bellied Flycatcher*																
Pacific-slope Flycatcher*																
Cordilleran Flycatcher*																
Eurasian Skylark* (I)																
Horned Lark*																
Tree Swallow*																
Violet-green Swallow*																
Purple Martin*																
Bank Swallow*																

Species	1	2	3	4	J	F	M	A	M	J	J	A	S	O	N	D
Northern Rough-winged Swallow*																
Cliff Swallow*																
Barn Swallow*																
Scrub Jay (acc)																
Blue Jay*																
Steller's Jay*																
Gray Jay*																
Clark's Nutcracker*																
Black-billed Magpie*																
American Crow*																
Northwestern Crow*																
Common Raven*																
Black-capped Chickadee*																
Mountain Chickadee*																
Chestnut-backed Chickadee*																
Boreal Chickadee*																
Bushtit*																
Brown Creeper*																
White-breasted Nuthatch*																
Red-breasted Nuthatch*																
Pygmy Nuthatch*																
House Wren*																
Winter Wren*																
Bewick's Wren*																
Marsh Wren*																
Canyon Wren*																
Rock Wren*																
Golden-crowned Kinglet*																
Ruby-crowned Kinglet*																
Blue-gray Gnatcatcher (acc)																
Western Bluebird*																
Mountain Bluebird*																
Townsend"s Solitaire*																
Veery*																

Species	1	2	3	4		J	F	M	A	M	J	J	A	S	O	N	D
Swainson's Thrush*																	
Gray-cheeked Thrush*																	
Hermit Thrush*																	
Varied Thrush*																	
Dusky Thrush (acc)																	
American Robin*																	
Northern Wheatear (acc)																	
Loggerhead Shrike																	
Northern Shrike*																	
Gray Catbird*																	
Northern Mockingbird* (R)																	
Sage Thrasher*																	
Brown Thrasher (R)																	
American Pipit*																	
Spraque's Pipit (acc)																	
Red-throated Pipit (acc)																	
Black-backed Wagtail (acc)																	
White & (wagtail species) (acc)																	
Yellow Wagtail (acc)																	
American Dipper*																	
Bohemian Waxwing*																	
Cedar Waxwing*																	
Crested Myna* (I)																	
European Starling* (I)																	
Hutton's Vireo*																	
Solitary Vireo*																	
Red-eyed Vireo*																	
Warbling Vireo*																	
Philadelphia Vireo*																	
Tennessee Warbler*																	
Orange-crowned Warbler*																	
Nashville Warbler*																	
Black-and-white Warbler*																	
Black-throated Blue Warbler (acc)																	

Species	1	2	3	4	J	F	M	A	M	J	J	A	S	O	N	D
Blackburnian Warbler (acc)																
Chestnut-sided Warbler (acc)																
Cape May Warbler*																
Magnolia Warbler*																
Yellow-rumped Warbler*																
Black-throated Gray Warbler*																
Townsend's Warbler*																
Hermit Warbler (acc)																
Black-throated Green Warbler*																
Bay-breasted Warbler																
Blackpoll Warbler*																
Palm Warbler*																
Yellow Warbler*																
Mourning Warbler																
MacGillivray's Warbler*																
Connecticut Warbler*																
Canada Warbler*																
Wilson's Warbler*																
Hooded Warbler (acc)																
Ovenbird*																
Northern Waterthrush*																
Common Yellowthroat*																
Yellow-breasted Chat*																
American Redstart*																
Painted Redstart (acc)																
Rose-breasted Grosbeak*																
Black-headed Grosbeak*																
Indigo Bunting (R)																
Lazuli Bunting*																
Green-tailed Towhee (acc)																
Rufous-sided Towhee*																
Grasshopper Sparrow*																
Baird's Sparrow (acc)																
Le Conte's Sparrow*																

Species	1	2	3	4	J	F	M	A	M	J	J	A	S	O	N	D
Sharp-tailed Sparrow* (R)																
Vesper Sparrow*																
Savannah Sparrow*																
Song Sparrow*																
Lark Sparrow*																
Black-throated Sparrow (R)																
Sage Sparrow (acc)																
American Tree Sparrow*																
Chipping Sparrow*																
Clay-colored Sparrow*																
Brewer's Sparrow*																
Dark-eyed Junco*																
Harris' Sparrow																
White-throated Sparrow*																
White-crowned Sparrow*																
Golden-crowned Sparrow*																
Fox Sparrow*																
Lincoln's Sparrow*																
Swamp Sparrow*																
Chestnut-collared Longspur (acc)																
McCown's Longspur (acc)																
Smith's Longspur*																
Lapland Longspur																
Snow Bunting*																
McKay's Bunting (acc)																
Rustic Bunting (acc)																
Dickcissel (acc)																
Lark Bunting (R)																
Bobolink*																
Western Meadowlark*																
Yellow-headed Blackbird*																
Red-winged Blackbird*																
Rusty Blackbird*																
Brewer's Blackbird*																

Species	1	2	3	4	J	F	M	A	M	J	J	A	S	O	N	D
Brown-headed Cowbird*																
Common Grackle*																
Great-tailed Grackle (acc)																
Northern Oriole*																
Scarlet Tanager (acc)																
Western Tanager*																
House Sparrow* (I)																
Pine Siskin*																
American Goldfinch*																
Lesser Goldfinch (acc)																
Red Crossbill*																
White-winged Crossbill*																
Pine Grosbeak*																
Common Redpoll*																
Hoary Redpoll																
Rosy Finch*																
Purple Finch*																
Cassin's Finch*																
House Finch*																
Evening Grosbeak*																
Brambling (R)																

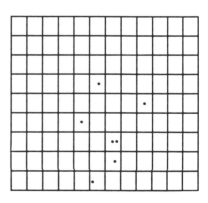

ADDITIONAL SPECIES	1	2	3	4	J	F	M	A	M	J	J	A	S	O	N	D
California Condor past remains																
Mongolian Plover (acc)																
Black-tailed Gull (hypo)																
Passenger Pigeon extinct																
Oriental Turtle-Dove origin?																
Gray Wagtail (hypo)																
Blue Grosbeak (sight record)																

STATUS	
▬▬▬	Hard to miss
▬▬▬	Should see
———	May see
· · · · ·	How lucky can you get

	LOCALITIES	Season			
1	Georgia Depression and Pelagics	s	s	f	w
2	Southern Interior	s	s	f	w
3	Peace River Parklands	s	s	f	w
4	Northern Boreal Mountains	s	s	f	w

CALENDAR

J-F-M-A-M-J-J-A-S-O-N-D

J-January   F-February

M-March A-April   etc.

SYMBOLS

(acc)-Accidental ·

(R)-Rare ·

(hypo)-Hypothetical

(l)-Introduced

(ext)-Extirpated

Index
The Birder's Guide to British Columbia

H

O

Oldsquaw 29, 42, 45, 48, 65, 197, 198, 221
Oriole
   Baltimore 186, 188, 189, 191, 198
   Bullock's 49, 87, 98, 99, 106, 110, 111, 118, 124, 125, 139, 152, 158, 159,
      177
Osprey 66, 80, 86, 97, 98, 99, 100, 101, 110, 117, 121, 125, 136, 139, 140,
      141, 144, 150, 152, 153, 177, 203
Ovenbird 36, 181, 183, 186, 188, 189, 198, 203, 204, 205, 206
Owl
   Barn 28, 29, 44, 52, 54, 57
   Barred 95, 112, 113, 136, 154, 161, 169, 188, 189, 203, 206
   Boreal 32, 35, 36, 37, 116, 134, 169, 174, 201, 204, 207, 208
   Burrowing 32, 59, 110, 157
   Flammulated 32, 101, 112, 120, 151, 153, 157, 159
   Great Gray 34, 100, 154, 160, 174, 188
   Great Horned 29, 32, 44, 51, 54, 57, 86, 98, 106, 110, 112, 117, 124, 136,
      139, 153, 154, 159, 188, 191, 198
   Long-eared 29, 31, 51, 54, 57, 86, 99, 110, 136, 156, 174
   Northern 29, 32, 51, 54, 57, 110, 120, 124, 154, 159, 161, 188, 218, 221
   Short-eared 29, 36, 43, 44, 56, 57, 87, 110, 128, 139, 155, 156, 210, 222
   Snowy 22, 29, 46, 54, 125, 126, 139, 195, 222
Oystercatcher
   Black 29, 59, 72, 74, 75, 79, 220, 222

P

Partridge
   Gray 31, 32, 111, 118, 126, 129, 130
Pelican
   American White 34, 115, 124, 154, 175
   White 24, 34, 100, 115, 124, 154, 175
Petrel
   Mottled 27, 38, 216, 218
Pewee
   Western Wood 32, 63, 67, 79, 84, 96, 99, 106, 113, 115, 117, 121, 136,
      139, 167, 169, 183, 198, 203, 205, 206
Phalarope
   Red 38, 42, 58, 60, 216
   Red-necked 36, 37, 38, 51, 58, 67, 119, 124, 129, 154, 190, 196, 199, 209,
      216

R

Rail
   Virginia 50, 54, 66, 67, 76, 79, 85, 86, 88, 102, 112, 116, 124, 138, 153
   Yellow 194
Raven
   Common 36, 38, 84, 89, 95, 98, 101, 102, 123, 161, 164, 169, 204, 208,
      211, 222
   Redhead 29, 53, 59, 67, 75, 106, 118, 121, 124, 127, 128, 140, 151, 161,
      174, 192, 193, 198
Redpoll
   Common 37, 43, 54, 101, 126, 156, 182, 188, 195, 209
   Hoary 22, 36, 126, 182, 188, 195
Redshank
   Spotted 29, 47, 53
Redstart
   American 31, 65, 87, 88, 118, 125, 126, 133, 140, 141, 143, 161, 162,
      163, 167, 168, 175, 177, 189, 194, 206
Robin
   American 32, 38, 67, 96, 98, 101, 117, 135, 145, 161, 167, 168, 188, 204,
      206, 208, 222
Ruff 29, 47, 57, 190, 219, 222

S

Sandpiper
   Baird's 29, 46, 47, 49, 53, 58, 99, 129, 138, 154, 190, 196, 210, 222
   Buff-breasted 29, 47, 57, 158, 190, 199, 219
   Curlew 29, 57, 218
   Least 36, 46, 47, 49, 53, 58, 65, 99, 124, 129, 138, 190, 196, 199, 209,
      219, 222, 224
   Pectoral 46, 47, 53, 58, 99, 124, 129, 185, 190, 196, 199, 219, 222
   Rock 21, 22, 29, 42, 58, 59, 72, 74, 75, 220
   Semipalmated 29, 49, 99, 124, 129, 138, 190, 196, 199, 222
   Sharp-tailed 29, 47, 53, 57, 158, 190, 193, 222
   Solitary 36, 53, 58, 99, 129, 168, 185, 199, 203, 210, 222
   Spoonbill 29, 57
   Spotted 53, 58, 65, 80, 96, 99, 117, 129, 136, 137, 169, 190, 196, 199,
      210, 219, 222
   Stilt 29, 58, 74, 129, 158, 185, 190, 196, 222
   Terek 29
   Upland 29, 35, 57, 192, 194, 219

V

W

Biography

Keith Taylor began his interest in birds as a boy growing up in Saskatchewan and Ontario. Immigrating to Australia, he worked as a field researcher studying the distribution of Queensland's rainforest birds. Returning to Victoria, where he continues to reside, Keith joined the staff of the Royal British Columbia Museum as an illustrator and curator of ornithological collections.

Recently, Keith has been self-employed as a freelance bird illustrator and has published birding guides to Costa Rica, Thailand, Ecuador, British Columbia and Vancouver Island. He has also written numerous articles for birding and natural history magazines and has led birding tours.

Semi-retired, Keith has been touring the world with birding trips to Hawaii, Costa Rica, Tahiti, Jamaica, South Africa, Great Britain and Mexico. North America's birding hotspots still hold his most intense interest and Keith holds the highest ABA list of any Canadian - 744 species.

NOTES & OBSERVATIONS

NOTES & OBSERVATIONS

NOTES & OBSERVATIONS

NOTES & OBSERVATIONS